D0991365

GAME MISCONDUCT

GAME MISCONDUCT

HOCKEY'S TOXIC CULTURE

AND HOW TO FIX IT

EVAN F. MOORE
and JASHVINA SHAH

TRIUMPH
BOOKS

Copyright © 2021 by Evan F. Moore and Jashvina Shah

No part of this publication may be reproduced, stored in a retrieval system, or transmitted in any form by any means, electronic, mechanical, photocopying, or otherwise, without the prior written permission of the publisher, Triumph Books LLC, 814 North Franklin Street, Chicago, Illinois 60610.

Library of Congress Cataloging-in-Publication Data available upon request.

This book is available in quantity at special discounts for your group or organization. For further information, contact:

Triumph Books LLC
814 North Franklin Street
Chicago, Illinois 60610
(312) 337-0747
www.triumphbooks.com

Printed in U.S.A.
ISBN: 978-1-62937-920-3
Design by Sue Knopf
Page production by Patricia Frey

If you walk through life and don't help anybody, you haven't had much of a life.

—Fred Hampton

To the ancestors. To the players who put up with racism, xenophobia, sexism, classism, ableism, and homophobia from teammates, journalists, parents, coaches, and opposing players. To those who love a sport that doesn't love them back. To the kid who is reading this book and decides he/she/they want to stand up for themselves and their teammates/homies. To the people who believe in Jashvina's and my work. More importantly, I dedicate this book to my family and friends, along with the People's Republic of the South Side of Chicago.

And to my daughter, Savannah: ask for forgiveness, not permission.

—E.M.

To everyone who's loved hockey but has never felt it love them back. To all the people who believed in Evan and me. To all the good people in hockey who have had my back, extended kindness beyond measure, and made me feel like each rink was my home. To BU hockey for giving me my first, and my permanent, home. To my mom and dad for their constant belief in me. To my best friends, Erica, Kim, Sandra, Chris, and Laura—not only for getting me through the toughest times, but for listening to my endless hockey stories and always encouraging me. To my nephews, Niam and Ira—I want you to be able to play this sport and I want to make it better for you. To Darren Stafford—I once said I didn't know what to do with my life and you told me to cover hockey. I hope I made you proud. Lastly, to all the amazing Black, Indigenous, women, and non-binary people of color in hockey.

—J.S.

Contents

Authors' Note

THE THEMES DISCUSSED THROUGHOUT *GAME MISCONDUCT*—BY design—are uncomfortable at best and triggering at worst.

Racial and homophobic slurs will be spelled out in their entirety, rather than partially obscured by dashes. Most of the time, if we are reprinting a racial or sexual slur it's because it is contained in a direct quote, and we don't believe it is our duty to protect that person by censoring their language. In the spirit of what Black Girl Hockey Club founder and executive director Renee Hess says, we urge those who hold privilege and have the power to effect change to "get uncomfortable."

This book speaks about hockey in very binary terms because that is how organized sports are structured. However, it is important to understand that non-binary people are also present in these spaces, especially since women's leagues have become a catch-all for those who are not cis (like in the WNBA, where Layshia Clarendon came out as non-binary). *Non-binary* is a broad term that could encompass anyone who does not identify as fitting in the binary of man or woman. When discussing bigotry like transphobia and sexism, we did not include non-binary people because we did not want to lump them in with women or with trans people (some people who are non-binary do identify as trans while others do not) when that act itself is transphobic against non-binary people in general.

There are also detailed instances of racism, sexism, homophobia, rape, sexual assault, and bullying, among other issues holding hockey back from being the sport it could be. We understand certain words and accounts may be triggering, and we mean no disrespect to anyone.

Foreword

Breaking Down the Untenable Institution of Racism in Hockey: Reading *Game Misconduct* by Jashvina Shah and Evan F. Moore

ANTI-RACISM WORK SHOULDN'T BE ON THE BACKS OF BLACK AND Indigenous People of Color, but oftentimes, it is. In hockey, BIPOC fans, executives, players, media, and staff do the groundwork to grow the game at the grassroots level and in marginalized communities while also asking ourselves, "What's the point?" We do the educating; we are the ones speaking up for ourselves and for others, even though it can feel futile to love a sport that doesn't always love you back. For every public display of diversity and inclusion by a professional league, there are hundreds of BIPOC folks working in our own schools, newspapers, cities, and organizations to make sure that hockey is truly for everyone, including us.

As journalists and as fans of the game, Shah and Moore have spent years using their work to bring hockey to a more equitable place. You'd be hard-pressed to find a critical fan of the game who does not recognize their names, as sports journalists and agitators of the status quo. Examining race in hockey from the locker room to social media, their book, *Game Misconduct: Hockey's Toxic Culture and How to Fix It,* looks critically at the sport and leaves no puck unturned. Using a combination of anecdotal and research-based information, the text takes an extensive look at the precarious culture of hockey, asking readers to face the pervasiveness of white supremacy from the top down. With voices like those of Dr. Courtney Szto, author of *Changing on the Fly: Hockey Through the Voices of South Asian Canadians* (2020), members of the Madison Gay Hockey Association, and numerous BIPOC players, parents, and fans, *Game Misconduct* is more than a collection of stories about race and hockey; it is archival evidence of the character of the sport. The text illustrates the deep desire of marginalized fans to shift hockey culture to be more welcoming, more discerning, and more accountable for BIPOC and LGBTQ+ folks involved in all aspects of the sport.

For those of us who are non-white, non-cis, non-male, or any combination of those identities, we do not always have a safe entry point to the game of hockey, whether it is to play, to watch, to coach, or to work in and around the sport. There is little representation, whether it is behind the bench, in the stands, or at the front office. *Game Misconduct* addresses the need to create space in hockey for the "non-traditional market" (code for non-white, non-cis, non-male) and reminds readers that equity for all is more important than the feelings of those who uphold systemic racism in sports.

In 2020, the murders of Breonna Taylor, George Floyd, and Ahmaud Arbery, the shooting of Jacob Blake, and the public reaction of athletes on the subject of police brutality pushed professional sports, including hockey, to acknowledge that the phrase **Black Lives Matter** is not meant as a divisive statement, but a plea for safety and accountability. Black death, the consequences of peaceful protest, an attempted coup on the American government, and the hard-hit Black and Brown communities during the COVID-19 pandemic forced many to acknowledge that racism and white supremacy run rampant throughout all of our institutions. *Game Misconduct* reveals the rotting foundations of racism in hockey and offers stark evidence that the system is broken.

So what's next?

When we use our voices, the marginalized gain strength. *We gain power.* By telling our truths, we shine a light in the dark, shattering the untenable institution of racism in hockey that balances precariously on the silence and submission of its victims. *Game Misconduct* asks readers to pay attention, to stand up, and to do right by BIPOC folks in hockey. In order to build a sport that is more equitable for all, those in power must acknowledge their mistakes, get uncomfortable, and make a change—or else they must move aside, and let those of us who truly love hockey grow the game.

R. Renee Hess is the founder and executive director of Black Girl Hockey Club, a nonprofit organization advocating for Black women in hockey.

Introduction

The way to right wrongs is to turn the light of truth upon them.
—Ida B. Wells

My love affair with hockey was solidified in the last place you'd think: an African American lifestyle magazine named *Jet*. As a kid, I flipped through the February 18, 1991, issue, and saw something I had never seen: a hockey player who looks like me—kind of. My hometown Chicago Blackhawks traded for winger Tony McKegney. Even though his stay on the team was short, it was cool to see a Black hockey player.

Despite growing up on the South Side of Chicago—a predominantly Black area—I became a hockey fan when I watched the 1988 Calgary Olympic Games. Over the years, I became a fan of the Chicago Blackhawks and several other players across the NHL. Years later, I started to write about the game and how it affects my heritage.

In 2013, I wrote an article for a now-defunct Chicago website (ChicagoSide) called "Black Man, Hockey Fan," in which I discussed my struggles of being a hockey fan in an area where the sport wasn't accessible. In the article, I mentioned that I would like to play hockey one day. A hockey player who read the article contacted me and offered me used hockey gear. I accepted the gear and started my journey as a hockey player.

I wasn't aware of what hockey culture consisted of until I started playing hockey myself. I quickly immersed myself in the nuances of the game and the culture that surrounds it. The camaraderie of the sport is matched by no other; it was a selling point for me. I joined a team of players who were learning the game. We practiced together. We drank together. A case of Miller Lite magically appearing in the locker room after a rat hockey game was considered the norm. Our friends and families knew each other. But another cultural norm was the loud minority: pro-racism, anti-gay, pro-bullying, and misogynistic.

Hockey says it wants to diversify its ranks, but without addressing the aforementioned issues, the sport will never be truly great.

Hockey isn't for everyone until *everyone* shows up.

—E.M.

I wouldn't be co-writing this book if it weren't for hockey. And I don't mean because this book is about hockey—I mean because I owe my life to hockey.

I wasn't born into this sport. I didn't start watching until I was 15. But the love I found for the sport was enough to carry me through two harrowing years of deep depression. And when that was done, it was BU hockey in undergrad that pulled me through and taught me that I could be happy again. Actually happy. When my family friend died, it was covering Princeton hockey that I clung to, Princeton hockey that supported me.

Hockey is my family. But through all of this, I could see the things that weren't right.

In 2017, after Donald Trump was elected, I promised that I would no longer be complicit in sweeping hockey's problems away and hiding them so desperately. As a college hockey reporter, I'd contributed to ignoring the problematic behavior. That is something I can never take back.

I had already started feeling so alone. But in 2018, I was alone.

In November 2018, I was sexually assaulted. I didn't want to leave my apartment after that, and the only reason I did was because I had to cover an Ohio State–UConn game that weekend. So I pulled myself up and drove to Connecticut, physically in pain and almost getting into an accident because I was crying so hard. But as soon as I got there and I saw Ohio State warming up, I felt so at ease.

Less than a month later, I was covering the New England prep hockey tournaments. And that was when I realized how truly isolated I was. I cried—for the first time ever—in a hockey rink. I cried in three of them, locking myself in bathroom stalls. I had to call my good friend Catherine to talk to me so I could pick myself up off the gym floor at Milton during the Flood Marr Tournament. I literally cried in the rink at one of the smaller schools.

As a Brown woman, I never belonged in this sport. My presence there was fringe at best, and only welcomed as long as I upheld the narrative of how great hockey was—and provided I left the Brown and woman part of myself at the door. But when that tournament hit, I truly realized how alone I was. Because I couldn't tell a single person who was there. I couldn't tell them what happened. I couldn't ask for support. My insides were being eaten and all I had to do was stand in the cold for 12 hours a day.

I knew that hockey would not accept me as a survivor of sexual assault.

The thing that hurts me the most is I know how great sports can be in healing. But I also see how many people, like myself, it fails.

People like to say if you love the game, it will love you back. But that isn't true.

That isn't the only reason I'm co-writing this book, though. I'm co-writing this book because one of my now-closest friends, and the one person who checked in on me daily after I was sexually assaulted, is a friend I have only because of hockey.

Hockey isn't great, but it can be.

—J.S.

1

What Is Hockey Culture?

WHILE HOCKEY SHARES SOME ASPECTS OF ITS CULTURE WITH other sports, like toxic masculinity, there are others unique to hockey. It thinks of itself as a sport that imparts positive values and creates better people, especially in making "boys into men." It champions respect, teamwork, niceness, and coachability. While those values are good, they are often twisted into something more sinister. These "values" are converted into actions that control and shape how players think, feel, and act.

Hockey exists in its own bubble, literally and figuratively. It's composed mostly of boys and men who are white, cishet, straight, and upper-class. And those who play often become coaches and teach the same values to the next generation.

"There is a lot of upside of this whole idea of being on a team, having shared mental models and shared values of what does it mean to be a member of this team," said Riley Fitzgerald, coordinator of sports psychology services for Boston University athletics. "Because it can, and it does, teach some valuable stuff about what it means to work with other people and to be a part of something that's bigger than yourself."

But hockey turns teamwork into extreme groupthink. It morphs from being a team player on the ice into being like everyone else off the ice. This creates a culture of silence—anyone who is different is afraid to speak out. Anyone who is different is afraid to be different. And if you aren't white and cishet, you're expected to leave those other parts of yourself at the door—you will not be accepted for who you are.

When Sunaya Sapurji, who has covered major juniors for a variety of outlets, including Yahoo Sports and, currently, The Athletic, wrote a story on Dan Boyle, a former player who is now a roadie for a rock band, she asked how he got into music that was vastly different from typical locker room music.

"Conformity is huge," Sapurji said. "I wanted to know, 'How did you still like this music and not be forced to conform?' And he said, 'It's crazy the amount of bullshit I had to go through to listen to this music. But I'm a really strong person. And so, it didn't bother me. But how crazy is that you need to be a strong person to listen to the music you want to listen to? That was crazy to me.' That's toxic culture."

The toxicity is present at all levels, including college hockey and major juniors.

"Your players are individuals first and people first," Fitzgerald said. "Hockey is just something that you're doing; it's a part of who you are, but not who you are. But playing at 16 AAA, even at that age it was suits and ties at games, slacks and polos on planes. It's that conformity, and I don't think that's the intention behind it all the time."

Instead of simply being polite, respect means never questioning the coach or going against the team. Respect means listening to coaches with no questions or pushback—even if what they're telling you is questionable.

The emphasis on hard work pushes the limits, shared Jordan DeKort, an Ontario Hockey League goalie and founder of GameChangers Workshop, which aims to shift the culture in sport.

"Being chastised and sometimes not even allowed to stay back at the hotel to work on schoolwork because it was more important to go to the mall with the team to watch a movie," DeKort said. "And that's what's crazy, is that it's not surprising that it goes back to that value system.... A lot of guys I played with were not very academically driven or focused. But the coach would buy into that and say, 'Hey, we're here for hockey. This is what's important. You can do schoolwork later on your own time when we get back.'"

The Merriam-Webster dictionary lists a few definitions for *culture*:

"The customary beliefs, social forms, and material traits of a racial, religious, or social group." "The set of shared attitudes, values, goals, and practices that characterizes an institution or organization." "The set of values, conventions, or social practices associated with a particular field, activity, or societal characteristic."

Okay, but what happens when you add hockey, the world's greatest sport, to the mix? Is hockey culture different from state to state? How about from the U.S. to Canada? Why do hockey stans act so nutty over it?

"I think it varies only slightly; I think the base is very similar, but I would say that hockey culture in Minnesota is far different than it is anywhere else, and there are a couple of different reasons for that," said former ESPN hockey scouting reporter Chris Peters. "Obviously we know how popular the sport is there for high school hockey—like football in Texas. Part of that is also hockey in Minnesota's similarity to how it is in Canada.

"I think hockey is such a community thing in Minnesota. There's a community aspect to it; the quality of the hockey program is tied to community pride. And it's not like that really anywhere else in the U.S., so, again, it just kind of comes back to it's this very niche thing with a small group of people playing.... But when you look at Minnesota and Canada, where it is such a community-based sport... it matters to the larger majority of people in those communities. That's where I see differences in terms of how hockey is viewed and how it is celebrated, and how the culture is formed."

Jaslyn Lim continues to experience hockey culture on multiple levels as a player, coach, and administrator. Lim, a former University of Iowa women's hockey club team member who coaches youth hockey in Chicago, is a member of Singapore's national hockey team.

"I know hockey brings everyone together in some way," Lim said. "In my building, I just met some dude who was playing, I think, at Fifth Third [Arena]. He came back with his gear. I had a hockey T-shirt on with a hockey mask. And it's like a connection, if that's a good thing, but the bad thing is it's a very competitive culture, where I see you're from another team, and we play in the same league, but I'm from this team. If I see you wearing your shirt, naturally we're going to be competitive, even with a T-shirt. And then the negativity comes within just playing on a different team. If you're not from that team, you're looked down on. I was talking to another coach about just, you know, being kids in general. It's like politics, right? You can hear your parents say something, naturally, you'll learn, and the negativity just starts from there."

And how do parents intermingle with hockey culture?

"Just go to the rink. Just hear parents shouting at the kids on the ice, shouting at the coach, shouting at the refs," Lim said. "I mean, that's the start of things, but when you're talking about parents being too into sport, when they start wanting to take charge, usually as coaches or they've got a board, running the club and stuff. When parents aren't happy with the board's coaching, they tend to step in. I understand, with how the sport is, you want your kids to play at the highest level. And if you take a look at the elite teams, they don't want anyone outside of the circle to come in; they want to stay competitive with the people they already know. So, say you're a new kid coming in. It's tough. You're not integrated with the already good kids. And change is something that I guess...you know, parents aren't gonna like it.... If it's just a little tweak within a club itself, they'll pull the kids out."

Black former pro hockey player Rane Carnegie believes the way hockey culture is set up actually hurts teams when they don't exhaust all their resources in finding players.

"[Without] a culturally diverse scouting team within your organization, it becomes difficult to get rich data to inform your general manager or ownership," Carnegie said. "You don't know what you don't know, right? So I find that one of the steps that we need to take in terms of penetration is getting more people that look like me or visible minorities in positions where they can influence decisions or where they can give another perspective that other people just aren't able to give, because they've never lived that experience.

"I can't talk for a white person, because I've never been white. I can't talk for an Asian person, because I've never been Asian. So I think that it's important to have a diverse network you can lean on for resources and information in order to put together teams that can help you find success. And I think that what's happened at all levels of hockey is that there hasn't been enough diversity, which is what we're trying to draw awareness around in positions of power. And believe it or not, positions of power starts at the scouting level. You have a predominantly Caucasian scouting field out there going to different arenas around the world, not only in North America, Europe, and the like. If they have any bias or racial bias based on how they were raised, and if the organizations don't do a background check on who they have in positions, it's a trickle-down effect. Oftentimes, what I found is that if you have a hockey resume and you know somebody in the right spot, chances are you're probably going to get a decent job. And there's very little background because they just look at your hockey resume, but there's a lot more to an individual than just their hockey resume."

Carnegie believes that hockey needs to include voices from every community the sport touches—not just the white ones.

"I think that because, from my own perspective, I didn't have a voice of somebody that looked like me that could articulate that our cultures are different," Carnegie said. "I think it's important that there's a culturally responsible way for the organization to hire more culturally diverse people in positions of power at the scouting level. At the back office, anybody can throw it out through the coaching level, as well. Because I don't want to be alienated as a Black player because my coach might not understand our cultural differences. So it's either you get culturally responsible and bring professionals in there to educate your predominantly non-diverse staff, or you try to find people that are diverse, that have the resumes that can help you be more inclusive and diverse within your organization."

When Hemal Jhaveri covered hockey for USA TODAY Sports and first started to notice the nuances of hockey culture, she saw a lot of things normalized that would be deemed outrageous anywhere else.

"Once I really started taking a look at it, I felt like I was a crazy person," Jhaveri said. "I felt that a lot of it is kind of gaslighting, the stuff that we are taught to just look at as normal. And when I started to be like, 'Wait, this is wrong,' I felt like I was the crazy one, because it was so accepted.... This is not normal. And nobody else around you seems to share that...like, the players didn't think it was weird."

She recalls covering a player who played through an injury when he shouldn't have.

"After morning skate, I just casually kind of overheard people talking about their injuries and stuff like that, and I'm like...'That's not good,'" Jhaveri said. "And so you kind of gain trust in yourself and you're like, 'No, actually, this is wrong.'"

The player in question played minor league Canadian hockey. "He was telling me about these injuries," Jhaveri said, "and he was like, 'Well, you know, I got chucked into the bench one time,' and he was really feeling like shit, but he's a hockey guy, so he's like, 'Well, I'm gonna go back out there.' Then he kind of told one of the assistant coaches, 'Hey, I don't feel good, like I think there's something really wrong with me.'... It turns out that he went back onto the ice. He finished the game, went home, and told his girlfriend, 'I think I'm fucked up,' and she was like, 'You're a hockey guy, you'll be totally fine.' So...this guy told multiple people there was something really wrong with him, and nobody believed him until the next morning when apparently he had a collapsed lung and he couldn't breathe, and they had to rush him into the ER to get that taken care of. It was just this crazy story of a person not able to trust their own judgment—[who] could have been taught, so deeply, to think about what other people were saying and to disregard his own pain that it seriously endangered his life."

Andrew Sobotka, Chicago Gay Hockey Association board member, says hockey is like no other sport.

"It is kind of the ultimate team sport. I think it goes beyond being on a team and playing together. When someone's on your team, it's like family," Sobotka said. "And I think hockey's unique in that most hockey players seem to want to be socially engaged; a lot of them have their own charity and they, you know, do all sorts of volunteer work. I think for the most part hockey players are good people who maybe need a little help in education, and making sure that they're being as inclusive as they can be. But I think it's a very close-knit community and it goes beyond just being players or friends with someone, it really becomes like a very sacred bond. And I think one of the reasons why is because hockey is a commitment."

Sobotka believes what separates hockey from other sports is the sport's emphasis on "investment."

"It's not like other sports where you can just [say], 'Oh, you know, I'll try it this season.' It is a financial investment. And taking that investment requires a level of commitment," Sobotka said. "There's also a level of respect among other people on the team. They know you're making a commitment to the team, they know you're going to show up to play a game."

Steve Lorenzo, the board secretary for the New York City Gay Hockey Association, explains the difference between gay hockey culture and others within the sport.

"The gay hockey culture that I sort of ascended in is very different from hockey culture as a whole," Lorenzo said. "Going to games, even college games on an enlightened progressive college campus like the University of Wisconsin, you would hear it was mostly homophobic slurs being yelled by people in the stands. Also, it was very easy to notice that there was a tremendous disparity on the ice, in terms of the racial constitution of the teams. You know, mostly blond-haired white kids.

"It just wasn't a game that I ever thought I could have access to as a player. I thought it was something that was violent and ubermasculine, and going to these games certainly didn't do anything to dissuade me of that notion. That wasn't until a friend of mine said, 'Hey, come watch one of our hockey games. I know you like hockey.' I went to my first game. And I saw, first of all, that it was a level of play that was very, very different from college hockey, but also that it was really about the notion of community-building, and about people having a good time and finding their common interests, based in hockey. So, it's really two very different worlds."

Lorenzo sees hockey culture's faults starting with youth hockey clubs, which makes sense, since kids are often influenced by their peers at this stage.

"Just playing at Chelsea Piers, there are youth hockey clubs that play there and sometimes there's a little bit of an overlap. We'd be in adjoining dressing rooms and there was no sound barrier, and the language that you hear from these adolescents.... I know growing up that we certainly weren't angels in locker rooms, or whatever, but the way that these kids were talking about women, were making anti-gay slurs, all these things that, you know, hockey is supposed to be better, and the culture of hockey is supposed to be better," Lorenzo said.

"You hear these kids talking in a locker room, I don't know if their coaches were present or not, I assume probably not, but the fact [is] that these are, you know, little crucibles where these attitudes toward women, toward gays, toward minorities are starting to ferment and nobody's challenging these kids. These kids are mostly kids of privilege, and they're recklessly asserting that privilege in ways that could manifest itself in antisocial behavior later. And it's really disappointing to see that, because these are their formative years and people should be challenging that. It's not our job as somebody in an adjoining locker room to say, 'Hey, stop that.' You know, there should be adults and people in these kids' lives monitoring that, and trying to be better role models."

Hockey culture for Black folks—and anyone else who is marginalized—is a peculiar place in terms of how players, fans, parents, and coaches aim to fit in. But what happens when these folks receive overt and covert pushback from the sport's gatekeepers? Maybe a form of respectability politics sets in.

Black hockey players are in a spot their counterparts in the NBA, the WNBA, and the NFL don't have to worry about. Players in those leagues have an immense support system—they get shit done.

When the Chicago Blackhawks traded for winger Anthony Duclair, a Black man, a local blogger who works for a well-known sports media company tweeted:

Every time the Blackhawks win the Cup they have a black guy.

Evan quote-tweeted:

That's not how you welcome someone.

Of course, a lot of back-and-forth ensued, but what Evan tried to tell this person that day was that Black hockey players, by definition, are already "othered." Every time they step into a rink or a locker room, on the bench, and on the ice, their teammates, coaches, opponents, and fans already know.

The golden rule that all of us ought to live by: don't tweet something about someone you aren't prepared to say to their face.

And that "othering" isn't exclusive to white people. Black folks have a long history of sizing each other up when it comes to someone being down for the cause or not. As a Black man who is a hockey fan, Evan has been at the shit end of assumption when it comes to the sport he loves. While he hasn't been called an "Uncle Tom" directly, his Blackness—or a perceived lack thereof—has been questioned over time.

Why you like that white boy sport?

Why you wanna be one of them?

Evan remembers one time when he was walking toward the rink with his gear and a group of men saw him and asked, "They let Black people in there?" Normally, he would've thought, *Here we go with this shit again*, but he knew what homie was saying was loaded with context.

The Blackhawks used to practice at a facility in Chicago, Johnny's IceHouse West, where the neighborhood has a reputation for violence and poverty. Hockey is a white sport. What had these gentlemen seen in their lifetimes that led them to decide that a hockey rink in their own neighborhood wouldn't be welcoming to them?

Lots to unpack, eh?

When Boston Bruins goalie Tuukka Rask made a TV appearance wearing a Boston Police cap after the team issued a statement calling for an understanding of social justice issues, Evan tweeted this:

> Tuukka Rask wearing a "Boston Police" cap after his team releases a statement about social justice is all one needs to know when it comes to hockey culture.

Evan went on to say that he didn't care what Rask wears, but he ought to know that it appears he has chosen a side, much like Chicago Cubs slugger Kyle Schwarber did a week earlier when he wore a Chicago Police cap while wearing a Black Lives Matter T-shirt.

Outraged members of Hockey Twitter were not happy with the tweet.

Many of them believed Evan was disrespectful to the police officers involved in apprehending the men who were responsible for the 2013 bombing that took place on Patriots' Day during the Boston Marathon. None of them brought up that their fellow Black Bostonians, who make up 25 percent of the city's population, made up 70 percent of traffic stops made by Boston's police department, according to WGBH News: "According to a WGBH News analysis of more than 7,000 stops conducted by Boston Police between January and September 2019, only 3 percent resulted in a summons being issued to black individuals, compared to 4 percent for white people, even as black people were stopped at a rate nearly triple their proportion of Boston's population."

What people seem to forget is that in many Black communities in America, the police are feared and/or hated; that's something that a lot of white people have a difficult time understanding. Law enforcement in America started out as a way to catch enslaved African descendants and protect property, so those stories, along with the recent unrest, weigh on the minds of a lot of Black folks. And Police Lives Matter and Blue Lives Matter were created in response to Black Lives Matter, which was created after George Zimmerman was acquitted in the shooting death of Trayvon Martin. These folks routinely expose themselves as hypocrites because they often yell, "Stick to sports!" when shouting down social justice in sports. But when a player on their favorite team appears to have similar political leanings as they do, exceptions are made.

There is also a strong connection between first responders (cops, firefighters), conservative politics, and hockey culture. Either they play the sport or their kids do. In Chicago, at the rinks where Evan has played, the Chicago Police have a team; so does their union, the Fraternal Order of Police Lodge 7, which is often outspoken when it comes to activism and progressive politicians.

John Catanzara, Chicago FOP's president, was not only stripped of his police powers, he was recommended to be fired by two different police superintendents. The FOP endorsed President Trump's failed reelection bid.

"During his first four years, President Trump has made it crystal clear that he has our backs," said FOP national president Patrick Yoes in a press release. "Our members know that he listens to the concerns of our brothers and sisters in uniform and is able to make tough decisions on the issues most important to law enforcement. President Trump is committed to keeping our communities and families safe."

In the aftermath of the January 2021 insurrection in Washington, D.C., where Trump supporters—some of them armed—stormed the Capitol, breaking and destroying property while members of Congress were inside the building, Catanzara defended the terrorists: "There was no arson, there was no burning of anything, there was no looting, there was very little destruction of property," he told WBEZ, Chicago's NPR affiliate, in a phone interview. "It was a bunch of pissed-off people that feel an election was stolen, somehow, some way."

White supremacists—who refused to accept an election result—killed a cop. If this were Black Lives Matter or another group, the energy would be different. Blue lives don't matter to the people Catanzara—a police lodge president—temporarily provided a rest haven for.

Catanzara later walked his words back, saying, in part, "I was in no way condoning the violence in D.C. yesterday. My statements were poorly worded. I certainly would never justify any attacks on law enforcement. After seeing more video and the full aftermath, my comments would have been different."

IN A 2019 CHICAGO PROTEST, police union members and white supremacists gathered at the Daley Center to criticize Cook County (Illinois) State's Attorney Kim Foxx—the first Black woman to hold the post—over her handling of actor Jussie Smollett's alleged hate crime. Catanzara was photographed by the *Chicago Tribune* shaking hands with Brien James, co-founder of the Vinlanders Social Club, a known white supremacist group the Anti-Defamation League describes as "a hardcore racist skinhead gang…that has had a high association with violence." The group's members are connected to multiple murders, according to the Anti-Defamation League. As of July 2020, James is affiliated with the American Guard and the Proud Boys of Indiana.

A few days after the 2020 U.S. election, New York Rangers defenseman and Trump supporter Tony DeAngelo continued his quest to let his political beliefs get in the way of reality. The OHL had handed DeAngelo an eight-game suspension in 2014 for violating the league's harassment, abuse, and diversity policy when he directed slurs toward a teammate, and the NHL mandated a three-game suspension without pay after attempting to push away a referee following an on-ice scrum.

DeAngelo tweeted:

> My home state of PA is trying to RIG it. They don't want our president to declare victory tonight. Well Michigan /Arizona/ Wisconsin let's make it happen for him anyway!

And amid Trump supporters storming the U.S. Capitol, DeAngelo announced he left Twitter, which had decided to ban Trump's account for life for inciting violence. DeAngelo said he planned to take his talents to Parler, a conservative-friendly app widely criticized as the place where January's insurrection was planned. (Apple, Google, and Amazon have since pulled support for the app from their platforms.)

Political beliefs—for some—aren't an issue, but what should the NHL do when a player utilizes their platform to full-throatedly endorse a philosophy—supported by white supremacists—that includes making up arbitrary rules about contesting the results of an election in a country where most of the league's franchises operate; calling for the lynching of Vice President Mike Pence; Black journalists and Black police officers being called "niggers" repeatedly; theft and destruction of the Capitol building; multiple arrests; and being responsible for the murder of a Capitol Police officer?

Don't forget how legendary defenseman Bobby Orr took out a full-page ad in the (New Hampshire) *Union Leader* to support President Trump's reelection, writing, in part, "That's the type of teammate I want."

Trump support in athletics isn't exclusive to the NHL—but it's widespread, and it won't go away just because No. 45 has left office. In the last days of the 2020 election, Evan was listening to local Chicago sports talk radio when he heard a political ad in which former Blackhawks and Red Wings defenseman Chris Chelios endorsed Pat O'Brien, the Republican candidate for Cook County State's Attorney, over the incumbent Foxx.

When announcing the endorsement, O'Brien tweeted:

> I am proud to have the endorsement of Chris Chelios, three-time Stanley Cup Champion, Blackhawk great & NHL Hall of Fame. Chris grew up in Chicago, lives in Cook County & sees the destruction that Kim Foxx policies have had.
>
> Chris Chelios standing up for his beliefs and to help the residents of Chicago and Cook County against the Kim Foxx program to put criminals before good people and law-abiding citizens. Are you willing to help?

During the ad, Chelios, a Hall of Fame blueliner, utilized the usual "tough on crime" platitudes, saying, "Our city has many wonderful things to offer, but sadly it has also become known for rampant crime and violence. This election, it's time to make a change. We need a Cook County State's Attorney who will restore safety to our neighborhoods. We have that in Judge Pat O'Brien.... So everyone in Chicago and all of Cook County, let's restore security to our families, friends, neighborhoods, and businesses. Enough is enough. Vote for Pat O'Brien, State's Attorney."

But here's where conservative criminal justice talking points and someone's checkered past are in direct competition with each other, allowing them to catch unintended strays. In 1983, Chelios, a second-round draft pick of the Canadiens, was arrested in connection with a woman's purse being stolen while he was training with Team USA, according to the Associated Press.

Years later, as a member of the Blackhawks, Chelios said this during the 1994 lockout about NHL commissioner Gary Bettman: "If I was Gary Bettman, I'd worry about my family, about my well-being right now. Some crazed fan or even a player—who knows?—might take it into his own hands and figure if they can get him out of the way, this might be settled. You hate to see something like that happen, but he took the job."

And here was the *Chicago Tribune*'s analysis of the blueliner's words: "If the hockey player's words had been uttered about the president of this nation rather than about the commissioner of the NHL, Chelios would face felony charges."

Here was Chelios' non-apology apology: "I was emotional and flew off the handle. I'd just come off the ice after practice. I'd had a bad week, and you keep hearing all week, this guy saying we're not going to play, we're not going to play. I just got mad. In 11 years, I don't think I ever said anything like that."

How about when members of Team USA—captained by Chelios (while he was the Blackhawks' captain) during the 1998 Nagano Winter Olympic Games—caused property damage in the Olympic Village in the aftermath of a disappointing showing?

Or when, in 2010, he was charged with a DUI in a Chicago suburb?

Wild stuff, eh?

In defense of Rask's Boston Police cap, stans said players have a right to their opinions and we live in a "free" country. If a Black hockey player wore a "Fuck 12" cap, the energy would be different—keep it a buck. There would be zero conversations about respecting their politics. And for hockey to do proper engagement with non-traditional hockey communities—Black and Brown communities—its stakeholders have to understand that not everyone in said communities views cops as heroes.

A few years ago, Evan wrote two stories for the *Chicago Reader* in which he interviewed six Black police officers from several municipalities across the Chicago area. When word got out about the background of Kyle Rittenhouse (a police/Blue Lives Matter supporter and wannabe cop who often posted photos of himself with guns), the Kenosha, Wisconsin, shooter who allegedly killed two and wounded one in shootings during street protests in the aftermath of Jacob Blake's shooting, Evan thought of what one of the cops he interviewed told him about the type of people police departments hire these days: "White cops just don't understand what it is to be Black and live under the veil that all people are treated equally when is it is far from true. We hire cops that just don't give a fuck about the communities—they want the action and the thrill of the hunt."

In the aftermath of the Kenosha protests, where Rittenhouse was seen fraternizing with cops before shooting protesters, *New York Times Magazine* reporter Nikole Hannah-Jones tweeted:

> Black man with no weapon walks away from Kenosha police and is shot 7 times in the back. White teen with assault rifle who just shot 3 people and KILLED 2, walks by Kenosha police with his gun & they offer him a water and he gets to go home. No greater summary of America exists.

Here's what former Illinois Republican congressman and Republican presidential candidate Joe Walsh tweeted on the subject:

> Here's the deal: I'm a white guy. I'm pro Cop. But it's up to us white people to take the first step here. It's up to us white people to admit the truth. And the truth is that Cops don't treat black lives the same way they treat white lives.
> Can't fix things until we do that.

NHLers, led by the de facto Edmonton NHL bubble spokesman, Vegas Golden Knights forward Ryan Reaves, decided to sit out the Thursday and Friday games that week in protest of the police shooting of Blake. Steve Grammas, president of the Las Vegas Police

Protective Association police union and Las Vegas cop, wasn't happy with the team.

Here's his statement, in part, on how the Golden Knights ought to be "educated" on the issues at hand: "When our officer was senselessly shot and paralyzed, you signed some sticks and sent them to his family. No boycott, no postponing of games. When hundreds of my officers were hit with rocks, bricks, bottles, edged weapons, and even had guns fired at them, the only concern for VGK was figuring out how to finish the Stanley Cup. Again, no threat of cancelling the remainder of the season unless the violence against officers stopped."

Grammas' statement is a microcosm of why and how many police officers view themselves the way they do, along with many Black people wanting nothing to do with the current iteration of the police.

There are layers, as they say.

ESPN senior writer and author Howard Bryant believes there is a connection between conservative politics, hockey culture, and staunch support for first responders.

"Let's not forget, the legacy is September 11; it's everywhere," Bryant said. "It's in every sport, so therefore in hockey, obviously, it's much, much easier. Much easier to adopt that first responders thing because there are no Black people there. If you look at the numbers—Gallup numbers—and look at all the polling numbers, one of the greatest gaps in this country attitudinally is the Black/white split between how they view the police. 9/11-type tributes land very differently at TD Garden [during Bruins games] than they would at TD Garden for a basketball game, especially now post-[Colin] Kaepernick and post-Ferguson [Missouri] and all of that."

A September 2020 study by Morning Consult titled "Demographic Data Shows Which Major Sports Fan Bases Are Most Likely to Support or Reject Social Justice Advocacy" backs up Bryant's hypothesis regarding conservative politics and hockey fandom.

The study says NHL fandom on average is "whiter and more Republican" than that of the other three major North American sports leagues (MLB, the NFL, and the NBA).

According to the study, "Three NHL teams have a larger share of Republican fans than Democratic fans—the Nashville Predators, Vegas Golden Knights, and Dallas Stars—while another five teams' fans are evenly split between the two parties. Fans of the Los Angeles Kings, New York Rangers, Florida Panthers, San Jose Sharks, and New York Islanders are the most likely in the NHL to identify as Democrats. The Los Angeles Kings have the largest percentage of nonwhite fans by a significant margin, followed by the Florida Panthers, Arizona Coyotes, Dallas Stars, and Washington Capitals."

Bryant, a native Bostonian, participated in the Sharks season ticket package while he worked in the Bay Area as a reporter in Oakland.

"It was actually really enjoyable to be a hockey fan out there because you didn't have all those East Coast borders," Bryant said. "And there's all kinds of different people at the games...Latinos and whites, and you can see Black people at the games. Because it was just a sport; the sport was so much more accessible in California, and more hostile on the East Coast. And it makes sense because it was a new sport. It was a new sport out there, but the Sharks were an expansion team and they pretty much belong to everybody.

"And that may be changing a bit more now, obviously, because I'm talking 20, 25, 30 years ago. And so now you start to have more than a handful of players, guys like Mike Grier who were Black American players playing in the early '90s. And, obviously, Anson Carter was Canadian, but you started to see the numbers go up. But I'm not sure that was necessarily accessible or translatable to Black fans feeling more welcome. Certainly more accessible for the players, but not as accessible for the fans.

"I think that just adds to the idea of the hostile territory, right?" Bryant continued. "When you go in, and you go talk to [Boston Bruins winger] Brad Marchand or you're watching TV and he's got a Blue Lives Matter hat on, how does that make you feel about watching Brad Marchand, especially with all this going on? Are we 'Skating for Black Lives?' Are we? And you've got a dissenting voice now in terms of a lot of the players talking about how the game is becoming more multicultural, and I think that's really a fascinating new space. And [former NHL winger and inaugural executive board member of the Hockey Diversity Alliance] Joel Ward isn't by himself—there are more of them. I always thought that the whole Blue Lives Matter thing and the weird thing with P.K. Subban when he went to Nashville, his Blueline Buddies [program to bring together youth and law enforcement]; it was incredibly tone-deaf. But once again, you have to look at the environment he's in."

No matter what Subban has done during his career, hockey culture seems to find ways to pick at him. Not all of the vitriol toward Subban is all about race, but cultural and generational differences also play into how he's viewed.

He's not a part of the club—but he seems to align himself with these folks.

"And that's what happens when you spend all your life trying to accommodate people," Bryant said. "What are you supposed to do in that world? I mean, you're constantly 'othered' and, on top of that, he's a big personality in a place that doesn't like big personalities. And then [he got] drafted by the Montreal Canadiens.... I remember I was in Montreal last year [2019], and I was talking to a cab driver and immediately the conversation came up about P.K.," Bryant said. "The conversation went to how he was just always bigger than the team, and the fans loved it, but the team didn't love it. And culture changes you before you change the culture."

The Montreal Canadiens, the hockey club with the most iconic brand in the sport with 24 Stanley Cups and 67 hall of famers—players and builders—appeared to say no to Subban, who won a Norris Trophy as a member of the team.

"Talk about a huge opportunity to be the front line when you're the most famous team in the sport. You've got an opportunity and they just didn't take that opportunity. And obviously, they [Canadiens] weren't quite sure he was as good a player as they thought he needed to be as well...to trade him for [Nashville Predators defenseman Shea] Weber was a complete example of smothering a personality," Bryant said. "Whatever deficiencies he did have in his game, the bottom line was...they had trouble dealing with his personality. If P.K. had a different personality, maybe he's still in Montreal."

During Subban's time in Montreal, he dealt with constant questioning by Canadiens coaching and team legends, fans showing up to games in blackface while wearing his jersey (this happened while he was on the Olympic team, too), and racism from Boston sports fans (stop us if you've heard that one before.)

Hockey culture mantra is all about the team and never showing individuality.

Subban's coach, Michel Therrien, broke one of hockey's unwritten rules to call his player out after a 3–2 loss to the Colorado Avalanche during the 2016 season after Subban fell at the blue line, allowing the Avalanche to score the game-winning goal. If one were to look at the play, as the Avalanche headed back up the ice on an odd-man rush, it didn't necessarily mean a goal was guaranteed.

Therrien said this after the game: "It's too bad that an individual mistake cost us the game, late in the game. As a coach, I thought he could've had a better decision at the blue line. He moved the puck behind and he put himself in a tough position. Unfortunately, at the end of the game, when we don't play as a team, we could be in trouble, and this is what happened."

Team captain Max Pacioretty chose not to speak to the media after the game. Even if Pacioretty's decision could've been due to another reason, the captain is the official spokesperson for a hockey club.

In 2014, when Subban scored the game-winning goal for the Canadiens in a game against the archrival Boston Bruins, some Bruins fans were so enraged at Subban for scoring a game-winning goal that the word "nigger" was trending on Twitter. This incident took place while Black players Jarome Iginla and P.K.'s brother, Malcolm Subban, were members of the organization.

The CBC reported fans were tweeting things like: "That stupid nigger doesn't belong in hockey #whitesonly."

The CBC also reported Influence Communications, a Montreal media monitoring and analysis company, said the word "nigger" and Subban's name were used in conjunction on 17,000 tweets after the game.

When Rask wore his Boston Police cap, here were some of the things Bruins fans tweeted:

> Showing solidarity for BLM was spot on. Does that mean we want ALL police to be hated and feared? The people of the Boston Marathon bombing are grateful for the city's officers. To say one hat on one player shows "hockey culture" is just ignorant. Stop creating divide.

> let rask have his opinion. i think he has his right to support the police and the org has the right to support the other side.

Good glad to hear someone supports the police over the Marxist BLM movement who constantly riots and causes damage and is trying to abolish the safety to society.

Arguments like this are why the far left (yes, the far left) will give Trump a chance at re-election. Black Lives Matter, and police brutality needs to be curbed and policing needs to be reformed. All true. But to say you can't also support good people at BPD is absurd.

He likes to support all those brave men and woman, who sacrifices their health and life because of your safety and wellbeing. Only thing it shows about hockey culture is, that hockey players are above others.

Here comes cancel culture for Tuukka Rask because he is an adult who can make his own choices but because people dont [sic] like it he is such a bad person.

If another 9/11 situation happens on American soil, I hope the #police and all emergency responders just let everything and everyone burn. Why should they do a damn thing for an ungrateful, hateful society? #BacktheBlue.

And our favorite:

I'm old enough to remember when people would use sports to escape politics.

A few weeks after wearing the hat, Rask left the NHL's Toronto bubble to spend time with his family.

"I want to be with my teammates competing, but at this moment there are things more important than hockey in my life, and that is being with my family," said Rask in a statement released by the Bruins. "I want to thank the Bruins and my teammates for their support and wish them success."

Some of the same fans who championed Rask's opinions then questioned his commitment to the team.

Here's what then NHL analyst Mike Milbury said about how Bruins fans viewed Rask's sudden decision to leave the team to be with his family: "This puts Tuukka Rask in a unique, if unusual, position. Others have opted not to enter the bubble; some mostly with health reasons, but others have left the bubble for childbirth or for health reasons or various reasons, but nobody has simply opted to just leave the bubble because they didn't want to be here and they needed to be with their family—I would not have done it. The rest of the league's [NHL] players have not done it. I think this will be...in a city that hasn't really embraced Tuukka Rask despite his success—a city that I grew up in, I played and coached there for 20 years and live there now, this is going to be a difficult decision to swallow for Boston Bruins fans."

Here's what Bruins general manager Don Sweeney said about Rask leaving the team: "In Tuukka's case, he has a newborn at home with two other young girls and he just felt that he needs to be home with them at this particular time.... Give Tuukka a hell of a lot of credit for trying to persevere through this and intiaite the process to come up and be with his teammates because, first and foremost, that's what he wants to do, but the priorities are in the right order and this is what he has to do at this time."

It's fair to say Milbury spoke for a lot of fans in Boston, and Rask isn't a bad guy for prioritizing his family over hockey—both statements can be true.

And after the Bruins were eliminated from the 2020 Stanley Cup playoffs, some Bruins continued to blame Rask for leaving the team when it needed him most.

Normally, when someone has to leave their job due to family issues, no one questions the importance of family. Rask's responsibility as a father and a husband trumps his "responsibility" to the Bruins—everyone should honor that.

Boston radio host Marc James appeared to believe Rask should not honor his responsibilities to his wife and children when he tweeted:

> Dear Tuukka:
> As a lifelong Bruins fan, I'm disgusted by your cowardly decision to give up.
> You QUIT on:
> •Boston
> •Your Coaches
> •All of Your Teammates
> •Yourself
> •Every Bruins fan
>   I hope that I NEVER have to see U in a Black & Gold Sweater with the spoked "B" Again!

And, in a surprise to no one, former NHLer Brandon Prust—who had a racist meltdown on Twitter in spring 2020—also joined in on Tuukka Rask slander season, tweeting:

> Ya he's a pussy. Don't ask for 8 million if u want to go home to cuddle.

2

The Structure of Hockey

ONE OF THE FACTORS—POSSIBLY THE MAIN FACTOR—THAT MAKES hockey so complex is its structure. Hockey is vastly unlike any other sport, and its organization is key to understanding how the system upholds and incubates toxicity as well as presents challenges for improvement. The three main bodies we address in this book are the NHL, USA Hockey, and Hockey Canada. But there are many more bodies involved.

Even without going into youth hockey, there are multiple pathways to the NHL. It isn't as simple as in, say, the NFL, where players play college football and then turn professional. There are multiple ways to make it to the NHL. The most popular routes are NCAA college hockey or major junior leagues—the 60 teams in the Ontario Hockey League (OHL), Quebec Major Junior Hockey League (QMJHL), and Western Hockey League (WHL) that make up the Canadian Hockey League (CHL).

The NCAA considers major juniors, where players receive a stipend, professional leagues. This renders those players ineligible for NCAA play, effectively pitting the two routes against each other. But aside from those two pathways, players also come from Russia, the Czech Republic, Finland, and Sweden—playing in one of their native leagues before jumping to the NHL. (American superstar Auston Matthews elected to spend his draft year in Switzerland, an unprecedented move for a high-end, North American prospect). Then there are also the minor leagues in North America, primarily the American Hockey League (AHL) and East Coast Hockey League (ECHL).

In both Canada and the U.S., hockey organization is complex due to the multiple leagues, levels, and teams that exist, not always in a clear hierarchy. After youth hockey (where, in the U.S., classifications once included peewee, bantam, midget, etc., but are now referred to much more logically by age categories), players have the option to continue playing through high school hockey, prep hockey, junior hockey (which offers players in Canada and the U.S. aged 16–20 space to develop their game without losing NCAA eligibility), or to play in the major juniors. In Canada, there is the youth level and then there are hockey academies, roughly the equivalent of prep schools in the U.S.

Now, not all leagues, amateur or not, are affiliated with either Hockey Canada or USA Hockey—the governing bodies for organized hockey in North America and members of the International Ice Hockey Federation (IIHF)—which is where things get very complicated.

Two of the main non-professional paths to the NHL are major juniors and NCAA hockey. While traditionally college hockey can be viewed as an American pathway and major juniors are considered Canadian, players from both countries can take either path. Historically, major juniors have been the primary NHL feeder, but college hockey is increasing the percentage of players it sends to the NHL.

The leagues are similar and also drastically different. Major junior teams, consisting of the OHL, QMJHL, and WHL, span three areas of Canada, while college hockey is mostly based in the Midwest and East Coast. Major junior players can join as young as 14 (in the WHL with exceptional player status), while in college hockey, players can't be recruited until January 1 of their sophomore year of high school (around 15–16 years of age). Verbal commitments are non-binding and there is no contractual commitment until students sign a National Letter of Intent. (Certain programs, like Ivy League schools, do not have NLIs).

Players who go the college hockey route tend to spend a few years in either USA juniors—the Tier I United States Hockey League (USHL) or Tier II North American Hockey League (NAHL)—or Canada's Junior A Canadian Junior Hockey League (CJHL). College Hockey Inc., the promotional arm of NCAA Division I men's hockey, reported that in 2019–20, the youngest college hockey team by average age was Minnesota at 20 years and 240 days old, and the oldest was American International College (AIC) at 22 years and 294 days. Comparatively, the maximum age for major juniors is 20 (players can turn 21 once the season has started).

Thus, for two completely different reasons, both major juniors and college hockey result in players being sequestered away from the rest of the population. This structure of hockey is crucial in understanding why the culture has been so resistant to change. (See photo insert for a graphic detailing the various structures of hockey leagues.)

Hockey Canada

Hockey Canada is the national governing body for hockey in Canada, including ice hockey and ice sledge hockey. Olympic and Paralympic ice hockey fall under its umbrella. The organization is composed of 13 members, representing provincial, regional, or territorial associations/federations that in turn regulate amateur ice hockey in their geographic regions. Each member is supposed to follow Hockey Canada's bylaws, regulations, and playing rules.

As a professional organization, the Canadian Hockey League (CHL)—which, as you'll recall, houses the three major junior leagues: Western Hockey League (WHL), Ontario Hockey League (OHL), and Quebec Major Junior Hockey League (QMJHL)—does not fall under the Hockey Canada umbrella. The Canadian Junior Hockey League (CJHL), which maintains a player's amateur status, also does not fall under this umbrella. Both are partners of Hockey Canada. However, it's slightly more complicated than that, because while those leagues don't fall under Hockey Canada, there are teams within the leagues that fall under province governing bodies, which fall under Hockey Canada. This is important because these leagues house a good number of players who are subject to rules made outside of Hockey Canada.

Other Hockey Canada partners include Aboriginal Sport Circle, Canadian Amputee Hockey Committee, Canadian Armed Forces, Canadian Ball Hockey Association, Canadian Deaf Ice Hockey Federation, Hockey Canada Foundation, the NHL, NHLPA, Roller Hockey Canada, and U Sports (the national governing body of university sports in Canada).

What control Hockey Canada does possess is diluted by passing off power to the provinces and territories. Take BC Hockey, for example. It is a member of Hockey Canada, but delegates to its member leagues, like the British Columbia Hockey League (BCHL), which is a member of the CJHL. (In April 2021, the BCHL announced its intention to leave the CJHL.) Then there's the Ontario Hockey Federation (OHF), a member of Hockey Canada and home to the Greater Toronto Hockey League (GTHL), one of the largest minor hockey associations in the world. The bylaws, however, grant the OHF jurisdiction everywhere except for Hockey Eastern Ontario and Hockey Northwestern Ontario. But the bylaws grant the OHF jurisdiction over major juniors (the OHL is in the OHF), as granted by Hockey Canada.

So, the CHL is an affiliate, not a member, of Hockey Canada. But the OHL, which falls under the CHL, is a member of the OHF, which is a member of Hockey Canada. So by the transitive property, the OHL is a member of Hockey Canada, even though its parent organization, the CHL, is not.

This makes it really hard to find out exactly which policies each organization has and who's ultimately responsible for carrying out said policies.

"This is how sports has been designed," said Courtney Szto, an assistant professor at Queen's University whose doctoral research focuses on South Asian experiences within hockey in Canada. "It's extremely fragmented on purpose to some extent because you can always pass the buck. It exists in tennis. I know it exists in all other sports as well. Any complaint that is lodged within any organization, nobody else has to take responsibility for them and they can say, 'Well, you know, the officials belong to this organization or that. We don't really oversee them.' It's the perfect system for these [problems] to manifest because no one is willing to take accountability for everybody.... I get that certain provinces and states should have a level of autonomy, but when we're talking about conduct, that should be very clear and it makes sense for everybody to have the same blueprint and accountability. I think they're just really trying to avoid lawsuits and things like that that they wouldn't want to pay for."

USA Hockey

USA Hockey's 2020–21 membership guide states that it is the official representative for the United States Olympic & Paralympic Committee (USOPC) and the IIHF. USA Hockey oversees youth, junior, and adult hockey programs and works closely with the NHL and college hockey on "matters of mutual interest."

The organization is made up of 12 geographical districts throughout the U.S., which are made up of 34 affiliates combined that "provide the formal governance for the sport."

The districts vary between broad areas, like the Atlantic District, and states, like the Minnesota District. The affiliates are hockey associations within those districts, like Minnesota Hockey. The bylaws state:

> Except for Junior teams, and subject to the terms of its Affiliate Agreement, these Bylaws and the rules and regulations of USA Hockey, each Affiliate Association shall have the sole and exclusive power to determine the participation of its member teams, or other teams falling within its jurisdiction, in USA Hockey's district playoffs and national championships.

So, USA Hockey lays down the law and the associations that run youth hockey are supposed to follow them.

Junior hockey teams are certified annually by the Junior Council into Tier I, Tier II, and Tier III.

Now, the NCAA operates by a completely different set of rules, very much its own and very much not beholden to any other organization. And college hockey has its own set of rules—so this is an area in which USA Hockey does not have jurisdiction. However, college hockey players still interact with and influence members of the hockey community, including those that fall under USA Hockey's youth organizations.

Take both Massachusetts and Minnesota, two hockey hotbeds with thriving high school hockey systems. USA Hockey handles youth hockey, but it doesn't handle all high school athletics, which fall under the state high school athletics umbrella. And that's a separate entity itself from the prep schools, which compete under different banners.

Minnesota Hockey's bylaws state that it will "remain a separate entity with complete authority to conduct its affairs and programs, subject only to the express obligations and restrictions contained in this By-law and in its affiliate agreement with USAH."

For high school hockey it is similar, as some programs are run through the state, while others are overseen by USA Hockey. Avery Cordingley, a member of the Madison Gay Hockey Association, referees high school hockey games in Wisconsin, which fall under the Wisconsin Amateur Hockey Association. However, Cordingley played high school hockey in West Virginia under the USA Hockey umbrella.

Now, in the U.S., college club hockey falls under USA Hockey. Youth and adult hockey in each state fall under that state's jurisdiction. But high school hockey has its own organization— operating under that state's leagues and prep school hockey leagues, like the NEPSAC in New England and the Upper Midwest HS Elite League.

The lesson is that hockey's structure in North America is confusing, at best, and that leaves areas with foggy jurisdiction and a question mark regarding who is responsible for creating and enforcing the policies designed to combat bigotry and make hockey safe and inclusive.

3

Racism

A child that is not embraced by the village will burn it down to feel its warmth.

—African Proverb

WHAT FOLLOWS IS THE ONLY MENTION OF HATE SPEECH in USA Hockey's rulebook for junior hockey and, as you can see, words like *racism* are not used. The language is instead very vague:

> A game ejection/game misconduct penalty shall be assessed to any player or team official who is guilty of the following actions: Uses language that is offensive, hateful, or discriminatory in nature anywhere in the rink before, during, or after the game.

Racism also isn't mentioned under the summary of fines, which only includes financial penalties for players or team officials assessed a game misconduct, gross misconduct I, or gross misconduct II penalty.

The problem with not being white in hockey is that you can never tell when people who are friendly to you actually think you're subhuman. Those in hockey's power structures expect you to hide pieces of yourself—your race and ethnicity—as much as you possibly can until you're "white" like they are. But you can't change the color of your skin, so you'll never be truly white. You can't escape all of the coded language thrown your way, words laced with racism. You'll never belong. The burden will always be on you to prove you're "not like other" people of your race. You're one of the boys. You're quiet, not loud and outspoken. You're not flashy.

And people can be nice to you. They will be, all the while harboring thoughts about how you aren't good enough. You rock the boat too much. You aren't cerebral enough. You never know who they truly are—and perhaps that's the most dangerous part, until you hear them "accidentally" say a racial slur or tell you people should only speak English in this country. But even if you are an acceptable, white-on-the-inside person, there's no escaping racism in hockey and what it does to you as a person and as a player.

In 2019, former NHLer Akim Aliu revealed he was the victim of abuse and racial slurs from a former coach while playing with the Blackhawks' AHL affiliate. Aliu made the incidents public 10 years later, resulting in that coach—Bill Peters—resigning from his job with the Calgary Flames. Aliu talked a lot about feeling isolated and how no one would believe him. Even after it became public, Peters apologized to everyone except the person he hurt the most: Akim Aliu.

Hockey culture and media told us Peters' hate speech was a one-off incident. But at the rink, in the locker room, in the stands, in the press box, and on the message boards, people like Peters found a haven for their bullying and racism.

Racism is learned. Peters went around for a whole 10 years thinking what he said to Aliu was okay. When Evan wrote his "Icing

Racism" story for the *Chicago Reader*, players shared stories of immediately reporting what a coach, fans, players, and their own teammates said to them and how they got blamed instead.

Josh Brown, a biracial man, played Division III college hockey at Indiana Tech. He has had his share of racial incidents on the ice. In one instance with his AA travel team, he received a two-game suspension, while the other player received merely a game misconduct.

"And it was even on my home ice. Weird how that works, right? And still to this day, I'm more than confused," Brown said. "I was told by my coaches, who were all white, 'Come tell me when it happens, don't hurt the team and do something stupid.' As for my 'White American' grandfather who supported me my whole competitive hockey career, he wouldn't hear anything until after the game, but his reactions would be [worse than] mine; he would make sure to let anyone know racism shouldn't be a thing these days."

Chicago hockey parent Tony Rodriguez says his son, Frank, now a college student, played in juniors and through high school at Chicago's Lane Tech College Prep High School.

"As a peewee, his team played a game in Dyer, Indiana, where the racial trash-talking was rampant on the ice. His team boasted three players sporting Hispanic nameplates," Rodriguez said. "His team was not known for being hitters, they were just talented players who scored more than they hit; they also won a lot. But in the second period, our center, a Hispanic kid, was crushed by a pair of large opposition players. The rest of the team just snapped and lit the Indiana team up for the rest of the game. After the game, the Indiana parents howled at what thugs our kids were, but when given a chance to discuss it outside with a few of our parents, they all suddenly became pillars of peace and non-violence.

"I think those kids learned a lesson in teamwork and not standing by when someone is singled out by racism. In this very white sport of hockey, it's gonna be the nature of this wonderful game itself that makes it more diverse. Hockey is a game of shifts. My dad worked in shifts as a machinist in a factory. Hockey is a game you can't play better by simply spending more money. Hockey is a game of accountability. A game where an assist is honorable. A game we all have the right to play."

Historically, Aliu is right in believing white people wouldn't be sympathetic to his plight. Think of 2009–10, when Peters uttered his slurs to Aliu. The Blackhawks were up-and-coming. Before the season—the team was a Stanley Cup favorite—winger Patrick Kane was accused of punching a cab driver. Later that season, the Blackhawks won their first Stanley Cup since 1961. Before that, the hockey world was focused on the 2010 Vancouver Olympic Games. Also, think about the demographics of hockey culture and its gatekeepers. Do you think there was a space created for Aliu to come forward with what he alleged?

Racism, real or perceived, doesn't have a time stamp. Let's be honest. Aliu is a Black man who would've gone to white people to say Peters, a man who was influential in his career, repeatedly used the n-word toward him. Also, Aliu stood up to it and believes he was demoted to the ECHL for doing so.

As for the people who like to say "Why now?" and "He's washed up," think about this: Aliu was a second-round draft pick, which means the Blackhawks once thought he was pretty good. Here's a selected list of former second-round draft picks: P.K. Subban, Duncan Keith, Chris Chelios, and Patrice Bergeron.

Later that year, Peters was hired by a KHL team; it's tough to say if he unlearned racism in the time since the Flames allowed him to resign.

In hockey culture, it's widely known that chanting "basketball" at a Black player is a racist slur. During a 2018 game between the Blackhawks and Washington Capitals, as Caps winger Devante

Smith-Pelly sat in the penalty box, a group of fans began to chant "basketball" in his direction. One of the first comments Evan saw on social media in the game's aftermath was from someone who tweeted: "Toughen up."

Let's unpack that comment. This fool said let's not condemn racism, but Smith-Pelly somehow ought to be expecting slurs to happen. In what situation should anyone expect to be ridiculed for who they are?

"It's pretty obvious what that means," Smith-Pelly told reporters after the game. "It's not a secret."

After the game, Evan tweeted:

> Over the past several years, I've written A LOT about diversity and hockey. Tonight, some kid who wants to play hockey was sitting at home watching tonight's Blackhawks/Capitals game, saw that incident and said "Naw, I'm good."

Remember, this happened during the NHL's "Hockey Is for Everyone" campaign, which also takes place during Black History Month. It appears those fans wanted to let Smith-Pelly know that hockey isn't for him. At that moment, those fans believed they were the gatekeepers of hockey we discussed earlier in the book. When someone holds such views publicly, they aren't the only ones who think that way; they have a group of people they bounce ideas off of. Pull up the video of the incident. Every Black person who has faced racism directly felt that moment.

"This has happened [to me] in hockey before," Smith-Pelly also said to reporters. "It's disgusting, that in 2018 we're still talking about the same thing, over and over. It's sad that athletes like myself, 30, 40 years ago were standing in the same place.

"You think there'd be some sort of change or progression."

LATER THAT SEASON, when Smith-Pelly was skating around the ice with the Stanley Cup raised above his shoulder after the Capitals won it all, Evan thought three things: *Is Smith-Pelly thinking about filling the Cup with the white tears of those racists? Is this one of the most unlikely Blackest moments of all time? He might have activated the kids who were on the verge of quitting the game due to racism.*

A month after his "Icing Racism" piece was published, Evan quote-tweeted:

> Since I wrote this, a 12 y/o goalie was the victim of racial slurs and a Red Wings prospect needed a police escort due to the slurs and death threats he's received. The main point of my "Icing Racism" piece is to show racism in hockey isn't a one off.

Gloria Wong-Padoongpatt is an assistant professor who teaches psychology at the University of Nevada-Las Vegas (UNLV). She is also an Asian woman, a mother, a hockey player (ice and roller), and a coach. Her research at UNLV focuses on the mental health of marginalized individuals—especially microaggressions. Wong-Padoongpatt, who started out as a figure skater, says her first experience with racism took place in her first roller hockey practice as a nine-year-old. She describes hockey culture as "toxic."

"It goes back and forth, but most days I'm kind of upset with the hockey culture. And, disappointed," Wong-Padoongpatt said. "I think those are the overwhelming feelings of hockey, and I get really frustrated with it. I'm a pretty good player in some of the co-ed spaces and it's just been...like I have a battle, kind of all my life. I've kind of just let it roll off me, with all the names thrown at me."

Over time, she's noticed how kids from non-traditional hockey communities are rapidly made to feel like they've done something wrong.

"I feel like, because I do this for a living, I am very racially conscious. I study microaggressions, I study systemic racism. I study white supremacy," Wong-Padoongpatt said. "So, intellectually, I know exactly what is happening in the sport. I can see it. I started a few girls' programs and it was never...my goal, it was just, I'm a woman playing hockey and then there's a lot of girls wanting to play all of a sudden."

As a coach, she sees her goal as creating community for the girls, protecting them, and educating them.

"I'm a psychologist by training," she said. "I'm really interested in self-esteem and self-concept and mainly how we can protect our self-concept from things like racism, like sexism. And one of the first steps and one of the most empowering things is to be able to label it, like white supremacy or a white space."

Wong-Padoongpatt knows from personal experience how marginalized hockey can make young girls and women feel. Helping them create that consciousness around the sport allows them to externalize what's happening to them.

"So, for instance, if I don't have these tools, and I'm a nine-year-old girl going into hockey and everyone's saying, 'Why are you here? You hit like a girl.' You hear all these things about their girl identity and with a girl not being able to process that there's patriarchy, there's sexism, they start to internalize that. They can't externalize it and put the blame on someone else or the system. What we default to is blaming ourselves and internalizing that hate. So as a psychologist working with racial consciousness for marginalized people, it's creating that consciousness first and then being able to, in that process, protect your own sense of worth."

How can the NHL start the conversation? It needs to say out loud what's happening—and mention its past in full detail. After all, when Major League Baseball celebrated the 100th anniversary of the

Negro Leagues, very few media outlets publicly discussed why the Negro Leagues were created in the first place.

"For starters, one has to be mindful of the fact that from the inception of the NHL in 1917, the 'hockey establishment' has been and continues to be made up of whites who, a, are team owners, hockey executives, and general managers, and b, hold racialized views and beliefs about Blacks that influenced how [Black players] were subsequently treated in the league," said Bob Dawson, a Canadian Black hockey player who played on an all-Black line (Dawson, Percy Paris, Darrell Maxwell) in 1970 at Saint Mary's University in Halifax, Nova Scotia.

"For members of the 'hockey establishment' to discuss the treatment of former Black hockey players, especially now with various initiatives to bring more Blacks into hockey, would cause them undue stress and publicity that would further sully the NHL's image as a league and sports institution," Dawson continued. "This could, among other things, have a negative impact on the NHL's efforts to grow the fan base among Blacks, particularly in the U.S., which in turn could potentially affect the league's bottom line."

Dawson, who often writes about hockey and its issues with diversity, says the NHL needs to reckon with its place in keeping the sport white. According to Dawson's research for an article with the Society of North American Sports Historians and Researchers (SONAHR), the NHL practiced an "unofficial policy of exclusion" of Black players from 1961 to 1974 in a similar fashion to what the NFL did from 1933 to 1945.

"As we know, Willie O'Ree was the first Black to play in the NHL in 1958. Between 1961—O'Ree's last year in the league with Boston—and 1974, there were no Blacks in the league, despite the fact that there were highly talented Blacks in the minor-professional leagues in Canada and the United States," Dawson said. "Players like Clobie Collins, Frank 'Danky' Dorrington, Stan 'Chook' Maxwell,

John Mentis, and Alton White, to mention a few, were passed over while white players with lesser talent went on to play in the NHL. It would appear that there was an 'unofficial policy of exclusion' against Blacks. Since the reintegration of Blacks into the league in 1974 with Mike Marson joining the Washington Capitals, they had to and still do today wage a personal battle for acceptance and respect. Some eventually received it while others never have."

During the alleged "exclusion" in 1967, the NHL expanded to 12 teams, adding the Los Angeles Kings, Minnesota North Stars, Oakland Seals, Philadelphia Flyers, Pittsburgh Penguins, and St. Louis Blues. In 1970, the NHL added the Buffalo Sabres and the Vancouver Canucks. Two seasons later, in 1972, the New York Islanders and the Atlanta Flames joined the league. More teams ought to mean more roster spots, right?

But wait, there's more.

In 1974, the Washington Capitals and the Kansas City Scouts joined the fold, with Marson, a Black man, suiting up for the Capitals. Keeping score at home, the NHL added *12* more teams before another Black player was signed. Here's what Dawson wrote about the NHL not having a Black player on any of its teams' rosters for 13 years:

> Contrary to the prevailing views, this writer is of the opinion that "racism" was the key factor in keeping the NHL an "all-white" league between 1961 and 1974. It's important to note that there were, in fact, a number of highly talented Black players, during that period, showcasing their skills in semi and minor-professional hockey leagues in both Canada and the United States (U.S.). They were grinders, smooth skating-playmakers, and goal-scorers, who dispelled the racist myths or beliefs about Blacks having ankles too weak to skate effectively and that they lacked both the intelligence and skills to play the game. Yet, they were systematically denied

the opportunity to play in the so-called "open and racist-free" NHL, while less gifted and talented white players moved on to play in hockey's premier league.

Scouting

A scene from the 1995 film *Canadian Bacon*:

> **Roy Boy:** How come you never see any Black guys playing hockey?
>
> **Kabral:** Now, do you think it's easy to just gradually take over every professional sport? Let me tell you something, man; Brothers have started figuring out this ice thing. Hope you enjoyed it!

Brothers—and sisters and non-binary folks—have figured it out, as Kabral predicted. But hockey's gatekeepers low-key balked at that notion.

In 1950, *Ebony*, a Black American lifestyle magazine, published an article detailing the possibility of Black hockey players making the NHL titled "Can Negroes Crack Big League Hockey?" Clarence Campbell, who was the league president from 1946 to 1977, told *Ebony*, "The National Hockey League only has one policy: to get the best hockey players. There is no tacit or otherwise, which would restrict anyone because of color or race."

The NHL's Western Conference Championship trophy [*don't touch it!*] is named after Campbell. He told *Ebony* there is "no Jim Crow in Canada," and went on to say racism doesn't exist in the country.

"Hockey is essentially a Canadian sport, and color discrimination is as foreign to us as and to the game itself.... There are Negro amateur hockey players of talent in Canada," Campbell told *Ebony*. "And they will be given an equal chance to compete for a job in professional hockey. Their color will be counted when the test is made. The only question that will be asked is: Can they play hockey well? Negro players are being scouted along with the others, and their opportunities will be no less. What will be stressed is their playing ability, not their color."

Six years before *Canadian Bacon* hit theaters, bestselling author Jeff Pearlman was a high school journalist when he interviewed Joe Bucchino, then assistant general manager of the New York Rangers. Pearlman asked Bucchino why there were so few Black players in the NHL. Bucchino began to answer Pearlman's question by saying the quiet part out loud, disregarding racism—stop us if you've heard that before—in hockey: "Hockey is not a big Black sport. With only four Black players in the league, it's shown that Blacks don't have strong enough legs. While they tend to be in physically better shape than whites, Blacks don't tend to play hockey."

Remember, Pearlman was a 17-year-old kid at the time, and the story went nowhere—in 1989. As Pearlman remembers it, Bucchino had no idea what he said could be viewed as racist.

"I was 17 or 18—so long ago. [Bucchino] was a very loud, jovial guy," Pearlman said. "He stated it as matter-of-fact."

Two years earlier, in 1987, Los Angeles Dodgers executive Al Campanis also said the quiet part out loud in an appearance on ABC's *Nightline* during a segment ahead of the 40th anniversary of Jackie Robinson's Major League Baseball debut. Ted Koppel asked, much like Pearlman did, why so few Black people were managers and executives in baseball.

Here's their exchange, which played out in front of millions, in its entirety:

> **Ted Koppel:** Why is it that there are no Black managers, no Black general managers, no Black owners?
>
> **Al Campanis:** Well…there have been some Black managers, but I really can't answer that question directly.

The only thing I can say is that you have to pay your dues. When you become a manager generally, you have to go to the minor leagues. There's not very much pay involved, and some of the better-known Black players have been able to get into other fields and make a pretty good living in that way.

TK: You know in your heart of hearts—and we're gonna take a break for a commercial—you know that that's a lot of baloney. I mean, there are a lot of Black players or a lot of great, Black baseball men who would dearly love to be in managerial positions.

[Campanis starts laughing]

TK: And I guess what I'm really asking you is to, you know, peel it away a little bit; just tell me, why do you think it is there still that much prejudice in baseball today?

AC: No, I don't believe it's prejudice; I truly believe that they may not have some of the necessities, to [be], let's say, a field manager or perhaps a general manager.

TK: You really believe that?

AC: Well, I don't say all of them. There's certainly a shortage. How many quarterbacks? How many pitchers do you have that are Black?

TK: I gotta tell you, that sounds like the same kind of garbage we were hearing 40 years ago about players when they were saying…you remember the days when they said 'Hit a Black football player in the knees,' and you know, that really sounds like garbage.

AC: It's not garbage, Mr. Koppel, because I played on a college team and the centerfielder was Black, and the backfield at NYU, with a fullback who was Black, never knew the difference of whether he was Black or white; we were teammates. So, it just might be that.... Why are Black people not good swimmers? Because they don't have the buoyancy."

TK: Or maybe they don't have access to all the country clubs or pools?

What Campanis said blew up, and he was basically finished in Major League Baseball. Since hockey is viewed in America as a lower-tier sport, however, bad behavior is often covered up. Campanis made those statements during the same year Dave Stewart, a Black pitcher, won 20 games for the Oakland A's. This is a hockey book; it seems like hockey and baseball could be interchangeable when considering Campanis' statement. It's a lot to unpack (Robinson and Campanis were roommates as Dodgers teammates at one point and Robinson was highly outspoken about the lack of Black MLB managers), but the main focus ought to be whether Campanis and Bucchino are the only ones who think that way about Black folks and other people from marginalized communities.

History says there's more like them—men who made racist decisions as team executives. If you follow sports and the intersectional racial/generational/cultural issues within, you've heard this before when it comes to Black quarterbacks. In hockey, some believe players, particularly Black ones, are forced to play defense or forward instead of center due to the amount of on-the-fly decision-making needed in the midst of game action.

Hockey scouts call it a lack of "hockey sense." Sound familiar?

We had this discussion not too long ago about Baltimore Ravens quarterback Lamar Jackson, when Hall of Fame general manager Bill Polian suggested the Heisman Trophy winner would be better off playing wide receiver.

Casual racism can influence how Black players are written about in scouting reports, further damaging their career before they get started. Ahead of the 2011 NFL Draft, Pro Football Weekly's Nolan

Nawrocki issued a sharp critique of Cam Newton, the quarterback many analysts viewed as the No. 1 pick, in a scouting report:

> Very disingenuous—has a fake smile, comes off as very scripted and has a selfish, me-first makeup. Always knows where the cameras are and plays to them. Has an enormous ego with a sense of entitlement that continually invites trouble and makes him believe he is above the law—does not command respect from teammates and will always struggle to win a locker room.... Lacks accountability, focus and trustworthiness—is not punctual, seeks shortcuts, and sets a bad example. Immature and has had issues with authority. Not dependable.... Can provide an initial spark, but will quickly be dissected and contained by NFL defensive coordinators, struggle to sustain success and will not prove worthy of an early investment. An overhyped, high-risk, high-reward selection with a glaring bust factor, Newton is sure to be drafted more highly than he should and could foreclose a risk-taking GM's job and taint a locker room.

Hockey analyst and blogger Chris Watkins crunched the numbers when it comes to race and hockey scouting in his post "Racial Bias in Drafting and Development: The NHL's Black Quarterback Problem." He reached three conclusions regarding the NHL's racial demographics: The NHL should have three times as many players of color. Racial stereotypes in coaching and scouting factor into why so few players of color ever get a shot at playing the center position. And Black players are traded twice as often as any other demographic.

Chris Peters, who covered the NHL Draft and prospects for ESPN, explains hockey sense as a "catch-all" term scouts utilize when evaluating whether would-be NHL prospects are up to snuff—making or breaking someone's pro hockey aspirations.

"The ability to process the game at high speeds; lots of things that are kind of tied to a vision," Peters explained to Evan. "The lanes that you're seeing in a path and the lanes that you choose in terms of backchecking, and the routes that you take to get to your man quicker."

Peters explains how hockey sense for Black players is often seen as a red flag in the eyes of scouts.

"Race technically has never come up. Now I think about it, I've had times when I have heard scouts say about a Black player that he lacked hockey sense," Peters said. "And sometimes I wonder if it's coded. Sometimes I wonder if it's legit. I think that there are a lot of scouts and I think scouting has done better; these are such high-level decisions that you can't really have...I think if you had those kinds of biases, they would come out and you wouldn't last very long. When it comes to a player's deficiencies, it usually comes down to decision-making."

Since players of color seem to be shut out of playing center in the NHL, what about the position makes scouts and coaches deem them unworthy of fulfilling its responsibilities?

The website How to Hockey breaks down the responsibilities of the centerman. In general, "the centerman is the support man," charged with helping out other players when they are in trouble. The centerman "is also considered the quarterback," tasked with winning faceoffs and leading breakouts. Unlike the wingers, who typically stick to their side of the ice, the centerman has more freedom to roam. Even though the centerman "covers the most amount of ice (and usually does the most skating)," in addition to winning faceoffs and leading breakouts his general duties are to cause trouble in front of the other team's net, stop players and pucks in front of his own net, score goals, make passes, help out the wingers, and back-check.

We also asked Peters how these thoughts can factor into hockey clubs' decision-making during the draft.

"In the last few years, we've had top prospects like K'Andre Miller and Quinton Byfield," Peters said. "I think nobody questions [Byfield's] hockey sense, and if they do that would raise a red flag for me because I think he's a highly intelligent player and [a] guy that is going to play a long time in the NHL. But you know, I think in terms of K'Andre, there's a little bit of a difference there because he was just learning how to play defense."

He also brought up a tweet he saw from a blogger who anonymously quoted a "[senior] scout," who had doubts about Columbus Blue Jackets defenseman Seth Jones' hockey sense—and toughness and attitude—while Jones was having an "average" interview at the draft combine. Jones, who was seen as the presumptive No. 1 overall pick of the 2013 draft, slipped a bit to No. 4 instead. Somehow, he overcame those concerns, becoming an elite blueliner and one of the Blue Jackets' alternate captains.

"I had known Seth for years and had covered him and had been around him; he was a captain at the national team program," Peters said. "I saw that and my blood started to boil, because I was like, if there's ever been a person who did not have character concerns of any kind it would be Seth Jones. I just know he was all about the team and so dependable in every single way on and off the ice. And so I saw that and I was like, okay, well, that is clearly some sort of dog whistle there because that is so far from the truth."

One of the first racist incidents Evan remembers in the NHL took place in 2003. John Vanbiesbrouck, a former 20-year NHL goaltender, was the coach and director of hockey operations for the Ontario Hockey League's (OHL) Sault Ste. Marie Greyhounds when he chastised team captain Trevor Daley, a Black man, by using racial slurs when speaking with two of Daley's teammates. Once the incident came to light, Vanbiesbrouck resigned his positions as head coach and general manager and sold his ownership stake in the Greyhounds. Canadian journalist Bill Montague, a Black man, broke the story. Here's what Montague told us in regard to the events leading up to breaking the story of Vanbiesbrouck's racist remarks toward Daley, and the aftermath:

"It was a Sunday morning, and I got a phone call from Sam Biasucci, who was a part-owner of the Greyhounds with John Vanbiesbrouck. They're very good friends. It was probably 9:00 AM, which was pretty early for them to ask to call at my house, and they asked if I could come down to the rink. Of course, I said, 'Well, what's it about?' and they said Trevor left the team. I said, 'Trevor left the team?' I mean, he was one of their star players.... I'm like, 'Okay, well, why'd he leave the team?' And they said that's why they wanted me to go down to the rink. So I said, 'Yeah, okay, give me about 40 minutes; I'll be right there.'

"When I get down to the rink, I meet with John and Sam Biasucci in the Greyhounds' press room, and it's just the three of us.... I said, 'Well, why'd he leave? What happened?' and they said they'd rather just keep that internal...they don't want to discuss it. To me, it's a pretty big question that has to be answered, and I asked [them] about five different ways.... They said that after the game—it was a 6–1 loss to the Guelph Storm—John was very upset, and he said some things that he should not have said and some of it was directed at Trevor. So it kind of made it sound to me like something happened in the dressing room after the game, the coach goes crazy on his players, and, you know, poor Trevor kind of couldn't take it and he went home because he got yelled at. That's kind of how they made it sound to me. Then I said, 'Well, what did you say?' and again they wanted to keep that internal, so in my mind after asking five different times; and I really remember this very vividly, I [thought], *Don't worry...once you leave here, you'll find out.*

"By the time I got down to the parking lot—Memorial Gardens parking lot—I made a phone call to...one of the players. They said, 'Don't use my name, but this is what happened. You know, Coach basically kind of referred to him as a "little nigger,"' and my mouth is open. And [it happened another time too], allegedly. So then I called to talk to another player where it happened—he confirmed that. And then I remember getting into work and reporter Brian Kelly yells 'Bill, he just walked in,' and it was Darren Dutchyshen from TSN. Now, Darren's son played on that hockey team. And when I said 'Hello, Darren,' he said, 'Can you believe it?' So right away, that's like the third pretty good source that confirms that this happened.

"So we come up with a plan; the Hounds play that night and we'll certainly approach John after the game. We waited 'til the other media left...and I went into his office and basically told him here's what we got and here's what you allegedly did. He came clean at that point...and he looked obviously stressed out over that thing. How can you not be, you know? We questioned him as to how this could happen. This is a guy who's a coach, a GM, a part-owner, the guy who's supposed to lead these men not only on the ice but to be good people and have a good value system. And I remember specifically, he looked at me. He apologized to me because I'm Black as well. I told him no apology was required because I'm here to do a cover story on Trevor and this isn't about me, but I asked him where this come from. He said, 'My background, I guess, Bill. I guess where I grew up.' And right away I thought, Detroit, because that's where he grew up, and obviously must have been surrounded by racists and stuff like that. The story just went viral.... But he was a little bit arrogant still at the time.... We asked him if he was gonna resign. And initially, the answer was no. And you know, it wasn't until the OHL obviously got involved and basically forced him to resign and sell his ownership shares. But he did, and the unfortunate part was he finally resigned and then Trevor agrees to come back to the team, and on his first game back to the team who's sitting behind the Greyhound bench like a spectator? It was John Vanbiesbrouck. And here's Trevor, who went through a hell of a lot there and then he finally returns...and the cockiness, as far as I'm concerned, of John and Sam Biasucci, knowing what this young kid has been put through."

Let unpack what we just read. A team owner calls a player—the team captain—a "nigger" on at least two occasions, and after he gives up his job and ownership of the team, he's sitting behind the bench. The team tried to hide what happened. Vanbiesbrouck also apologized to Montague, the nearest Black person—but not Daley. Just imagine if Los Angeles Clippers owner Donald Sterling would've sat courtside at a game behind the team's bench in the immediate aftermath of selling the team due to his racist comments. People would've lost their shit.

When racist incidents happen in hockey, one of the first rebukes by hockey people is, "There's no place for this in our sport." Seems that there is a place for racism in hockey, since it happens pretty frequently.

Remember when NBA superstar LeBron James said something similar about how "there's no place for racism in basketball" and the NBA got Sterling out the paint quick, fast, and in a hurry? Also, there haven't been any similar incidents since.

Hockey often operates in the cut—a place where there's not a whole lot of scrutiny. Some folks love not to know, and they'll engage in mental gymnastics when the subject matter makes them feel uncomfortable.

"He's apologized."

"That was a long time ago. Why are we still talking about this?"

And our personal favorite:

"Let's move on."

Vanbiesbrouck told a local newspaper, "I told Trev this is an old wound with me. I grew up with it. I'm as sorry as anybody that it's stuck with me."

Thankfully, former NHL goaltender Kevin Weekes, a Black man, was not here for the play play when hearing about Vanbiesbrouck, a former Florida Panthers teammate: "I think it is very classless. It leads me to now wonder what he thought about me the whole time that I was in the [Florida] system. It makes you wonder."

And his response to Vanbiesbrouck's apology: "I don't understand how you are going to play in New York City for 12 or 13 years, and being a member [of] the New York Rangers, playing in Madison Square Garden, and have those sentiments, and have those feelings and thoughts? Ironically, he ended up going to the Ice Hockey in Harlem [functions]. What was he there for? Just to be there. It just shows me the high level of trash and not any class or any refinement. It's uncalled for."

Apologists for racist behavior spend a lot of time centering the feelings of racists while ignoring the people who are the most uncomfortable when racial slurs are made public: the victims of racial slurs. But Evan can imagine what players like Aliu, Daley, Simmonds, Smith-Pelly, and so many others have gone through, because it happened to him.

Evan remembers the first time he was called a racial slur. This was in 1994, and he was 14 years old. It was at football practice—and it was by a teammate.

After team warm-ups, everyone dispersed to their individual position drills. In Evan's case, he went over to the linebackers area. As he was heading over, a teammate, also a linebacker, walked up to him, said "nigger," and jogged off. At this point, Evan was in complete shock, but also not surprised. For his first two years of high school, he went to De La Salle Institute—then an all-boys Catholic school— where some of his fellow Black classmates often struggled, because it was the first time many of them had been the minority in their schools.

What does Evan do? Start to kick this guy's ass and tell the coaches he attacked him unprovoked? Ignore it? Or does he find his own way to retaliate, where the coaches are none the wiser?

Evan remembers a good amount of racist incidents that were swept under the rug due to a classmate who was "connected" through law enforcement, politics, an alumnus, or the mafia. Many of his white classmates were from Bridgeport and Canaryville, two Chicago neighborhoods where a lot of cops and firefighters live—areas that have a long history of racism.

Evan decided to save his "get back" for a tackling drill. When it was his turn to line up against the guy, he balled up his fist, squared up his shoulder, and buried his forearm right into his chest. As he fell back, his feet went into the air. When this guy hit the ground, Evan stood over him and gave him a nasty look. Everyone on the team *oohed* and *ahhed* thinking Evan had just delivered a random vicious hit. Nope, it was purposeful.

But his "get back" was short-lived because of the secret he had kept all those years.

Why didn't Evan tell a coach? Shit, he didn't even tell his parents. What would've been the consequence? Buddy gets suspended for a couple of days? And in that time period, he unlearns his racist ways?

Hell naw.

Here's the thing when it comes to the privilege of racism: we'd bet a dub ($20) that his former teammate has *zero* recollection of what he said to him that day. But if you were to ask Evan, he could probably tell you which way the wind was blowing that day, the top R&B song on the Billboard music charts, and where the White Sox were in the pennant race, among other things.

Evan completely understands why Aliu held on to what happened to him for all those years. It's extremely painful, and from what we've seen in the aftermath of his announcement, white people often struggle when Black folks call them out when it comes to racism. Not a soul moved on what went down until a few of Aliu's white teammates confirmed Peters' racism.

Perhaps it's time to believe us when we tell you something's happening?

Perhaps someone creates a space where racism is dealt with sooner than later?

And in Aliu's case, his tormentor held his career in his hands. And once someone labels you a "complainer," that's a wrap. Let's say Aliu had a long NHL career and a coach chastises him for not making a play or something. In that coach's head, he may be thinking, *If I get after Akim, he's going to say it's because he's Black.*

Evan has written about this incident before. Some of his former teammates and classmates reached out asking for the identity of the racist. He told them; they weren't surprised. Admittedly, Evan looked him up on Facebook when we were writing this book. To the surprise of no one, he had a meme on his page that reads, "The way my life is set up, I speak my fucking mind. I'm too old to hide my feelings."

On that day in practice, he spoke his mind in saying what he thought about Evan. Evan is glad he put him on his ass; he's glad everyone saw it. An ass-kicking is temporary, but the sting of racism lasts forever.

And years later, Evan wrote about a group of kids who went through something similar at Kennedy Park on Chicago's Southwest side.

When it comes to children spewing racism, we think about where they most likely learned this behavior from: the adults in their lives. These adults can be parents, teachers, coaches, aunts, uncles, friends, an older sibling, cousins, and neighbors—the places young, impressionable minds find their activation. After all, Vanbiesbrouck blamed his "upbringing" when the world got wind of his racism.

In April 2018, Evan was a couple months removed from starting out at the *Chicago Sun-Times* when he saw a tweet from a former Chicago Now (*Chicago Tribune*'s blogging community) colleague whose son played a Little League game at Kennedy Park, located in an area that's well-known for overt and covert racism.

In the tweet, Ray Salazar, a Chicago Public Schools English teacher, claims the team they played against, Kennedy Park Cobras U11, called the West Lawn Southwest Pride—a team composed of Latinos—"Taco Boys." And in a second incident, the Pride, who won the game 10–7, allegedly heard one of the Cobras tell his teammates during a pep talk that they were going to "build a wall around home plate."

Remember Evan's "Icing Racism" piece he wrote for the *Chicago Reader* when he mentioned that an opposing player called his teammate a "nigger" during a game? That incident took place at a rink two blocks away from Kennedy Park. And this took place in the only Chicago ward to overwhelmingly vote for Donald Trump during the 2016 presidential election (70 percent of the 19th Ward's 54th precinct voted for Trump). In the 2020 election, the same precinct once again voted for Trump (76 percent), according to City Bureau, a South Side Chicago–based nonprofit civic journalism lab.

In a surprise to no one who knows better, during the 2018 midterm elections, 10,695 Chicagoans (3,860 of them from the 19th Ward, where scores of first responders live) voted for Republican congressional candidate Arthur Jones, an outspoken white supremacist, an anti-Semite, and a Holocaust denier who founded the America First Committee, the membership of which is limited to "any white American citizen of European, non-Jewish descent."

Evan attended Morgan Park High School, which is located near this area. Some of his former classmates have a lot of stories of racial shenanigans from that area.

In the aftermath of Evan's two stories detailing the incidents and the "discipline" of the Kennedy Park team, he heard from a lot of people from the Kennedy Park area who claimed he had gotten his facts wrong. They wanted to know when he was going to write about the racism from the West Lawn team. He also heard from people who believe nothing has changed in the neighborhood.

Looking back on things, there's no way to know if the kids or the coaches involved learned a lesson. The community is also known for its insular nature, so we have no idea if the coaches and players were actually suspended. We have no idea if anyone involved faced any actual sanctions.

One of the incidents happened *after* one of the rules from the house league was violated.

Evan quoted the league's policies in his story: "If coaches and/or players use 'foul or abusive language,' they are ejected from the game and suspended one game. A second infraction, which the team from West Lawn is also alleging took place, warrants a 'suspension for the balance of the season and reinstatement at board discretion.'"

Some facets of hockey culture operate in a similar manner: instead of looking inward to undergo a self-check, blame everyone else by lashing out and saying, "We aren't the problem; it's you."

Hockey needs therapy. In a lot of cases, when talking things out in therapy, the layers are peeled back in order to get to the cause(s) of the root issue.

Darren Andrade, who wears many hats as a Canadian, the son of Jamaican immigrants, a basketball writer, a father, a brother, and a parent, saw how hockey culture can have an adverse effect on kids from nontraditional hockey backgrounds. His brother took a lot of racial abuse from fans and parents as a youth hockey player in the Toronto area.

"When a sport and a culture can be so embedded in a country's fabric, in a country's identity, I think it has a great power when it becomes that. And hockey culture, to me, for too long has represented a sort of an abuse of that power," Andrade said. "And its inability to find equality, its inability to find a common ground with not just the citizens or the people that popularized this game, but the ones that came to add to it [and were] turned away at the door.

"So when you say, 'What is hockey culture to me?' I guess it's not that simple, but [at its simplest] it's represented an abuse of power. Even though it still represents an opportunity, I believe in the power of sport. And so I can believe in the power of hockey. But I think it knows its own power. I think it knows its place in that fabric of Canadian society...a little bit less in the States, but North American society is big.... And I think for far too long it's used it to maintain that idea of what it wants to be instead of what it has to be and what it should be."

When Andrade and his family went into the arena to watch his brother play, they observed an "invisible" line between people in the stands. They'd hear racist remarks in the stands or walking out of the arena; his brother would experience racism right there on the ice. "There were parents shouting the n-word every single game," Andrade said. "There were kids on the ice screaming that word from their bench. And there [were] no repercussions for those parents."

Andrade says his family continues to live near the arena, and they want nothing to do with it.

"That was the major turning point as a family," Andrade said. "But even as a kid, you know, my father didn't put me or my second-oldest brother into hockey after the incidents."

He loved the sense of rebellion he felt as he stood up for himself.

"It really did represent a bit of a divide in that way...and that experience for me, my brothers, and a lot of my friends and...people in the community [shaped] the way we view hockey," Andrade said. "And, again, it was regrettable because there was a love, and I think now you're seeing a resurgence of that love. Just seeing a few more players getting through, but you're also seeing a lot more details of what's been happening and why it's been slowed and why Black people haven't been given those opportunities in hockey."

Despite his experience in youth hockey, Andrade's brother still watches hockey—but his kids aren't involved.

"He's a big Maple Leafs fan, so his love, I would say, is the love that kind of remains the strongest because he was the one taken out," Andrade said. "I don't think he wanted to leave. I don't think he wanted to stop playing. But, again, my dad was like, 'Fuck this. I'm gonna kill someone.' We kind of wanted to go into it...we weren't that heartbroken, but I think he still holds on to it. My brother's got a son right now, and hockey wasn't even on the radar for him. He's into baseball, football, and basketball. Also, when we talk about the little ripple effects, here's a man that still loves hockey, but was just like, 'No, we're gonna go this way.'"

Of all the words Vanbiesbrouck could've used to dress down his players in the aftermath of an embarrassing defeat, he—a grown-ass man—chose to say "nigger." In those moments, Daley's Blackness was the main point of contention in Vanbiesbrouck's mind—not losing a game. Years later—after he, and his racist behavior, left the news cycle—Vanbiesbrouck was named USA Hockey's assistant executive director of hockey operations—a decision Daley reportedly fumed over.

Here's what USA Hockey President Jim Smith said after the organization hired Vanbiesbrouck, a known racist: "It is really exciting to get someone with John's background."

It appears that racism is only seen as a series of problems—not something institutional, according to a scholarly article written by Elizabeth "Betita" Martinez titled "What Is White Supremacy?" In it, she writes:

The most common mistake people make when they talk about racism is to think it is a collection of prejudices and individual acts of discrimination. They do not see that it is a system, a web of interlocking, reinforcing institutions: economic, military, legal, educational, religious, and cultural. As a system, racism affects every aspect of life in a country.

By not seeing that racism is systemic (part of a system), people often personalize or individualize racist acts. For example, they will reduce racist police behavior to "a few bad apples" who need to be removed, rather than seeing it exists in police departments all over the country and is basic to the society. This mistake has real consequences: refusing to see police brutality as part of a system, and that the system needs to be changed, means that the brutality will continue.

In 2018, during a game against the Sault Ste. Marie Greyhounds, Kitchener Rangers winger and Red Wings prospect Givani Smith skated toward the Greyhounds bench and extended his middle finger, flipping off several members of the team. The OHL suspended Smith two games for the gesture.

In typical fashion, Smith was attacked on social media with racism and insults after the incident, according to the *Waterloo Region Record*. (One man sent a photo of Smith to his personal Facebook account with HOCKEY NIGGER in the caption.) He also received a death threat, needing a police escort out of the building.

But there was an impetus to Smith lashing out the way he did. Smith's teammates heard racist comments coming from the Greyhounds' bench.

"It's heartbreaking, to be honest," Rangers general manager Mike McKenzie told the *Region Record*. "He shouldn't have to endure it. He did a good job of turning the other way. I think the unfortunate part—and it pains me to say this—is that he's probably used to it by now. He's probably heard things before, which is brutal."

When then San Francisco 49ers quarterback Colin Kaepernick began kneeling during the national anthem before NFL games in 2016, the hockey world made it quite clear that kneeling would be unacceptable. John Krupinsky, an assistant coach for the Federal Hockey League's Danbury Hat Tricks in Connecticut, said if any of his players knelt, they could grab their gear and "get the fuck out now."

He said, "First day of camp. Something really important. We're not women's soccer. We're not the NFL. If there's anybody here that's gonna be disrespectful to either the American or the Canadian national anthem…. You'll never see the ice in this arena. We don't have that problem in hockey. We're better than that. But there's no sense in wasting anybody's time if that shit was gonna happen. I don't believe it would happen here. We're the most patriotic sport that they have out there. Just keep that in mind, thank you."

His comments contained an added bit of sexism, just for good measure. This coach is, of course, ignoring what the protests are about.

In March 2019, an incident in college hockey involved a Boston College player making a racist remark to a Providence player. An official heard the comment and reported it. No punishment was issued, as the league said it could not determine who made the remark.

In April 2019, The Athletic reported a Los Angeles youth team suspended three coaches and 15 players for an anti-Semitic video. TSN's Rick Westhead has written about the rampant racism in the GTHL.

Diversity: An Old, Old Wooden Ship Used During the Civil War Era

It is not our differences that divide us. It is our inability to recognize, accept, and celebrate those differences.

—Audre Lorde

During Black History Month 2020, Evan interviewed former NHL player and Chicago Blackhawks community liaison Jamal Mayers for an NBC Sports Chicago podcast. Evan asked him for his thoughts on whether the NHL's Black players or the league's players of color would one day form a group similar to the Players Coalition, a group of NFLers who bring light to social justice issues through "advocacy, awareness, education, and allocation of resources."

Mayers was skeptical, because NHL players tend to shy away from anything that would be viewed as them separating themselves from the team.

"I can assure you, since they were 14 they just wanted to be one of the guys; they just want to be another player," Mayers said. "So the idea of creating a separate situation goes against their whole mind-set right now, and I can assure you that [Columbus Blue Jackets alternate captain] Seth Jones is thinking: *Why would I do that? I'm with my guys; these are my teammates....* I think we shouldn't lose sight of the fact that the game...although it is a microcosm of what's going on society, in that locker room I can assure you that he's respected. He has a voice and people love him and they want to be his teammate and they love being around him. They look up to him. Younger players look at Seth Jones like, *I want to prepare like that guy. I want to show up like that guy. I want to be like him.* And...that's been my experience as well, and I would be surprised if guys feel like they need that. You know what I'm saying?

"If there's big things that happen, there needs to be a way for them to communicate that on a bigger scale, in the sense that something happens that shouldn't be happening, there should be a resource which I think they're developing, creating a platform...so that stuff isn't taught and isn't tolerated. And I think it's happening now and I think the league understands that needs to happen, and they're doing a good job, but as far as us creating our own...I don't know if I said it correctly but I don't think that the players playing today feel there's even a need for it."

Evan asked Mayers about a possible NHL players–led coalition in February 2020, before the COVID-19 pandemic and the police killings of George Floyd, Breonna Taylor, and Rayshard Brooks, and the hate crime murder of Ahmaud Arbery. Then the world changed—and the NHL, which often benefits from a lower profile due to the popularity of the three other major North American sports leagues, could no longer hide in the cut as social justice issues are now on the league's doorstep.

In June 2020, the Hockey Diversity Alliance (HDA) was formed by current and former NHL players of color Trevor Daley, Evander Kane, Wayne Simmonds, Matt Dumba, Chris Stewart, Joel Ward, Nazem Kadri, and Akim Aliu.

"It's about both [diversity and racism]," Kane told The Hockey News. "I'm Black and I'm white, so maybe I tick off both boxes. When you talk about women in our sport, there are so many powerful voices in that area. We're seeking out those types of players and all players from all different forms of background. It's about diversity and creating a more welcoming culture, but at the same time, there's clearly a racism problem in our sport. It's been pushed aside and covered up ever since I started playing hockey, and that is a major issue we need to suppress in a major way. If you don't get rid of the racism, how are you going to create a more diverse game? That doesn't make any sense."

The August 2020 police shooting of Kenosha, Wisconsin, man Jacob Blake provided the NHL its first opportunity to step up as the

WNBA, the NBA, NASCAR, Major League Baseball, the English Premier League, and Major League Soccer have. In a surprise to no one, the NHL offered a "moment of reflection" instead.

The HDA called the league out on its shit. Here's how Minnesota Wild defenseman Matt Dumba reacted to the NHL lagging behind the other major sports leagues in response to the Blake shooting, per Sportsnet 650 in Vancouver:

"It's kind of sad and disheartening for me and for members of the Hockey Diversity Alliance, and I'm sure for other guys across the league. But if no one stands up and does anything, then it's the same thing, that silence. You're just outside, looking in on actually being leaders and evoking real change when you have such an opportunity to do so."

And it sounds like Dumba is already resigned to the fact that the league's players of color will be the ones holding the bag—as Mayers told me—when it comes to racism in hockey:

"You're just relying on the minority guys to step up and say it. But what would really make the most impact is to have strong white leaders from teams step up and have their two cents heard. All the other white kids who grow up watching them, who might be their biggest fans, can look up and say, 'Wow, if he's seeing this and trying to stand up and to listen, then why am I not as well? Why am I continuing to hold on to this ignorance or hate that I feel toward a subject that I maybe don't know everything about?'"

The NHL eventually postponed games after the players pushed it to do so.

Vegas Golden Knights enforcer Ryan Reaves seems to have undergone the same self-check as many other notable Black folks with a platform: examining how they are going to call out systemic racism while garnering support from white colleagues. Speaking to Gary Lawless of VegasGoldenKnights.com, he relayed his experience prior to the NHL postponing games:

"[Wednesday] night…we went out for dinner with a couple of the boys, and then Brayden McNabb asked if we were going to play [Thursday]. I said, 'Yeah, why not?'" Reaves said. "I then came upstairs and asked myself if we were really going to play. Are we not going to support what's going on here? You have to think we are. Honestly, I was up all night. I ended up calling Marc-Andre Fleury—I texted him at 12:00 AM to see if he was still up. He called me back and we had a decent conversation. In my head, I was thinking about how there were only a couple players of color in the bubble. How is this going to look? Am I just going to walk out to support my Black community? Am I going to be the one or two or three out of the eight teams doing it? Am I not going to support and just go play and act like everything is fine? I was back and forth, but in my head I felt like we shouldn't play. I felt like this was something that we needed to support.

"Lo and behold, I wake up after an hour or two of sleep and I have a text from Kevin Shattenkirk asking me to call him. I called him, and he said he had players from the teams out East and they wanted to hear what I had to say. I said I feel like it's a strong message and a very powerful message if a sport like hockey, which is predominantly white, can stand up and say, 'I don't know what you've been through and never will, but I see what's going on in this country and I don't think it is right.' Every single player said they would stand behind it and that we should not play. I got another text that Vancouver wanted to talk about [it]. I get outside their locker room and every one of those guys thought we should sit for two days and said they'd stand behind it. It was a big exhale for me because I felt like I was alone in it, but it was the exact opposite. I couldn't have felt more in a group than I did [that] morning. It was great because it was such a powerful message to see that people really see what is going on in this country. As white athletes, they don't want to stand for it anymore. To take that stance, I applaud every single NHL player right now. I really do."

This was the NHL and NHLPA statement in regard to postponing games: "After much discussion, NHL Players believe that the best course of action would be to take a step back and not play tonight's and tomorrow's games as scheduled. The NHL supports the Players' decision and will reschedule those four games beginning Saturday and adjust the remainder of the Second Round schedule accordingly.

"Black and Brown communities continue to face real, painful experiences. The NHL and NHLPA recognize that much work remains to be done before we can play an appropriate role in a discussion centered on diversity, inclusion, and social justice.

"We understand that the tragedies involving Jacob Blake, George Floyd, Breonna Taylor, and others require us to recognize this moment. We pledge to work to use our sport to influence positive change in society.

"The NHLPA and NHL are committed to working to foster more inclusive and welcoming environments within our arenas, offices and beyond."

Dallas Stars president and CEO Brad Alberts announced that the team lost some of its season ticket holders due to protests and the hockey club's support of Black Lives Matter. This is a team and fan base that houses winger Tyler Seguin, one the first white NHLers to attend a protest.

San Jose Sharks winger Evander Kane was satisfied that the NHL and some of the players seemed to be listening, saying on the *NHL on NBC* broadcast, "It was great to see that the players came to the realization that this was an important period of time and moment in time to make a statement and come together. I think the biggest thing I stressed along with Matt [Dumba] was that it can't just be one or two teams or three or four teams—it's got to be everybody. And the fact that everybody came together, I thought, was great."

While it's great that current and former NHLers have been loud and proud when it comes to the aims of the Hockey Diversity

Alliance, the group may have already failed in one glaring area: initially, no women members served in decision-making roles.

It should be noted that Kane, in 2016, was sued in Erie County State Supreme Court (New York) for sexual assault.

Groups that achieve a measure of racial and ethnic diversity have a long history of leaving women on the fringe—or completely out of the picture. Amid all the activism we've seen in the past several years, women of color, particularly Black women, have stepped up in many ways before the men did.

Thanks to the WNBA, they've often shown the other sports leagues what to do when it comes to athlete activism.

And when the league rolled other initiatives out under the HDA banner, such as its fan inclusion committee, a Twitter user pointed out that 11 of the 18 members are white, four out of 18 are women, and only one of 18 is a woman of color.

Also, Korn Ferry, the firm the NHL hired to help the Executive Inclusion Committee make diversity recommendations, is as white as a hockey team, with a few people of color sprinkled in.

Why not give the women who've been involved in so many areas in the sport a say in a moment that could change hockey culture for good? And why not involve the people who are the victims of racism?

In many cases, resistance to change comes from the top. In America's case, the then leader of the free world, former president Donald Trump, not only bristled at diversity training, he threatened to pull federal funding from schools who teach the *New York Times Magazine*'s "1619 Project," a Pulitzer Prize–winning project that details how slavery continues to have an adverse effect on America—and Canada. (Which is hilarious when you think about how many ancestors of formerly enslaved Black people ended up in Canada and were instrumental in creating ice hockey as we know it.) Low-key, if you think the way former President Trump does, you'll mostly find a way to follow suit in his lack of effort to keep up with a constantly changing workforce.

The memo issued by Russell Vought, director of the U.S. Office of Management and Budget, reads, in part: "All agencies are directed to begin to identify all contracts or other agency spending related to any training on 'critical race theory,' 'white privilege,' or any other training or propaganda effort that teaches or suggests either (1) that the United States is an inherently racist or evil country or (2) that any race or ethnicity is inherently racist or evil."

The memo goes on to say that federal agencies "should begin to identify all available avenues within the law to cancel any such contracts and/or to divert Federal dollars away from these un-American propaganda training sessions."

In the meantime, we tracked down Raychel McBride, an Illinois-based diversity, inclusion, and affirmative action manager. In her capacity, McBride is often tasked with consulting and coaching companies that aim to change workplace culture, which includes diversity training; inclusion practices; and diversity, equity, and inclusion analysis and strategies.

She has some advice for the NHL and the HDA.

"I've gone to the Blackhawks games and I'm like, 'Oh, it's like a sprinkle of Black and Brown people here.' It doesn't feel like it's the most welcoming environment, and so I have always wondered, 'What does that feel like being the person out on the ice, who is actually living in that environment?' So I definitely think that what they're doing is necessary," McBride said. "I think they really do need to stay focused on their call to action. I think that the WNBA is doing a really great job of being very strategic and [focused]."

McBride lauds the WNBA for its activism. After all, the players were at the forefront of getting Rev. Raphael Warnock elected to the U.S. Senate over Kelly Loeffler, the right-wing former co-owner of the Atlanta Dream.

"The WNBA continues to put out statements about what their call to action is…. They're asking you to call your local officials, they're asking you to get out and vote," McBride said. "So, I think [the NHL and the HDA] have to figure out what it is they're looking for…is the call to action for players, or is the call to action for the community? What are we hoping to see? What does success look like for us? They really have to identify that."

McBride also pointed out that the NHL has to decide if it's comfortable with the HDA leading the charge, or of it wants someone in an executive decision-making role within the league to be part of it, as well, and help drive the change. After all, the necessary changes may involve the actual processes and policies of the league. (The NHL did hire Kim Davis as executive vice president of social impact, growth initiatives, and legislative affairs, in November 2017.)

"That's a different conversation," McBride said. "I don't know if what they're looking for is a change of culture of their environment and their teams…or if they want someone to just respond to what's happening externally."

McBride believes when women are left out of diversity and sensitivity training, not as many essential points of view are considered when changing workplace culture.

"I do think you need to have as much perspective at the table as possible, and that's something I talk a lot about, especially when I talk about boardrooms," she said. "For example, my organization just got our first female board member in its history [in 2020], and I'm thinking, 'You gotta be kidding me!' And at the same time I'm like, 'This is wonderful; we needed this.'"

McBride thinks the NHL needs to go beyond traditional thinking when it comes to diversity. Perhaps someone within the NHL has a seen or unseen disability or considers themselves part of the LGBTQIA+ community. These viewpoints bring something to the table and ensure the league is getting as full a perspective as possible.

McBride was nice enough to walk us through the times when diversity and inclusion training has had mixed results. For example, *Harvard Business Review* looked at why mandatory diversity programs often fail.

Employees are "going to go into that with a not-so-good mind-set," McBride said, of "I'm being made to do this," not "This is available to me and I'm really passionate about it and I'm gonna sign up." That's why she personally is a big advocate of not mandating diversity training. However, she stresses, organizations still need to provide some foundational training. That might look, she says, like "a conversation each year about inclusion, and how it's important that we make each other feel welcome and that people can show up authentically as who they are."

Race, specifically, continues to be a polarizing topic for companies and corporations to grapple with, McBride says. In her view, it's important to begin with the decision-makers.

"I think when you get started talking about diversity in terms of race and maybe even diversity in terms of mind-set and having opinions that are different from yours, that's a different conversation because not everybody is ready to have that conversation and [be] open-minded and willing to hear it," McBride said. "So a lot of times, I will push back and say, 'You don't really need to start doing anti-racism training and some deep diversity training until you have maybe a group of folks that can start the charge.' So maybe you start with your managers and your leaders, and you take them through the training, and they start to kind of go out and drive those conversations, and then you start bringing more people in.

"And I think you have to expect that some people will just say, 'I don't want to be a part of this,' and move on."

Indeed, diversity and inclusion initiatives have a history of failure.

In the U.S. and Canada, spaces in journalism, education, and the corporate world, among others, are often doomed to fail because a white power structure often leaves people of color and women to do the heavy lifting, shouldering the task of fixing the work culture they did not create.

In many cases, these initiatives exist in name only. A lot of these folks who drag their feet when it comes to common decency often conflate equality with supremacy. Common decency should not be a partisan talking point.

"The labor goes on them. The pressure goes on them. The critiques are on them, too," Wong-Padoongpatt said. "And I don't know [if] it's sustainable. And I know that [hockey culture is] just so toxic. And when it comes down to it, I don't see it lasting very long. But I commend them for trying,"

Wong-Padoongpatt had been working with the Golden Knights on a women's program to introduce girls and women to the sport.

"It was a great program," Wong-Padoongpatt said. "Once they changed the hockey director, they completely wiped it out without even consulting me, [cut] all the women- and girls-specific things and just folded it all into adults [learning] to play.... The rationale is that the girls and women don't need these spaces by themselves.

"To be honest, I didn't have time to explain it to them and I didn't want to. But I was just seeing all the work that we were putting in just disappearing without consulting us, without having a conversation."

Hockey, historically, has dragged its feet at every turn when it comes to social justice. In January 2021, *Sports Illustrated* reported on the internal strife between the HDA and the NHL, citing an explosive meeting the group had with NHL commissioner Gary Bettman in June 2020 in which he propped up several league-mandated diversity initiatives while questioning what the players were doing during that time. *Sports Illustrated* reported Bettman had quickly backtracked his statement.

Bettman's clapback is often utilized by white men when their motives are questioned when it comes to diversity measures. If Bettman had done his job back when initiatives were launched, there wouldn't be a need for the HDA. The HDA rightfully called Bettman out on his shit—and he pulled a sucka move. And, as McBride said, the league diversity council is left to do the heavy lifting.

By October 2020, it seemed the HDA had had enough of the NHL failing to act. An October 7, 2020, statement read, in part, "Unfortunately, the support we hoped to receive from the NHL was not delivered and instead the NHL focused on performative public relations efforts that seemed aimed at quickly moving past important conversations about race needed in the game."

This statement shouldn't be a surprise to anyone who knows the history of uncomfortable conversations around race. Are we expecting hockey—an institution wholly owned and operated by white people—to do the right thing?

One of the main incidents that told us hockey—and hockey culture—hasn't learned a damn thing since the police murders of George Floyd and Breonna Taylor was when the Arizona Coyotes drafted Mitchell Miller, a player who has a history of racism, bullying, and not taking responsibility for his actions in a tangible way. He all but admitted to committing a hate crime against Isaiah Meyer-Crothers, a Black, developmentally disabled classmate, and promptly received 25 hours of community service. For some of the league's teams, for USA Hockey, and for the University of North Dakota, Miller's repeated use of the word "nigger" and smashing a Black, disabled classmate into a brick wall wasn't a deal-breaker. To be fair, some teams and draft experts took Miller off their boards, but why didn't others? Remember how the Coyotes were on the forefront of battling racism in hockey, but drafted Mitchell anyway?

"Our fundamental mission is to ensure a safe environment—whether in schools, in our community, in hockey rinks, or in the workplace—to be free of bullying and racism," said Coyotes president and CEO Xavier Gutierrez in a statement, per *The Arizona Republic*. "When we first learned of Mitchell's story, it would have been easy for us to dismiss him—many teams did. Instead, we felt it was our responsibility to be a part of the solution in a real way—not just saying and doing the right things ourselves but ensuring that others are too. Given our priorities on diversity and inclusion, we believe that we are in the best position to guide Mitchell into becoming a leader for this cause and preventing bullying and racism now and in the future. As an organization, we have made our expectations very clear to him."

Once again, the HDA found itself in the familiar position of calling hockey culture out on its shit. Its NHL HDA Pledge, which it asked the league to sign, states: "We will not support, partner with, or accept support from any organization that has engaged in, promoted, or failed to appropriately respond to racist conduct in their organization of any kind (including, without limitation, the proliferation of hate speech, discrimination in the provision of goods, services and facilities and other areas such as employment)."

After receiving pressure from all sides, the Coyotes renounced their draft rights to Miller.

"We have learned more about the entire matter, and more importantly, the impact it has had on Isaiah and the Meyer-Crothers family," Gutierrez said in a statement. "What we learned does not align with the core values and vision for our organization and leads to our decision to renounce our draft rights. On behalf of the Arizona Coyotes ownership and our entire organization, I would like to apologize to Isaiah and the family. We are building a model franchise on and off the ice and will do the right thing for Isaiah and the Meyer-Crothers family, our fans and our partners. Mr. Miller is now a free agent and can pursue his dream of becoming an NHL player elsewhere."

Miller's lack of punishment shows why white kids often get the benefit of the doubt that Black kids rarely receive when it comes to the criminal justice system—you know, one of the reasons we've seen a different tone in the recent worldwide social unrest.

While Evan was in college, he received *50 hours* of community service for cracking open a beer in public (he was playing basketball at a friend's apartment complex) a week out from his 21st birthday. He had to check in with a probation officer and clean up trash on the side of the road with dudes who broke into people's homes and hadn't paid child support. Miller did *a lot* more than Evan did and got half. A college student drinking beer on a Saturday afternoon isn't breaking news, but it's easy for Black teens to end up in the criminal justice system after minute infractions. And let's not forget how 12-year-old Tamir Rice was murdered by a white police officer or how 17-year-old Trayvon Martin was murdered by a neighborhood watch volunteer who went on to auction off the gun he used for $250,000.

"All you have to do is watch a hockey game between now and the first hockey game ever in the NHL, [and] you can see it right away. The guys that look like me don't get the same opportunities," Rane Carnegie said. "And if they do get the same opportunities, because they are just that undeniable with their talents, they have a much shorter leash than the Caucasian peers they play with.

Carnegie, who is Black, says he knows all about the "short leash." He claims it factors into his exit from the OHL's Plymouth Whalers.

"I was at a team party. I lived with another player on my team. We were all smoking weed. Some of my teammates left roaches in the ashtray," Carnegie said. "There's no video camera footage showing I was the only one smoking weed. We had 15 players on my team there. So now what happens is [I] get suspended and get curfew—nobody else does. Why is that?"

Years later, Carnegie ran into one of his former Whalers teammates, who inadvertently dropped a bombshell in regard to Carnegie's dubious exit from the team.

"I found out...that they voted me off the team," Carnegie said. "I'm like, 'Why did you vote me off the team?' He's like, 'Rane, you stole a car.' I'm like, 'What are you talking about?'.... Well, our coach, Mike Vellucci, had a team meeting. And he told them that he had to send me home because I stole my billet's car. So they didn't even have to vote. My former teammates told me, 'We just knew that [you were] being sent home because you stole your billet's car.'"

Carnegie, who denies any theft, says he borrowed the car to pick up his girlfriend from the bus station and then he brought the car back.

"So the head coach and general manager, Mike Vellucci, who is now coaching in the NHL, lied to these 18-, 19-year-old boys that didn't want me on their team because I'm there to steal their ice [time] anyway. So he traded for me and told them a Black kid stole the car. I'm now wondering…when I was dominating in Halifax and getting close to 100 points, why I never got an opportunity to play in the AHL. Why did I never get an opportunity to talk to NHL teams? Is it because NHL scouts were talking to Mike Vellucci, and Mike Vellucci [was] telling everybody that I stole a car? I don't know, but I just know that we get treated differently. We don't get treated the same; as soon as we mess up, we're gone."

When the need for change is apparent, various groups have various ideas on how the goal ought to be achieved. In hockey's case, some folks want to work with the NHL, while other hockey advocates want to burn down the system. The folks in the latter category question why they work with an institution that has had more than enough time to set hockey culture straight. And some folks want to work with the stakeholders in the hockey world while keeping context in mind.

Kwame Damon Mason, who directed the 2015 film *Soul on Ice: Past, Present, & Future*, which details the story of Nova Scotia's Coloured Hockey League of the Maritimes and the history of Black hockey players, believes everyone who cares about the future of the sport ought to work together to ensure hockey reflects a diverse society.

"It's interesting, where we are right now, compared to when the film dropped in 2015," Mason said. "I knew that things were going to change and it's not always gonna be like this. So it's just trying to adjust all that we see and it's a lot different than what I expected, but I didn't expect it to go down like this. But sometimes you're making changes that have to get a little ugly before it gets pretty," Mason said.

Then NHL commissioner Gary Bettman saw the film—and he loved it.

"Sometimes it's one of those things where you've got to see it to understand it because, you know, when somebody says to you [they're] making a film about the history of Black hockey, and you're…deep in hockey, you might just have to have your back up against the wall. I think Gary…understood the magnitude at least [of] what that film could do," Mason said. "I was trying to say to people, 'This is a great starting point for conversation'.…All these different little pockets [of hockey fans] might have been having conversations, but no one was really thinking, 'Is everybody thinking the same thing I'm thinking?' There's a lot of information there that people didn't know, which was great. And there [were] a lot of people that were opening doors."

Mason's film achieved cult status. Evan found out about the film from social media, and other folks saw it based on word of mouth. While Mason remains positive in regard to the NHL's diversity efforts, he's aware that *Soul on Ice* only achieved cult status and was not roundly accepted by hockey insiders.

"When I first started asking around [there were] people who decided no, that's not gonna fly. 'You know you can't make a film that's going to go against the grain of hockey. They'll never let you make it,'" Mason said. "That made me think about all the guys that played in the NHL, especially in the '80s and '90s. I guarantee you that's what they [were] told.... I remember when I was in Edmonton, George Laraque was told, 'George, why bother playing hockey? You'll have a better chance playing football. There's no Black guys playing hockey.' So it's kind of the same mentality. People are saying [*Soul on Ice*] is not going to resonate [or] it's going to get shut down."

Fast-forward to years later, in the midst of a global pandemic and hockey trying to find its place in social justice reckoning, and people are starting to see where Mason was going with *Soul on Ice*.

Overall, Mason is content that some sort of dialogue is happening in hockey circles.

"I'm glad that the conversations are happening," he said. "I just think people need to give a little grace, in a sense that we need to just start educating people, at least, to understand why we are trying to get them to be empathetic because they've never known our struggle. So for a group of people who've never known a struggle, a lot of people are gonna say, 'Well, that's no excuse.' But it is what it is. All I could do is just be a support vessel for that cause. But I know when it comes to growing the game of hockey and making sure that there's a normalization between Black voices and faces in the game of hockey, I know what I can control. I can control a visual medium."

Hockey's White Backlash and the NBA

I can't believe what you say, because I see what you do.

—James Baldwin

In the aftermath of Evan quote-tweeting the Tuukka Rask tweet, one of the people who voiced their displeasure of Evan's allegedly sizzling-hot take found his Instagram post announcing the deal to publish this book.

The person said the following in their defense of hockey and hockey culture, while taking swipes at the two major sports leagues that have the most Black players, the NBA—the most frequent target of hockey fans—and the NFL:

> Hockey is literally the least controversial sport with the least drama... I saw your comment regarding Rask wearing a Boston Police hat. The Boston Police have nothing to do with what happened to George Floyd, also they are responsible for risking their lives and saving thousands of lives during the Boston Marathon terrorist attack. Generalizing every police officer as racist due to the actions of a few, is no different than generalizing every black man as a criminal due the criminal actions of a few. You want to talk about a sport that needs culture change, lets talk NBA/NFL where drug use, domestic violence, assault, robbery, and the occassional murder are committed by current and former players at an alarming rate.

There's a lot wrong with this statement. More than ever, people—based on their partisan politics—love not to know. They view facts like a supermarket hot bar: take what you want and leave behind what's undesirable. As we will explain throughout this book, hockey has just as many unreported problems with the law as any other sport—probably more. But when hockey guys show up in the police blotter, they make the most of their time in the spotlight. Hockey ain't the Rotary club the aforementioned commenter makes it out to be. And involving the NFL and NBA is dog-whistle rhetoric, at best. Opposition research doesn't necessarily need to be correct; it just needs to seem correct in the eyes of the people who have similar beliefs.

Hockey players have literally committed the same crimes as football and basketball players. Let's look at some of the NHL's high-profile incidents over the years:

In 2018, Nashville Predators forward Austin Watson pleaded no contest to a misdemeanor charge of domestic assault of his girlfriend. *The Tennessean* reported: "After the witness saw the couple fighting and flagged down a passing officer, the victim initially denied Watson had touched her. Later in the interview, she said Watson was responsible for causing scratches on her chest. The 31-year-old victim, who is also the mother of Watson's child, told police that 'sometimes he gets handsy,' although the report did not elaborate on what that entailed. The victim also urged police not to say anything because it could hurt his career, according to the report."

The NHL suspended Watson for 27 games; the suspension was later reduced to 18 games. A year earlier, Watson had been one of several Predators who participated in "Unsilence the Violence," the YWCA's public awareness campaign to end violence against women, while the Predators Foundation pledged $500,000. Watson later said the impetus of the arrest was an alcohol relapse. In an Instagram post, he said he's been dealing with anxiety, depression, and alcoholism since the age of 18.

A month before Watson's arrest, then Phoenix Coyotes forward Richard Panik was arrested by local police after he refused to leave a Phoenix-area bar. Panik, who told the cops on numerous occasions "I play for the Coyotes," pleaded guilty to criminal trespass.

The Chicago Blackhawks and their AHL affiliate, the Rockford IceHogs, let forward Garret Ross play 18 games after local authorities were ready to charge him with one count of nonconsensual dissemination of private sexual images, or "revenge porn." (The charges were later dropped.) The timing of Ross' benching appeared to be reactionary due to the charges making the light of day.

How about when then Los Angeles Kings defenseman Slava Voynov was arrested for abusing his wife? It didn't get much media attention and the Kings were fined $100,000 by the NHL for letting Voynov on the ice for an "optional" practice.

Or how about when then Colorado Avalanche goalie Semyon Varlamov reportedly stomped out his then girlfriend back in 2013? The team supported him and he went to practice before turning himself in to the police. Varlamov was released after posting bail. He played in the team's next game. (Varlamov was later acquitted of the charges.) Varlamov's coach and Hall of Fame goaltender, Patrick Roy, no stranger to domestic violence during his own playing days (in 2000, Roy was arrested after pulling two doors off their hinges during an argument with his wife), told the *Denver Post*, "It's a law thing and it's important for me as a coach that I keep my focus on my team and we keep our focus there and at the same time, let the law decide what's going to be."

Or how about when Coyotes center Mike Ribeiro was named in a civil lawsuit accusing him of sexually assaulting his children's nanny, and the media was filled with stories about his "redemption?"

Blackhawks legend Bobby Hull was abusive to two of his wives and pleaded guilty to assaulting a police officer who intervened when Hull was arguing with his second wife, Deborah.

Here's what Joanne, Hull's first wife, told ESPN's *SportsCentury*: "I looked the worst after that Hawaii incident. I took a real beating there. [Bobby] just picked me up, threw me over his shoulder, threw me in the room, and just proceeded to knock the heck out of me. He took my shoe—with a steel heel—and proceeded to hit me in the head. I was covered with blood. And I can remember him holding me over the balcony and I thought, 'This is the end, I'm going.'"

In 1998, Hull told the English-language *Moscow Times*, "I played the way I live; straightforward. I have no regrets about anything I did in life." And when asked if he had to do it all again, he reportedly laughed and said, "Maybe I'd drink a bit more."

Hull also said that America's Black population was growing too fast.

Chicagoan John Moore saw the elder Hull's racism firsthand during a charity golf tournament.

"I played in a golf outing and our foursome played with a legendary Blackhawk [Bobby Hull] and his son [Brett Hull], who was also in the league. For a couple of holes he [Bobby] kept telling jokes about 'darkies,'" Moore said. "The jokes continued until one of my buddies pulled the son aside and told them I was Black. The jokes stopped, but there was no acknowledgment or apology from the father or son. The interesting thing, a significant portion of the kids at the local orphanage are Black and Brown so it goes to the complicated relationship these guys have with racism. They are out here telling racist jokes as they are raising money for Black and Brown kids. They would use that as a defense against accusations of racism, but you and I know both know it does not make someone less racist."

Crowley Sullivan, ESPN Classic's former director of programming, told the *Chicago Tribune* this about telling Hull's entire story: "There have been whispers about Bobby Hull for years, but the full story has been swept under the rug in Chicago. Our focus is not just to show Bobby Hull the athlete, but Bobby Hull the person. If we don't chronicle the things he's done, we're doing our viewers a disservice."

Despite Hull's history of violence against women, the Blackhawks retired his number. And after a whole TV show documented his misdeeds, the Blackhawks named him a team ambassador and built a statue of him in front of the United Center. Hull also has a rink—with another statue—named after him in Cicero, a Chicago suburb. In 2016, knowing all of this, the Winnipeg Jets inducted Hull into their Hall of Fame.

Scott Brown, senior director of hockey communications for True North Sports and Entertainment, which owns the Jets, said this when the Jets' decision prompted backlash from a Winnipeg columnist: "It's largely a celebration or a nod to an athlete's accomplishments on the field rather than speaking to a larger issue or larger societal issue. For the hockey community of Winnipeg, we had to acknowledge the presence of the WHA and the role that they played in the existence of the current Winnipeg Jets. And Mr. Hull's accomplishments during that period of time on the ice, particularly playing with Ulf Nilssen [sic] and Anders Hedberg, just couldn't be denied."

Four seasons ago, the Hulls appeared in an NHL commercial during the Stanley Cup Final. And the duo represented the league at a ceremonial puck drop ahead of the 2017 Winter Classic.

In terms of popularity breakdown of the various sports leagues globally, the NHL is somewhere between the top tier (NFL, NBA) and the lower tier. But when a hockey team gets really good after being really bad for a long time, the dynamic changes, and many longtime fans vehemently bristle at the NHL's niche-sport status. As someone who is both a fan of basketball and hockey, Evan would call himself one of the few people who have noticed the inferiority complex some think hockey has with the NBA—which is extremely weird, because many Black Americans' entry into hockey was seeing their favorite rappers and singers wearing hockey jerseys. Take Tupac Shakur chastising the press while wearing a Detroit Red Wings jersey, Rihanna sporting an Ottawa Senators jersey, Snoop Dogg sporting a Pittsburgh Penguins jersey with GIN & JUICE as the nameplate (and later on in the "Gin & Juice" music video, he's wearing the AHL's Springfield Thunderbirds jersey), Wu-Tang Clan's Cappadonna wearing a Montreal Canadiens jersey in Raekwon's "Ice Cream" video, and Craig Mack wearing the iconic Charlestown Chiefs sweater from the film *Slap Shot* on his *Project: Funk da World* album cover. In 2020, Griselda's Westside Gunn wore a Chicago Blackhawks jersey in a video.

Evan noticed that hockey's inferiority (or superiority) complex usually seems to surface nationally in the spring, when the Stanley Cup Final and the NBA Finals are happening at the same time. He saw a meme on social media comparing the championship speeches of Chicago Blackhawks captain Jonathan Toews and the Miami Heat's LeBron James with the number of times each of them said "I" versus "we," with the caption, WHY I WATCH HOCKEY INSTEAD.

The meme claimed James said "I" 18 times (and Toews, 0), while Toews said "we" 14 times (James, 0). If someone were to take the meme at face value—and loved hockey—they would think NBA players are flashy and selfish, while hockey players are selfless individuals and upstanding members of the community. Based on Evan's research of both championship interviews, the T-shirt and the cap James wore in the meme appear to reference the Heat's 2013 championship team.

The first thing James did was thank his opponent, the San Antonio Spurs. ESPN reporter Doris Burke asked him questions only he could answer; necessarily, he said "I" because he was the only person who could speak to those questions.

In aftermath of the Blackhawks beating the Boston Bruins to win the Stanley Cup in 2013, The Hockey News senior writer Ken Campbell began his interview with Toews by saying, "Jonathan, there's one man in NHL history who can say that he's captained the Chicago Blackhawks to two Stanley Cups—and that man is you, Jonathan Toews."

Toews responded, "That's me...right on."

During nationally televised games, a commercial is shown featuring a montage of NHL players saying "we" over and over again, solidifying hockey as the ultimate team sport in the eyes of hardcore fans.

Hockey is a great game that doesn't need to pick on other sports to prop itself up. But why does the hockey community feel the need to constantly boast its supremacy over other sports leagues?

"White backlash" is why.

University of Iowa professor Dr. Nikolas Dickerson wrote a 2016 article titled "Constructing the Digitalized Sporting Body: Black and White Masculinity in NBA/NHL Internet Memes."

In it, Dickerson explains "white backlash":

> Whiteness is a reference to the social constructed nature of White identity, and the study of whiteness interrogates how understandings of whiteness shape societal norms and social institutions (Doane, 2003). Since the formation of the United States, society has been structured to privilege the White male body. Joe Feagin's [sic] (2010, p. 3) uses the term "the white racial frame" to refer to the manner in which our social world is interpreted through the perspective of White bodies. In other words, understanding of whiteness structures our cultural norms, but also demonstrates how social institutions are stratified to privilege White bodies. In this manner, whiteness can be understood to function as an invisible social norm. Thus, a central component of studies that examine how whiteness is constructed seek to expose how whiteness operates as the dominant lens of interpretation by making it visible through analysis. Yet, color-blind ideology helps to perpetuate the White racial frame through a refusal to engage with issues of race.

And according to Dickerson's findings, the racism in the memes isn't overt, it's implied:

> I believe these memes represent a form of White backlash politics. The notion of White backlash politics has consistently been linked to the cultural climate of the 1980s and 1990s. Anxiety about job security due to global outsourcing, affirmative action programs, and the States' role in protecting minority rights, all created a mis-conception [sic] that Whites would soon be the minority (Doane, 2003). This perceived crisis created what could be thought of as a White revolt. One of the ways this revolt was manifested was through popular culture.

The American exceptionalism rhetoric spewed by Donald Trump's "Make America Great Again" campaign slogan and "America First" banners plastered at rallies during his presidential campaign as President Barack Obama's second term came to a close back up Dickerson's research.

The research pertaining to white backlash makes a lot of sense in Evan's city of Chicago, as some Blackhawks fans bitched at local media for a perceived focus on the Bulls. In Chicago, when the Blackhawks were in the midst of their three Stanley Cup wins, some within the fan base openly believed the Bulls were not worthy of media coverage. These folks rallied around Patrick Kane amid his transgressions (including misdemeanor assault, theft, and harassment charges in 2009 and a sexual assault investigation in 2015 that didn't result in charges), while some of them viewed then Bulls guard and Chicago native Derrick Rose as a "thug." (This was before a civil rape suit was filed against Rose; he was later cleared by a jury.)

NBA players' activism continues to be viewed as a turn-off for some hockey fans.

For the uninitiated, in terms of the dynamics of basketball in Chicago, Evan would compare it to high school football in Texas, or hockey in Minnesota: extremely important. On top of that, not only are the Bulls synonymous with former player Michael Jordan, the most famous athlete of all time, but basketball culture in Chicago is unmatched.

These are just a few of the basketball players who grew up in the Chicago area: Isiah Thomas, Dwyane Wade, Derrick Rose, Candace Parker, George Mikan, Cappie Poindexter, Anthony Davis, Doc Rivers, Maurice Cheeks, Tim Hardaway, Mark Aguirre, Cazzie Russell, and Patrick Beverley.

As for hockey in Chicago, it's mostly a suburban sport, and the Chicago area can claim Chris Chelios, Tony Granato, Eddie Olczyk, Ryan Hartman, Vinnie Hinostroza, Kendall Coyne Schofield, and a few others.

Why do fans of hockey, which is such a dope sport all on its own, constantly feel the need to insert themselves into a rivalry that largely doesn't exist? We wondered if the same inferiority complex exists among fans in other cities with prominent hockey clubs and a strong local basketball scene like Los Angeles, Washington, D.C., Toronto, Detroit, New York, Philadelphia, and Boston.

Turns out, the inferiority complex is a thing.

We thought of how the documentary *The Carter Effect* gave an overview of the impact former Toronto Raptor Vince Carter had on the city, creating its basketball culture that produced so many NBA basketball players in the last 10 to 15 years (Tristan Thompson, Shai Gilgeous-Alexander, Kelly Olynyk, Andrew Wiggins, Jamal Murray, Nik Stauskas).

The documentary makes a compelling case that Carter's presence was the catalyst for so many Canadian kids picking up a basketball and, in some cases, basketball overtaking hockey in terms of interest. And some of those kids shunned hockey—hockey culture more so— outright due to a communal view of the sport as the "other."

Darren Andrade believes racism and bullying in hockey culture forced so many Toronto-area kids to not consider hockey, instead opting for basketball and baseball. As Andrade told us about why some Black folks up north view hockey as a white man's sport, we were reminded of the 2009 film *Invictus*, about how then South African President Nelson Mandela and the South African rugby team, the Springboks, attempted to bring together a country reeling from decades of apartheid.

In the film, soccer is viewed as a Black sport, while Black South Africans see rugby as a white sport. In one scene, a white woman offers what appears to be a secondhand Springboks jersey to a Black child, who recoils in fear at the sight of it.

Andrade knows that feeling.

In the aftermath of hockey analyst Don Cherry's xenophobic on-air comments, which got him fired, Andrade wrote about the racist incidents and bullying his brother underwent as a youth hockey player, forcing him to give up the sport for good, in a HuffPost Canada blog titled "Hockey Never Wanted 'You People' Like Us. Don Cherry Was A Constant Reminder."

"It was an outsider versus insider that devolved into the racist incidents that I detailed there [the article]; that was our introduction to the culture that we left behind really quickly," Andrade said. "During the BLM [Black Lives Matter] movement here, when you talk about racism, it's so ingrained in America that people think you're talking against America. Well, that's kind of like what hockey was [in Canada]; if you talked against hockey, you were anti-Canadian. So that was something that furthers the divide...sports was a big part growing up of the divide between races at school.... Whether you were a part of it or not—and a lot of immigrant kids, first-generation kids, Black kids, and Indian kids; we weren't a part of that. That's what hockey culture was to us growing up.

"From the inception of the Raptors 25 years ago, you saw that rise of basketball culture in a hockey country. And there's been some sort of deviation from the natural Canadian kids who get into hockey and, because of some of the culture and incidents that have happened, a lot of kids have gone the other way: soccer, basketball, baseball. There has been that sort of growth, and hockey has not seen that growth. And that coupled with the fact that a lot of the best athletes haven't traditionally been accepted into that hockey fold, and those athletes have gone on to bolster other leagues and other sports and, in turn, other cultures. Again, we go back to that circle of the divide."

Andrade points to the wave of Caribbean immigrants who came to Canada during the 1970s. "Assimilating in some ways, it was a big turnoff; it became a sort of a sore spot in some ways," Andrade said. "It was so Canadian that if you weren't a part of [it], it dispelled you, so I think the seeds were planted then, in terms of kids like me that grew up [and] never really related any love of hockey or hockey culture upon our kids. There's a ton of athletes up here that, if they were more welcomed into the culture of hockey, would have pursued it."

Andrade sees hockey as trying to play catch-up to the NBA in terms of marketing its stars.

"[There is] a definite narrowing of the gap," Andrade said. "And I think that they feel it. I think that's part of the resentment.... The personalities of the players are starting to come out a little bit more [in the NHL] because they're trying to play that catch-up game, but they've missed the point in terms of what's really made the NBA appealing, which is...they get ahead of certain social issues. I know they sort of address it in the way that hockey buries it. The resentment here [in Toronto] is that the Raptors and basketball culture is chipping away at that. And I think that's part of what's causing the NHL to be a little bit more conscious of the things that they're doing and be a little bit more involved in the conversation.... They look at it as good business now, because that gap is narrowing."

Over time, we've noticed that for many of us who have a hockey origin story, it's organic—unlike for other folks. In 2016, during Game 7 of the Stanley Cup playoff series between the Chicago Blackhawks and the St. Louis Blues, Hockey Twitter got to know a St. Louis man who watched a hockey game for the first time.

You may remember Anthony Holmes, better known as "Tony X," who live-tweeted what he was seeing:

> Yo deadass this the first time I've ever watched hockey and this shit has been LIT for these first 45 seconds
>> Wtf is a power play
>> White people been hiding hockey from us for years bruh.
> This shit lit
>> I don't know who this dude kane is but we gotta stop him

And, upon seeing Blackhawks goaltender Corey Crawford head to the bench so the team could bring in an extra skater, Tony tweeted:

> The goalie just said Fuck it and left?

A few years removed, Holmes, a Black man, is still a fan of the Blues, and even got to watch them win a Stanley Cup in 2019. Unfortunately, he too has noticed the seedy underbelly of hockey fandom's infatuation with the NBA, which he believes is why some Black folks are keeping hockey at arm's length.

"Hockey and NBA fans, they like to compete against each other," Holmes said. "They basically want to 'up-one' another; they want to have their sport [be] better than other sports. Hockey tries to be like, 'We're tougher; we don't have any injuries, we just played through it,' and basketball is like, 'Oh, we're more entertaining, we have bigger stars.' I mean, it's an all-white sport versus an all-Black sport, to be honest. That's how it is; I like both.

"Even, to get that far, you got to be into the game. I just don't think that Black people are into the game. Yes, there's ones that do get that far and start watching the game and there are ones who won't. I mean, this is something you don't want to see. You don't want to see 'Back the Blue' on the ice, you don't want to see police caps. But before that, it's just a matter of eyes on the product. It's a major problem because I see it all the time."

Hockey Culture and Media

If you're not careful, the newspapers will have you hating the people who are being oppressed and loving the people who are doing the oppressing.

—Malcolm X

On July 4, 2019, football player and activist Colin Kaepernick quoted abolitionist Frederick Douglass in a tweet saying, "What have I, or those I represent, to do with your national independence? This Fourth of July is yours, not mine...There is not a nation on the earth guilty of practices more shocking and bloody than are the people of these United States at this very hour."

Kaepernick seemed to want to remind the masses that at that time in American history—July 4, 1776—Black folks were still enslaved. A member of the Chicago Blackhawks beat responded—in a since-deleted tweet—to Kaepernick with the all-too-familiar retort to any alleged dissenter in America:

> If you hate America, then move.
>   Anywhere.

If someone on the hockey beat, who is a trusted media member and is expected to be accurate, tweets a statement that is empty of thought, history, empathy, and context, they can't be the only one who thinks that way. In fact, they are not.

Toronto Star reporter Ken Campbell, in a 2006 article titled "Emery Marches to a Crazy Beat Sens Don't Hear," wrote this when describing the attire of then Ottawa Senators goaltender Ray Emery, a Black man: "Then along comes a cockroach-eating goalie who dresses like a gangsta rapper and shows up at practice doing a Dennis Rodman impersonation."

Can we expect that person to accurately report on the issues that are important to a demographic within hockey fandom?

Canadian sports reporter Bill Montague, a Black man, had similar gripes on how hockey media handled John Vanbiesbrouck's hire with USA Hockey, knowing his history of racist behavior.

"I really believe there are a lot of weak reporters/journalists out there who are afraid to ask the tough questions," Montague said. "I did see that even at that teleconference they had a guy from The Athletic and then maybe one other guy from ESPN or something may have asked him a question about it. But to me, he should have been bombarded with questions about that. Where does it come from? How could you ever utter those words? Have you ever reached out to Trevor Daley? What did you mean when you said it was your upbringing? I've always felt like this; I used to be a real hard-nosed reporter, and I just feel there's a lot of soft reporters out there today who are scared and nervous to ask the tough questions. I mean, you still have some good hard-hitting ones, but all that should have been front and center and should have been so much more of that story."

We expect a lot of white people to struggle with racism, since it doesn't affect them on the scale it does people of color. When journalist and activist Ida B. Wells wrote an editorial about lynching, the *New York Times* described her a "slanderous and nasty-minded mulattress."

As journalists Juan González and Joseph Torres wrote in the 2011 book *News for All the People: The Epic Story of Race and the American Media*:

> [N]ewspapers, radio, and television played a pivotal role in perpetuating racist views among the general population. They did so by routinely portraying non-white minorities as threats to white society and by reinforcing racial ignorance, group hatred, and discriminatory government policies. The news media thus assumed primary authorship of a deeply flawed national narrative: the creation myth of heroic European settlers battling an array of backward and violent non-white peoples to forge the world's greatest democratic republic.

In the United States and in Canada, journalism, especially sportswriting, is a predominantly white, male, suburbanite-driven profession. In America, newsrooms rarely reflect the demographics of the areas they cover. The *New York Times* and the *Wall Street Journal* are both 81 percent white, while the *Washington Post* is 70 percent white, according to numbers compiled by the Columbia Journalism Review.

Hemal Jhaveri, USA TODAY's former race and inclusion editor, says she was fired in March 2021 over a tweet she wrote in the aftermath of the Boulder, Colorado, massacre where 10 were killed in a grocery store. Jhaveri, who has written about race and inclusivity issues in hockey, appears to have been "canceled" by right-wing media and by her then employer. While she was incorrect in hypothesizing the shooter's race, white men continue to be the driver of violence with weapons while enforcing white supremacy. According to the Violence Project, a nonpartisan research group that tracks U.S. mass shooting data dating back to 1966, white men, more than any other group, are disproportionately responsible for mass shootings.

Let's break this down. Jhaveri was the *race and inclusion editor*, which means it shouldn't have been a shock to anyone she would wade into these waters. And what message do USA TODAY's actions send to whomever fills Jhaveri's position?

"So many newsrooms claim to value diverse voices, yet when it comes to backing them up, or looking deeper into how white supremacy permeates their own newsrooms, they quickly retreat," Jhaveri said in a Medium post explaining her departure from USA TODAY.

Newsrooms—per their history when it comes to bringing diverse voices into the fold—continue to tell on themselves.

Meanwhile, Susan Page, USA TODAY's Washington Bureau chief, kept her job after hosting an event for Trump administration employees at her home. The same newspaper that waxed poetic about objectivity when firing Jhaveri came to Page's defense, saying, in part: "USA TODAY is fully aware of these long-standing events that recognize the accomplishments of women and fall well within the ethical standards that our journalists are expected to uphold."

It appears that the game is rigged.

THE CANADIAN ASSOCIATION of Black Journalists (CABJ) and the Canadian Journalists of Colour (CJOC) authored a 2020 study titled "Canadian Media Diversity: Calls to Action" that explored similar issues in the country:

> The absence of representation in newsrooms across Canada has become impossible to ignore in light of recent events. The *Vancouver Sun*'s editor-in-chief apologized in September after the newspaper published an op-ed suggesting that ethnic diversity is harmful. Then, later that month, the

industry received widespread criticism for its reductive coverage of Prime Minister Justin Trudeau wearing blackface and brownface. Both of these incidents happened over the past few months—and that's on top of the barriers journalists of colour have faced for decades. Even at our national broadcaster, which prioritizes diversity as part of its mandate, people of colour (POC) and Indigenous people comprise less than 15 percent of staff, which is not representative of the more than 20 percent of people of colour who make up Canada's total population.

Normally, we wouldn't expect these folks to know much about Black life. But living in an era where information is readily accessible, it's clear they don't want to know. The aforementioned *Vancouver Sun* op-ed written by Canadian college professor Mark Hecht in 2019 suggesting ethnic diversity is problematic for Canadians says as much:

Many western nations assumed that increasing ethnic and cultural diversity through immigration would be beneficial. The dogma of diversity, tolerance, and inclusion assumed that all members of the society wanted to be included as equal citizens. Yet, instead of diversity being a blessing, many found that they've ended up with a lot of arrogant people living in their countries with no intention of letting go of their previous cultures, animosities, preferences, and pretensions.

Wow, this man basically said, "Shout out to Don Cherry! #sticktaps."

The cutline for the op-ed's photo reads, "Ethnic diversity can harm social trust and economic well-being of societies, studies have found."

Who greenlit that op-ed? And why was someone like that, who teaches at the college level, allowed to submit a column dripping with racism? When walking back the column amid criticism, the *Vancouver Sun* released a statement saying, "An opinion article by Mark Hecht published in Saturday's Weekend Review section and online contained views that do not meet the journalistic standards of the *Vancouver Sun* and do not represent the views of our editors and journalists." On the contrary, it seems like the column does indeed meet the journalistic standards of the *Vancouver Sun*, since an editor read it and hit publish.

The paper followed up with this: "The *Vancouver Sun* is committed to promoting and celebrating diversity, tolerance, and inclusion. Our vibrant community and nation are built on these important pillars."

Okay, but if the newspaper is committed to diversity, why publish an op-ed by a man who wants no part of it? Maybe the answer is above our pay grade, but we can continue to ask the tough questions, right?

But what do we do when journalists are unaware—or aware—that their writing is utilized to confirm stereotypes about people?

Campbell's article was written in the aftermath of the NBA's dress code mandate (2005)—the first of its kind for the four major sports leagues. Critics of the dress code held the belief that it was implemented by the NBA, which is composed of a majority of Black players, due to the 2004 "Malice at the Palace" Indiana Pacers–Detroit Pistons brawl.

Historians Stacy L. Lorenz and Rod Murray believed as much when they authored a 2011 article titled "The Dennis Rodman of Hockey: Ray Emery and the Policing of Blackness in the Great White North."

Under a subhead reading "Ray Emery: Hip-Hop Meets Hockey," Lorenz and Murray wrote:

Just as the NBA was concerned about defiant Black males in unsettling gangster gear, it appears that Emery's white teammates (and perhaps the reporters who covered them) thought they might be better off steering clear of the "rapper" goaltender. "The Ottawa Senators have worked furiously over the past 13 years cultivating an image as Canada's squeaky-clean bilingual franchise," wrote Ken Campbell. And Ray Emery threatened to undo all that work in just a few short months.

The Rodman comparison loses luster when we view it in the context of ESPN's Michael Jordan documentary *The Last Dance*. Despite his antics, Rodman was well-respected by teammates as he was a key part of the Chicago Bulls winning three championships while adopting a "leave me the fuck alone and let me do my job" persona along the way.

When a racist incident happens, the first people hockey media interviews are Black people. We've never understood why that is. Why not interview the group—white people—who are the main culprits in said racism? Beat reporters and bloggers have locker room access to these dudes. And when racism is framed as a problem that is exclusive to a certain group of people, everything stays in that area—sort of like something left out of sight in an attic.

In February 2020, Evan interviewed former Chicago Blackhawks winger Jamal Mayers for an NBC Sports Chicago Black History Month segment.

Evan asked him about the trend of white sportswriters interviewing Black players only when racist incidents come up. He said this: "I've lived in the locker room; I know what it's like, they would have asked everybody. Think about it. If I'm P.K. [Subban], and I'm in that room; that just happened. They're asking everybody about it. I guarantee they don't just ask P.K. They are asking the captain, they're asking other players, and then they only show P.K.'s response. But they have the other ones, too."

Mayers also had some words for our non-POC friends in hockey: "We have to also make sure that we bring white people into the process as well because it can't just be Black people. It can't just be me saying it; it's got to be everybody. Everybody's got to be [a] part of that."

Seems like straight talk about race scares the shit out of white journalists.

Studious hockey fans noticed the same. Chicagoan and hockey fan Gabriela Ugarte loves the sport, but in recent years she started to notice a disturbing trend: white sportswriters only speaking to Black athletes about the city's issues.

"The Bulls and the Blackhawks play in the same stadium, which is on the West Side of Chicago, and there was like this vast difference in the way that Black players on the basketball team are interviewed versus white players," Ugarte said. "So when Chicago has gun violence it is always a big topic in the city. You would constantly see Black players...not being held accountable but constantly being asked these questions, whereas people were playing in the same building who happened to be white and in the NHL were never asked the same things even though they technically belong to [those] communities."

Ugarte, who says she once worked at Chicago's American Indian Center when it had a partnership with the Blackhawks, says hockey—as a staff, as a label, and as a crew—seems to believe that racism in the sport is something new.

"This problem did not just start back in June [2020]," she said. "If you do even do a quick Google search on racism in hockey, you'll see that instances of racism faced by children playing hockey are quite common. I think it is purposeful. Like, they purposefully ignore these issues because it's very uncomfortable, right? Because talking about race or learning to talk about race is hard and it's uncomfortable. It requires you to do a lot of work."

As people of color, it scares us, too. But when the people who recoil at informing the masses about race issues refuse to tell the entire story, stereotypes continue on their merry way. We also need to call these issues what they are—racism—and explain exactly what it is and what it looks like, which is something a lot of white journalists are afraid to do.

Val James, the first Black American to play in the NHL, wrote a whole book in 2015 detailing the racism and indifference he received the entire time he played hockey. He has mixed emotions about how people—mainly white sportswriters who work at big-time media outlets—are starting to listen after he had been talking about racism in hockey for decades.

Again, the man wrote a whole book about racism the hockey media somehow missed.

"The thing is that when you do bring that back up, it is shoveled under the rug pretty quickly," James said. "You and I both know how the media and how upper-echelon companies tend to do that when they knew they were wrong in the first place.... My stuff happened from the mid-70s to probably the end of the '80s. And then it just seemed that someone else [Black hockey players] had to foot the bill from the '80s up to...the 2000s. So it's always been there. It's just a matter of why...no one really wants to listen to you when you're actually telling them at the time that it's happening to do something to make it stop.

"I guess what we should be doing is, like I said, we have to educate the adults, so that they can educate their own children and their children educate their children," James said.

Admittedly, Evan bristled a bit at what James said about how Black people are often forced into educating white people about racism when the information has been out there forever. Hockey media seems to put more research into finding stories that center racists in redemptive arcs while the onus is on Black folks to forgive white people when we were just minding our own business.

In the aftermath of Akim Aliu's allegations against coach Bill Peters, Campbell shared on Twitter a piece on how Graeme Townshend, a Black hockey player, was called a racial slur by his then coach, whom he later forgave.

"If you don't put forth a greater effort, the world will only see you as a stereotypical nigger," Rensselaer Polytechnic Institute coach Mike Addesa told Townshend and another Black teammate in 1989.

"Stereotypical nigger?" What the fuck is that? Where does that type of rhetoric come from?

Here's why white hockey media capes for problematic behavior created by hockey culture: finding a Black man who forgave a racist doesn't fix systemic issues in the sport. Just because one man was able to forgive doesn't mean we all should. After being outed as a racist and a bully, now former Calgary Flames coach Bill Peters resigned; the team never fired him.

Shireen Ahmed, a Canadian activist and sportswriter, believes that hockey media often utilizes different words to describe Black hockey players than their white counterparts.

"For instance, Evander Kane is an intense player. But Kane is Black and while he can be impassioned, his actions are interpreted as "rowdy" [e.g., fighting with officials]. [That] is far different than language used to describe, say, Jeremy Roenick when he physically abused the refs," Ahmed said. "There is an attempt to vilify Kane while words used to describe Roenick [include] 'outspoken.'" Kane is from Vancouver and although he has an impressive contract with the San Jose Sharks, most of the headlines are about his antics in casinos or elsewhere. We have seen that Black players are given unfair shakes from the media. For example, P.K. Subban, although giving the most generous contribution in history to a children's hospital in Montreal, was accused of showboating in his celebrations.

Ahmed believes that despite several instances of racism in hockey, the sport's press corps refuses to discuss it in a meaningful way.

"Black players cannot be joyous in celebrations or physically rough because they will be accused of being too boisterous and being brutal in their physicality," Ahmed said. "There are less than 30 Black players in the NHL. And the politics of sport are louder now than ever, despite a refusal for Canadian media—and hockey media—to discuss race in any meaningful way."

The shitshow that is the firing of Don Cherry, a known xenophobe and sexist, shows how predominantly white spaces in hockey are propped up and protected.

"It took an on-air racist rant from the 85-year-old Cherry to be fired—finally. And hockey culture reflects this in its overwhelming white male media, who act as gatekeepers and protectors of people like Cherry."

Hockey has always been thought of as Canada's game. And *Canada's game* implies *white Canada's game*—despite the history of the Colored Hockey League as well as the Indigenous impact on the game. This xenophobia has extended even to white players from other continents.

First, there was the CHL import rule in 2013 that banned drafting foreign goalies. The ban was lifted in 2018–19 because it made no sense. In 2017, then Arizona Coyotes forward Max Domi, who was born in Winnipeg, Manitoba, tweeted about stricter Canadian immigration policies after a Somali refugee was charged following a violent attack in Edmonton, Alberta. (Max's father, Tie, a former NHL player, is the son of Albanian immigrants. Internalized xenophobia exists.)

The tweet read:

> Really hope everyone in Edmonton is ok. We're behind you.
> This is why we have to be aware of some of the people we
> let into our country.

Cherry, on Remembrance Day, said on *Hockey Night in Canada*, "You people...love our way of life, love our milk and honey. At least you could pay a couple of bucks for poppies or something like that. These guys paid for your way of life that you enjoy in Canada."

It wasn't his first transgression. He's said worse, but for some reason that was the one that got him fired. Cherry spouted xenophobia for a long time, aimed against European players too. And he infamously said women don't belong in a men's locker room.

Sportsnet fired Cherry, but it took too long. He was given too many chances, with Ron MacLean standing by him, not rebuffing what Cherry was saying. By staying silent and not pushing back, MacLean has always been part of the problem—he represents the silent majority that does nothing to fight bigotry, therefore enabling it to grow.

In USA TODAY, Kevin Allen wrote, "The problem was that the same Cherry who could grow emotional telling a story about a severely injured youth player or about soldiers playing road hockey in a war zone could also make comments that sometimes came across as xenophobic."

There is no "comes across as." It either is xenophobic or it isn't, and the mainstream media's desire to create a middle gray area when there isn't one is just so it can appeal to "both sides."

In 2019, Chicago Blackhawks broadcaster Pat Foley said of Eisbären Berlin's Austin Ortega during a preseason game in Germany, "Ortega, sounds like he should be a shortstop." Saying someone with a Latino name should be playing baseball instead of hockey is racist. (We use the term Latino instead of the gender-neutral Latine or Latinx since this instance is referring to a man.) It's also worth noting Ortega isn't a no-name player; he was a prolific scorer when he played college hockey and was on Nebraska-Omaha's Frozen Four–bound NCAA team. It took two days for Foley to apologize to the organization. Ortega chose not to speak to him.

In August 2019, The Athletic's Justin Bourne tweeted:

> Have the leafs Nordic players (Nylander, Kapanen Engvall, Johnson) been good? Maybe not. But have they been outright awful either? Oh objectively yes. Yes they have.

It was completely unnecessary to lump all of the Nordic players together like that, but it shows how Canada considers anyone not from North America as an "other."

Hockey, though, does have a good number of European imports. Some of these players don't speak English. But in 2017, ESPN reported that some teams don't assign translators to players on purpose. The Washington Capitals' media relations director, Sergey Kocharov, is fluent in Russian, but he did not translate for Evgeny Kuznetsov. From the article: "The general rule on teams is for all players to speak English when it pertains to hockey. There's not much that needs to be said on the ice, so even if a player's English isn't great, he can find a way to get his point across."

In the article, Buffalo Sabres center Jack Eichel told ESPN, "We have a couple Swedish guys on our team. And they're always yelling at each other in Swedish. You want to know what they're saying, but they could be talking about you. You don't know."

(Thankfully, at least Kevin Shattenkirk said he "is OK" with players congregating and speaking in their own languages.)

The article demonstrates the fear of foreign languages, along with classic xenophobia. Removing a player's access to a translator is cruel and it puts them in a situation that makes it even more difficult to adapt. Moving to a new country is hard enough when you don't know the language—but having your own team take away access to a translator makes it hard for players to accurately control how they come across, and it's a way of forcing them to conform and leave part of who they actually are behind.

Eichel's "they could be talking about you" comment is the one that so often leads to "speak English!" comments that force those of other ethnic backgrounds into conforming. While one can argue that players do need to learn English if they plan on living in a predominantly English-speaking country, giving them tools instead of taking them away—like removing translators—is the way to do it.

IN 2019, WHEN the St. Louis Blues were in the middle of their Stanley Cup run, then San Jose Sharks reporter Paul Gackle found Islamophobic and racist tweets from Blues goalie Jordan Binnington from 2013 and 2014.

The tweets read:

> I was thinking. when people who wear the burqas are at the airport how is the security able to see if that's them in their passport... Srsly
>
> Also If you're underage & nervous of getting into a bar, throw the damn burka on. no way the bouncer will get into that awkward questioning
>
> Ya taxi man I'd probably rather listen to the radio than listen to you talk on the phone in another language

Binnington's tweets were Islamophobic and clearly xenophobic. Those of us who are not white also understand the look people give you when you speak in a language that is, well, Brown. (While

Jashvina was covering Princeton, a player on the team who had retired due to injuries and was serving as a student coach said he didn't like the Coca-Cola commercials in different languages. And in front of Jashvina, he said, "This is America. Speak English.")

For Yahoo Sports, editor Michael Hoad referred to Binnington's tweets as "controversial." The tweets weren't controversial; they were racist and Islamophobic. The media framing them as "controversial" minimizes the severity and invalidates the concerns of people of color—in this case, Muslims. Much like the word "offensive," it makes it seem as though it's only a problem in perception and not a problem in actuality.

The Canadian Press used the same word when writing about Binnington's response to questions about his tweets. Binnington told reporters:

"It was a while ago when I was a teenager and it was a little sarcasm, joking around."

"I was a teenager and that's what life's about. You live and learn and you grow as a human so, you know, I'm just here to play a couple hockey games."

Binnington did not apologize, and referring to his comments as a "joke" instead of something he did wrong illustrates that he actually hasn't grown to understand why they were wrong in the first place. And typically only white, male teenagers are afforded the defense of being young and ignorant—it doesn't apply to people outside that category. (Certainly not to people like Jashvina, who is used to being targeted in airports because of the color of her skin).

The NHL released a statement in which deputy commissioner Bill Daly said, "These are five-year-old social media posts from a Player who wasn't even a part of the National Hockey League at the time. While we certainly don't condone public comments that can be perceived as insensitive, we haven't seen anything to this point that would cause us to take any kind of action in response to these posts."

The phrase "perceived as insensitive" again mitigates the severity and dismisses concerns as trivial.

Members of the Blues organization, including head coach Craig Berube, Jaden Schwartz, and captain Alex Pietrangelo, all declined to comment.

The *St. Louis Post Dispatch* reported that when a reporter asked a follow-up question to Binnington, Mike Caruso—the team's president of media and brand communications—asked if anyone had hockey-related questions.

This is a classic example of hockey organizations protecting their players and preventing media that does want to hold them accountable from, well, holding them accountable. And members of the organization refusing to say anything and focusing instead on hockey exemplifies one of the virtues hockey loves to tout—the idea that staying silent about things that are perceived as "controversial" (even though they aren't) is good. It is what keeps players polite and nice.

IN MARCH 2019, *College Hockey News* and Jashvina reported that a Boston College player had directed a racist comment at a Providence player. Hockey East did not hand down any discipline, citing a lack of evidence.

The league said, "While we are aware some inappropriate remarks were made between players on the ice, we were unable to determine the source of the remarks with the degree of certainty necessary to take further action at this time. The matter is considered closed."

Boston College said in a statement, "There is much uncertainty regarding what may or may not have been said among players during the hockey game last Friday at Providence College. BC Athletic Director Martin Jarmond spoke with the BC hockey team and reiterated his and Coach York's highest expectations regarding their professionalism. He also reached out directly to the Providence player involved in the alleged incident. Based on the facts available to all parties, we consider the matter to be resolved."

The incident was reported because of a source, not because the league announced an investigation into the incident. Hockey East told CHN that there is no league precedent to announce supplemental discipline, and the conference usually only does that for physical incidents the public can see on the ice. The league followed its protocol in the referee reporting the incident to the league and the league investigating it.

However, the league went about the process incorrectly. If there wasn't enough evidence to find the perpetrator, the league should have punished the team or the coach. This is a good indication that our languages and our rules are not equipped with the right policies to handle racism. It's not as simple as an unsportsmanlike conduct penalty or yelling at a referee. It's unacceptable to not punish someone for something like that; by failing to punish someone, you demonstrate the behavior is acceptable—no matter how often you say it's not.

While this is referring to what was done after the incident was reported, another issue we often see is that there has to be proof something bigoted was said. Those who report these incidents are questioned. Their credibility and accounts are questioned, which they should not be.

And players seldom report bigoted remarks. In this case, they were reported by a referee because the referee overheard them. Players—or anyone else—don't report because they are not believed and because, usually, no punishment comes from it.

Anti-Indigenous Racism

It's been centuries since colonizers came and took this land from Indigenous people, but that racism and stripping of rights have continued to this day. There are too many instances of genocide in both Canada and the U.S. to name them all here. There was the Trail of Tears. There were the Osage Murders in Oklahoma. In Canada, there were the residential schools, where children were taken from their homes and placed into schools for forced assimilation between the 1880s and the 1990s. WBUR reported that thousands of students were tortured and killed. Kids were sexually abused.

One of those kids was Fred Sasakamoose, one of the first Indigenous people to play in the NHL.

"Hockey brought Fred joy. But he also remembers feeling sad," WBUR's Aaron Lakoff wrote.

At 15, Sasakamoose went back to his parents for just two months before he was sent to work for white men in the field. Then he was summoned to Moose Jaw to play junior hockey.

"A hundred thirty kids at training camp," Fred says. "A hundred thirty. All white. I was shamed—shamed at being Indian. I could never change it," Sasakamoose told WBUR.

That racism, of course, still exists for Indigenous players.

A First Nations player, Trey Lewis (who played in major juniors), never had conversations about racism on his teams growing up. It's something he attributes to the diversity of his neighborhood.

"It's almost like a split right down the middle. Maybe we were more used to playing with mixed teams and having to deal with that," Lewis said.

But when he played in First Nations tournaments every spring and summer, they had those conversations.

"We would talk about the regular teams we were on and how they might not like that because we were Native, we get the stereotypes. That we're troublemakers on the ice and off the ice and all that kind of sticks with us. I've seen that happen to like a lot of my friends; you know, they just get labeled early on," Lewis said.

"We Native Indigenous people have been talking about this for a while, and it's still something that's kind of pushed to the back burner in hockey. You know, mascots and the fans dressing up, and it's still happening."

As a member of a marginalized community, Lewis has experienced what an added burden it puts on Indigenous players.

"[Trying] to explain [it] to people too is just hard," Lewis said. "To be successful, whether that's hockey or whether that's any other profession, for Black people and I can speak for First Nations, it's a difficult road, and it definitely affects their careers. Even before, I was kind of a low-skill, meat-and-potatoes, hardworking kind of player. And growing up they labeled me as crazy, wild, and reckless. And I was, to some degree, but I think I kind of got in my own head and kind of tried to play to that for them. I almost took it as a compliment. Because I was Native, I was crazy, and so I had to act crazy and kind of be wild. And I mean, that is definitely part of my playing style, but I think it gets in your head and you can play to it. When you call somebody disruptive or a punk, if you tell them that enough, they're going to act like it. You know what I mean? It just kind of rubs off on them without them even realizing it. I didn't even realize it until I look back on things."

Lewis said he dealt with a few instances of blatant racism.

"But I was lucky enough my dad's heritage is from Wales. So I have got a lot of white genes. You know, I look white, and I really think I benefited from that…. I've definitely seen that happen to good friends of mine, whether it's in the classroom or on the ice, they get labeled immediately, or a lot earlier than I would, and we could be doing the same thing on the ice. You know, if a stranger saw me they might not even think I was Native at all. That's another thing that added to my privilege, for sure."

CBC reported that Terry Teegee, the regional chief of the British Columbia Assembly of First Nations and a Takla Lake First Nation member, called on the NHL to recognize violence against Indigenous peoples. (At publication of this book, the Mi'kmaq community is being targeted in racist attacks, and no NHLer has spoken about it, even those who chose to stay out of Black Lives Matter because they weren't American. This is a Sidney Crosby subtweet.)

Sports organizations being more inclusive toward and knowledgeable about First Nations people was one of the calls to action for the Truth and Reconciliation Committee.

"I really believe that would alleviate some of the issues of not just participating [in sports] but also in the higher levels such as coaching and administration," Teegee told the CBC.

In 2020, Edmonton Oilers defenseman Ethan Bear, who is from the Ochapowace Nation in Saskatchewan, became the first NHL player to have his name written in Cree syllabics on the back of his jersey. Before making the NHL, he played in the WHL for the Seattle Thunderbirds and billeted with Alan Sutliff, who became close to Bear's family. (Ed. note: While Ethan Bear's mother declined an interview for the book, she did grant permission for Sutliff to share these stories.)

At first, Bear didn't talk about his experience as a First Nations player. But in his second year in AHL Bakersfield, that changed as his girlfriend was researching her First Nations heritage.

"She was doing some studies on learning more about her heritage as well. And so, he was telling us all about, when he was 21, how he was helping and explaining to the guys on his team that 'That's not okay to do that and this is why,' and he was learning things from some of the older guys. He helping his teammates understand, you know, little bits and pieces of aspects about racism and helping open their eyes."

As an educator, Sutliff speaks to the players he billets about racism.

"I sometimes get really nervous when I see where a player of color has been placed. Because the billet treats them fine, because they're a hockey player, but they do not acknowledge that they might be struggling with some racism issues. And so I think billet parents should have some level of training around race issues as well. But I think that's not ever been part of it, because there are so few players of color," Sultiff said.

The racism faced by Indigenous and First Nations communities is often ignored. But the ramifications of centuries of genocide and residential schools have left a lasting mark. And it is often ignored.

In his book *Stickhandling through the Margins: First Nations Hockey in Canada,* Michael A. Robidoux wrote, "During the 1970s, the seemingly innocuous proposition by the federal government to fund Aboriginal sport in Canada was rife with assimilatory initiatives, and had less to do with funding Aboriginal sport, and more to do with transforming local sporting practices to fit into the mainstream Western system."

This is important because it gives another perspective into how white people often police the way non-white people play the game. It's a method of control and, as the author noted, of turning someone into their version of what a person should look like. It's the way in which hockey strips who you really are from you—you can be accepted, if you leave the other part of yourself at the door.

Robidoux further wrote:

> First Nations hockey is often portrayed as violent, reckless and dangerous. During my research in Kainai, I learned how neighboring non-First Nations minor hockey associations perceived the Kainai team. Claims of cheating and verbal and physical abuse in the stands and on the ice filled pages of complaints from parents that one hockey association filed against the Kainai association. The persistent complaints and the severity of the alleged offenses eventually led to Kainai's banishment from minor hockey, which was only remedied when Kainai joined a different league the following year.

> Stereotypical characterizations of First Nations people
> are not new; early European accounts were mixed with fear
> and contempt for what they perceived as a barbaric lifestyle.
> Descriptions of First Nations recreation are especially telling;
> early missionaries, colonists, and settlers openly described
> their disdain for what they saw as an excessively violent and
> overzealous approach to sport.

The author gives examples of his experiences of hockey tournaments that involved excessive drinking and heavy penalties on the ice—and how these aspects of tournaments are not in the least exclusive to First Nations tournaments.

"I offer this narrative to illustrate the strong connection that exists between recreational hockey and alcohol, and the pervasiveness of violent, unruly behavior in hockey—these aspects of the game are not specific to or more prevalent in First Nations contexts."

And on top of all that, Indigenous people must deal with racist team mascots—white people wearing headdresses to sporting events while doing the "Tomahawk chop" and telling Native folks they are honoring "tradition," so they should be fine with it. Native folks face a type of racism that Jashvina and Evan never have to deal with. Imagine a sports team named after a racial slur for Black folks with a blackface caricature as a logo. Never mind; you don't have to imagine that.

Blackface is seen a lot during Halloween. Evan once wrote about how Black people are often seen as costumes—not people. Our Indigenous brethren obviously feel a way about mascots and our country's celebration of "explorer" Christopher Columbus. While many Italian Americans view Columbus as the face of their ethnic pride, others see him as nothing more than a colonizer who claimed land that did not belong to him and wiped out Indigenous people and their cultures. Can an explorer be dubbed a "discoverer" of land or territory when it's already populated by a people and their culture? Hell naw!

And that version of history has an adverse effect on Indigenous kids, according to the American Psychological Association. Stephanie Fryberg, PhD, University of Arizona, writes this in the study "Summary of the APA Resolution Recommending Retirement of American Indian Mascots": "American Indian mascots are harmful not only because they are often negative, but because they remind American Indians of the limited ways in which others see them. This in turn restricts the number of ways American Indians can see themselves."

4

Sexism and Sexual Violence

Sexism, sexual assault, and domestic violence are not the same, but they are connected.

Sexism is threaded through hockey, whether through the presence of ice girls or through the comments of the sport's broadcasters, like Mike Milbury, who, in the context of the NHL's playoff bubble during COVID-19 in 2020, called women a distraction for hockey players. Women and non-binary people are judged by their clothes, how they speak, what they look like, how they act. Women in hockey are often harassed online in their direct messages and are often the recipients of sexist insults, questions about their hockey knowledge, or inappropriate comments. Those who are not cisgender men do not fit into this community.

The instances listed in this chapter are just a few that are public. There are many more that are not listed or that were never told.

LAURA ROBINSON, AUTHOR of the book *Crossing the Line: Violence and Sexual Assault in Canada's National Sport*, said she was never viewed as anything more than an accessory to a player—despite being an athlete herself.

"It was never, ever assumed that I was there as an athlete. I must be like a girlfriend or something, but not an athlete," Robinson said.

John Cyfko, who played AAA hockey and junior hockey and trained at one of the highest-level gyms in Canada, witnessed the way women were characterized by those within hockey's power structure when he was 15 years old. One of his coaches came into the dressing room and started talking about "like eating pussy or something."

"A lot of the things he said were very demeaning toward women and hyper-sexualizing women," Cyfko said. "The thing with all of that is that as kids, we can't say anything. It was putting all of the hypermasculinity on a group of rather innocent grade-time kids."

In 2020, the Washington Capitals' Brendan Leipsic was found to be involved in a misogynistic group Instagram chat that fat-shamed women, including teammates' wives, and called women "little whore cunt."

After screenshots of the group chat circulated, Leipsic tweeted an apology:

> I fully recognize how inappropriate and offensive these comments are and sincerely apologize to everyone for my actions. I am committed to learning from this and becoming a better person by taking time to determine how to move forward in an accountable, meaningful way. I am truly sorry.

Leipsic then deleted his account. The Capitals released him.

On the surface these may just be words, but words matter.

"Words have power," said Brenda Tracy, rape survivor and founder of Set the Expectation, a pledge aimed at male college and high school athletes to promote accountability. "Words can start wars, or words can end relationships. Words can trigger eating disorders. Words matter. Names have a lot of power. And so I think it matters. Before you can abuse someone, you have to dehumanize them. And one of the quickest ways to do that is through our language," Tracy said.

And this problem goes far beyond language.

"There's all kinds of metaphors that work in sport and war," Robinson said. "Rape, penetrating, and these words, there's a reason why they're interchangeable between sport, war, rape, and churches." It speaks to a "deeply embedded patriarchy," she says.

Hockey also has a history of a relationship with Barstool Sports. The site and its founder, Dave Portnoy, have a history of being both sexist and racist. In 2019, the Boston Bruins created playoff rally towels sponsored by Barstool Sports. In 2014, Portnoy harassed sportscaster Sam Ponder and called her a "slut" on his podcast.

At the time, Hemal Jhaveri wrote for USA TODAY: "Anyone familiar with the sports media ecosystem knows that this is how Barstool works. Any attempt to hold them accountable for their reprehensible behavior will be met with an onslaught of attacks from their fan base."

A more seemingly innocuous way hockey connects with Barstool is by associating with, retweeting, and promoting its hockey podcast, *Spittin' Chiclets*. Now, because Portnoy does not host the podcast, people often say it's fine to associate with it and retweet it.

The problem is that associating with and promoting any arm of Barstool enables Barstool to survive, which in turn enables its harassing behavior.

IN SEPTEMBER 2019, Toronto Maple Leafs star Auston Matthews faced charges for disorderly conduct stemming from an incident the previous May that the team had not been aware of. A woman security guard at Matthews' apartment complex, who had been sitting in her car, alleged Matthews and his friends tried opening her car door before walking away, with Matthews pulling down his pants (with his underwear on) and grabbing his butt. Per the police report, video surveillance showed Matthews walking away with his pants around his ankles.

In response, Toronto's coach Kyle Dubas said in a statement, "I think you always wish that whenever you're part of any organization, athletics or otherwise, that there's never going to be any issues, there's never going to be any errors in judgment and never going to be any distractions. Unfortunately, there often are.

"We have to use it as an opportunity to continue to educate our whole organization—every player, every staff member—about the way that we expect our organization to conduct its business here at the rink every day—in the weight room, in the community—and how they interact with every citizen that they come into contact with, because when they are doing so they're representing the Toronto Maple Leafs."

There's the problem of how Dubas framed it, calling the behavior "errors in judgment" and "distractions," phrases that center the team and the victim while minimizing the severity of Matthews' actions.

Once the charges were dismissed (the CBC reported the two parties settled out of court), Matthews did apologize, saying, "I just want to reiterate again how truly sorry I am for my actions and my behavior. I never meant to cause any distress to this woman and I can assure you that I've learned from my mistakes and my actions."

In the aftermath, we saw the media's role in mitigating violence against those who are not men. After the report, prominent members of the hockey community took to Twitter, making jokes or dismissing Matthews' conduct, like CBS Sports' Pete Blackburn tweeting:

> well it's certainly a story, but it's not a massive deal. just him being a drunk idiot it sounds like

There was Bruce Arthur's column in the *Toronto Star* in which he wrote, "If true, it's the kind of dumb, entitled, thoughtless thing that young men are prone to do, especially if they have power and money. Scaring a woman at two in the morning with a group of drunken men is menacing if you think of it from her point of view. Matthews doesn't seem to have done so."

It's not a "dumb, entitled, thoughtless thing." It's a harmful action. It's predatory in its nature. Framing it in this way, as a stupid thing Matthews did at night as a prank, is normalizing behavior that threatens women.

In July 2020, the Professional Hockey Writers Association nominated Matthews for the Lady Byng Memorial Trophy, awarded to the player who best exemplifies sportsmanship and gentlemanly conduct. What is so gentlemanly about his conduct in May 2019? By ignoring that event, the PHWA was essentially saying off-ice conduct doesn't matter—and therefore not holding players accountable.

In 2014, the Minnesota *Pioneer Press* reported that two USHL players, Thomas Carey and Brandon Smith, appeared in court facing "felony charges of using a minor in a sexual performance and possession and distribution of child pornography." Court documents allege Smith taped Carey having sex with a 15-year-old girl. Both men, who said they knew she was underage, claimed she consented to being taped. By Minnesota law, consent is not considered a defense in using a minor in a sexual performance. Per court documents, the alleged victim found out about the video after receiving messages from her peer group and other hockey players.

In 2015, the paper reported the players pleaded guilty to three counts of child pornography after agreeing to a plea deal that did not require them to register as sex offenders. They began serving time in Clay County Jail.

In 2017, the *New York Times* published a story looking at the work of researchers into perpetrators of rape. It wrote, "Heavy drinking, perceived pressure to have sex, a belief in 'rape myths'—such as the idea that no means yes—are all risk factors among men who have committed sexual assault. A peer group that uses hostile language to describe women is another one."

BEFORE WE BEGIN a discussion about sexual assault, there are important parameters to define. The Rape, Abuse & Incest National Network (RAINN) defines sexual assault as "contact or behavior that occurs without explicit consent of the victim," including fondling or unwanted sexual touching. The FBI defines rape as "penetration, no matter how slight, of the vagina or anus with any body part or object, or oral penetration by a sex organ of another person, without the consent of the victim." Legally, the definition varies by state. (Ed. note: this book's co-author went to RAINN following her sexual assault.)

Per the U.S. Department of Justice, there are 433,648 victims of sexual assault and rape aged 12 and older on average yearly in the United States. Out of every 1,000 cases of sexual assault, 995 offenders will go free. Just 46 reports will lead to arrest and 4.6 rapists will be incarcerated.

While women are more likely to face sexual assault than men, men can also be on the receiving end of sexual violence. And sexual violence affects trans, non-binary, and genderqueer people, as well as Native Americans, at the highest rates.

From 2005 to '10, victims chose not to report for a variety of reasons, including fear of retaliation, belief the police would not help, belief it was a personal matter, belief it wasn't important enough, or feeling that they "didn't want to get the perpetrator in trouble."

Victims of sexual violence can suffer from problems with work, school, or social relationships. According to a 1992 study published in the *Journal of Traumatic Stress*, "A Prospective Examination of

Post-Traumatic Stress Disorder in Rape Victims," 94 percent of rape victims suffer from post-traumatic stress disorder (PTSD).

The Department of Justice Canada reported that, as of a 2014 survey, 37 of every 1,000 women were victims of sexual assault. In addition, five out of every 1,000 men were victimized. And 83 percent of sexual assault cases were not reported to the police.

There are many misconceptions about sexual assault and many means used to discredit survivors. A common one is how survivors' stories shift or that they don't always give the same account of events.

"As a trauma victim, I'm not going to remember what happened to me in perfect sequence...that's not how my brain works, because of trauma," Tracy said. "So, if someone robbed your home, you'll be able to tell the police ABCD happened. And that looks credible to everybody because that's how we're supposed to remember things, Then, [as a] sexual assault survivor, I might remember L, M, and Q tomorrow. And then people are like, 'Oh, she's lying because she can't remember.' People don't even understand the dynamics of this violence and trauma, so it makes sense to me that they're not going to understand how victims' [minds] work, how any of that works really."

It isn't just that sexual violence happens in hockey. It's what is done—or rather, isn't done—about it.

Billy Tibbetts is one of the best examples. Per the *Hartford Courant* and the *Patriot Ledger*, in 1992, when Tibbetts was 17, he was convicted after pleading guilty to raping a 15-year-old. Despite calling the crime "brutal," the judge handed Tibbetts a suspended sentence of three to five years and four years' probation—a fancy way of saying that he never went to jail. Tibbetts eventually did go to jail, but only because in 1994 he was charged with assault and battery of a police officer. He received another suspended sentence and probation in 1995. Tibbetts then went to jail and was paroled on October 29, 1999.

Tibbetts was given many more chances and he was signed in 2000 by the Pittsburgh Penguins, where general manager Craig Patrick told the *Pittsburgh Post-Gazette*, "I wrestled a lot in making the decision [to sign Tibbetts]. He messed up as a young man, and nobody condones what he did. It wasn't something any of us would be proud of, by any stretch of the imagination. But we have a [rehabilitation] system in place, and he deserved a chance to live his dream. He served his time. Let's see if the system works. If the system doesn't work, he'll be back where he was and have a miserable life. But if it has worked for him..."

Committing rape goes far beyond being a "hurdle" to overcome. Words matter, and referring to a rape accusation as a hurdle centers the alleged perpetrator and decenters and ignores the plight of the victim.

The main point is that Tibbetts was convicted for rape and he didn't even go to jail. (If this sounds familiar, it's because Stanford's Brock Turner also did not go to jail despite an eyewitness account of him raping an unconscious woman in 2015.) There was no proof, ever, that Tibbetts had changed or grown. And there was no consideration for his victim. What kind of message does this send to a rape survivor?

Sunaya Sapurji, who has covered major juniors for a variety of outlets, including Yahoo Sports and, currently, The Athletic, said she thinks it's difficult for women to come forward after an assault.

"When the perpetrator is an athlete, it makes it even more difficult, even more frightening, even more traumatizing," Sapurji said. "That person usually has some form of status. They might have money. Look at the history of what's happened at least in the media in the past, some of the high-profile cases that have happened before and how the victims have been continuously re-traumatized. Unfortunately the thought can be, 'Is it worth it?'"

In a *Pittsburgh Post-Gazette* column, Sally Kalson wrote:

How nice for Billy Tibbetts that he got the chance to overcome his past and go on to a rewarding career with the Penguins. I wonder if the 15-year-old girl he raped in 1992 is doing as well.... And what of the rape victim? She'd be about 24 now, old enough to be graduated from college, working, married— or reclusive, depressed, alcoholic. Whatever she's doing, I'm guessing it doesn't involve a contract that pays about $140,000 for a 29-game season. That's the deal Tibbetts has with the Penguins—not bad for a guy on parole who has to register with police as a sex offender.... I would like to see a portion of every paycheck garnished. If the victims don't want the money, let it go to a rape crisis center or a juvenile court program that works with teen-age offenders. The next Billy Tibbetts is out there, waiting to erupt. If the current one had a hand in stopping him, that would be some form of justice.

Sexual assault, for the reasons noted previously, is not an easy topic to cover. Most reporters—especially sports reporters—are not trained in it. Attempts usually result in victim-blaming from the media, decentering survivors, or insinuating survivors are lying. According to the National Sexual Violence Resource Center, research shows that only between 2 and 10 percent of victims file false reports. Victims rarely lie. Without an understanding of the facts and how trauma affects our brains, it is easy for sexual assault allegations to be misreported.

In 2001, after Tibbetts had been signed by the Penguins and when he had been arrested again, the *Hartford Courant* profiled Tibbetts, who pleaded guilty to rape.

In 2006, James Mirtle, now editor-in-chief of The Athletic Canada, wrote, "Say what you will about Tibbetts' conduct on the ice and his demeanour off of it, he deserves whatever hockey career his talents dictate. I can do without any more self-righteous—and uninformed—blithering about why he deserves less.

"He's 31 years old and has clearly moved on. It's time we did so as well."

(The op-ed he referred to as "self-righteous" was Kalson's in the *Post-Gazette*.)

That last sentence is particularly callous, since survivors of sexual assault don't get to move on so effortlessly, if at all.

"Victim-blaming for me, No. 1, is lazy," Tracy said. "If we have figured out a way to make it the victim's fault, then I don't have to hold anybody accountable. I don't have to change anything. I don't have to create a policy. You don't have to do anything."

In *Time*, Shireen Ahmed, a sports activist and writer covering the intersections of racism and misogyny in sport, tackled the media's poor coverage of topics like sexual assault. She wrote, "I have worked with survivors of violence and have yet to meet or know of a victim who has enjoyed any of the bullying, shame, societal isolation, and mental health upheavals, and wanted to claim some type of infamy from an attack. And I won't even dignify the ridiculous notion of 'false accusations.'"

The piece centered on the coverage of rape allegations against soccer star Cristiano Ronaldo, but it still applies to the coverage of hockey players who've been accused of alleged sexual assault.

Ahmed wrote, "Predictably, the same sports media who initially had no interest in this story have become 'experts' in criminal law, and on sexualized violence. The vacuous reporting and unnecessary reflections are mostly done by men, and center the 33-year-old star. Opinions on due process (reminder: it's a legal system not a justice system) and about Ronaldo's athletic prowess and teams don't have anything to do with this case."

Yes, Tibbetts' case occurred nearly 30 years ago. But for a more recent example, look no further than Ben Johnson, whom the New

Jersey Devils drafted in 2012. In 2013, Johnson was charged with two counts of sexual assault for two separate incidents between January and March of that year. In 2016, Johnson was found guilty of the first charge and sentenced to three years in prison. The CBC reported that the judge, Kirk Munroe, said the victim couldn't give consent because of her blood alcohol level. The Devils terminated Johnson's contract not long after.

After his release from jail in 2018, Johnson was signed by the Cincinnati Cyclones of the ECHL in December after he became eligible for parole in November.

In a statement published in the *Cincinnati Enquirer*, the team said, "After an exhaustive and prolonged vetting process, we decided to sign Forward Ben Johnson. The decision was not one that was taken lightly and only after countless hours of research, internal and external candid conversations, and reflection was the choice made to proceed with the signing. The Cyclones do not condone or promote sexual assault in any capacity. The easy thing for us to do would be to not sign this player but we have found this to be a mature young man of faith and character that will be a contributor not only on the ice, but also more importantly in the locker room and community. We hope that this organization and setting proves to be the best environment for him to continue to grow personally and professionally."

Johnson was also named the ECHL player of the week in December 2019.

The Cyclones clearly stated they do not condone or promote sexual assault, but if that were truly the case, they would not have signed Johnson. Claiming they made the difficult decision is interesting, since in sports the easy thing is to ignore off-ice actions and focus only on on-ice performance.

This narrative always centers the alleged perpetrators and their redemption while giving little to no consideration to the survivors, or to others who have survived sexual assault. It sends a very clear message that two things—on-ice performance and the player's redemption—are more important than anyone harmed by off-ice conduct.

"He went to prison, got out of prison, and then was playing hockey, like, right away," said Jordan DeKort, Johnson's former teammate and roommate in Windsor who testified at Johnson's trial. "So, that's interesting to me. I guess 'interesting' is not the word I would normally use for that, but it makes me quite angry."

Two cases, nearly 30 years apart, of players being convicted of sexual assault and still finding a playing career in hockey.

And it isn't just the players who are protected. It's coaches, too. In December 2020, TSN's Rick Westhead reported that former AHL coach Jarrod Skalde filed a lawsuit stating the Penguins hired and retained a coach they knew was a sexual harasser. Skalde was a former assistant with the Wilkes-Barre/Scranton Penguins, Pittsburgh's AHL affiliate. A Penguins lawyer told TSN the team filed a motion to dismiss.

Skalde alleged that Clark Donatelli sexually assaulted Skalde's wife during a road trip. He also alleged that after bringing the matter to the attention of then Penguins assistant general manager Bill Guerin, Skalde was told to keep quiet. He was then fired on May 5, 2020, which he alleged was a violation of Pennsylvania's whistleblower laws. (The Wild, for whom Guerin now works, declined to comment to TSN.) Donatelli's lawyer also declined to comment.

In the motion to dismiss, the Penguins said the whistleblower laws don't apply because he did not report the alleged assault within 180 days, which, per the team, is required under state law. Skalde said he and his wife did not report it right away because they were unsure what to do and they were afraid of retaliation.

The claim said Skalde told Guerin on June 21, 2019. A week later, Dontaelli resigned for "personal reasons." In the claim, the Skaldes also claimed they learned of more sexual harassment by Donatelli, which the Penguins allegedly knew about but did not stop.

WHAT IS REFERRED to by the CDC as Intimate Partner Violence (IPV) and more commonly known as domestic violence includes physical violence, sexual violence, stalking, or psychological aggression. Per the CDC, about one in four women and one in 10 men will face sexual violence, physical violence, or stalking by a partner.

Per the Rhode Island Coalition Against Domestic Violence (RICADV), people abuse partners to create power and control. The coalition states, "The difference between domestic violence and a family dispute or argument is that batterers use acts of violence and a series of behaviors to establish ongoing control and fear in the relationship through violence and other forms of abuse."

But it's more than just physical violence, says Ruth Glenn, the CEO of the National Coalition Against Domestic Violence. Glenn worked for the Colorado Department of Human Services for 28 years and as director of the Domestic Violence Program (DVP) for nine of those years.

"You know, it's a shove up against the wall with my arm on your neck," Glenn said. "It's telling you that you're a worthless piece of shit—I'm sorry for the language. It's not allowing you to have access to finance, which I guarantee you that there are players' partners [whose] husbands are making money and that partner may not have access to any of that money. So it looks different."

The RICADV stated that abuse is a learned behavior that is reinforced when abusers "are not arrested, prosecuted, or otherwise held responsible for their acts." Abuse has long-lasting effects on women, harming their physical health, mental health, and possibly careers. Abuse also traumatizes children who witness it.

IPV, like sexual assault, is complicated. Some will point to a survivor's willingness to stay with or forgive their partner as proof that nothing happened, or that whatever happened was not bad. Per the National Domestic Violence Hotline, there are many reasons why survivors of IPV stay, including fear, normalized abuse, shame, intimidation, lack of resources, immigration status, and even love. The National Coalition Against Domestic Violence reported that women who leave abusive partners increase their chances of being killed by 75 percent.

According to the RICADV, "The problem is really with the question. The question implies that the violence is the problem of the woman who is the victim of the violence, and that it is up to her to solve it."

In Rhode Island, 83.3 percent of defendants in abuse cases are charged with misdemeanors, and most first-time abusers do not go to jail.

IN 1992, CHICAGO Blackhawks rookie Sergei Krivokrasov was charged by the Duluth State District Court with assault and disorderly conduct after he allegedly spit on and hit a woman after she asked him for money for an abortion, saying she was pregnant with his child. She had met Krivokrasov at Minnesota-Duluth's weight room while training in the offseason. Krivokrasov pleaded not guilty.

Four years later, the *Minneapolis Star Tribune* reported that Minnesota-Duluth athletic director Bruce McLeod had tried to bribe the woman, who was a student at UMD, not to testify against Krivokrasov, who was not nor ever had been a student at UMD. McLeod wasn't charged because money was never exchanged.

In 1999, Krivokrasov had to agree to counseling in order for a domestic violence charge filed by his wife to be dropped. His wife alleged that he slapped her and kicked her and pushed her down a few steps. Nashville general manager David Poile said the team would not assess further discipline: "We obviously don't condone the activity, but we do support the Krivokrasovs and we do hope and pray that their problems can be worked out."

In November 2014, Los Angeles Kings defenseman Slava Voynov was charged with allegedly attacking his wife. He was suspended indefinitely by the NHL in October 2014.

The *Los Angeles Times* reported that, per the police report, Voynov allegedly kicked his wife and choked her, at one point pushing her face into the corner of a wall-mounted television. In July, he began serving out his 90-day jail sentence and had to complete a 52-week domestic violence prevention program plus community service. He served for two months and then went back to Russia to avoid deportation.

However, three years after Voynov's probationary period ended, the judge dismissed his domestic abuse conviction. The NHL then faced a choice—allow Voynov back into the league or not. (Voynov still represented Russia in the Olympics.) Some called for a lifetime suspension, but instead Voynov was suspended for the 2019–20 season. The Kings said they wouldn't sign Voynov, regardless. But that left every other team in the league. And some teams considered it.

In 2018, Nashville Predators winger Austin Watson was arrested and charged with domestic assault. Watson, who had appeared in a domestic violence public service campaign the year before, was suspended for 27 games following a league investigation. Watson pleaded no contest and was released on bond and sentenced to three months' probation.

In a statement, NHL Commissioner Gary Bettman said, "Today's ruling, while tailored to the specific facts of this case and the individuals involved, is necessary and consistent with the NHL's strongly held view that it cannot and will not tolerate this and similar types of conduct."

That's interesting, considering that, as of this book's publication, the NHL still does not have a domestic violence policy. If something should not be tolerated, shouldn't the punishment for it be written into the rules?

ADDRESSING SEXUAL ASSAULT, gendered violence, and intimate partner violence is a large task—and it's complex. Society has a rape culture problem, and sports is a microcosm of society. Society also champions values like hypermasculinity, which results in championing violence—praising hockey fights, for example—or demeaning those who are not cis, straight men.

This is something that extends to other sports, as well—Jessica Luther's book *Unsportsmanlike Conduct: College Football and the Politics of Rape* provides a great look at the rape culture in college football—but hockey may be the sport that most glorifies violence. That hockey still has such a unique and insular culture with little room for dissent or for outsiders makes it an easy one to keep perpetuating and a difficult one to change.

As demonstrated earlier, a lack of consequences, a lack of informed reporting from the media, and victim-blaming allow this to keep happening. The best method is, of course, prevention. There are several groups and advocates working within the sports world to create a solution through prevention.

"It's been that way for decades in sports and there's a lot of things that support that culture," Tracy said. "One is just the stigma around sexual violence, rape, domestic violence, any of that stuff a lot of people don't want to talk about [or] don't know how to talk about. It's something that we've been told shouldn't be talked about."

DeKort said that, although he testified truthfully at Johnson's trial, it was framed as though he was against Johnson. Johnson was an NHL draft pick. DeKort was not. DeKort was later traded.

"I can't be 100 percent certain that that's the reason I was traded, but it probably played a part in it. Because we also weren't allowed to see each other outside of the rink...because I [testified] in his trial," DeKort said.

The events inspired DeKort to start the GameChangers workshop, where he teaches players to be active bystanders. It teaches leadership, communication, and how to be a successful team while shifting the culture.

The GameChangers website states: "Our main philosophy is to begin to shift the culture in sport. We want our clients to be leaders in social change, and to limit incidents in their organizations. We also hope to provide participants transferable skills for both sport and life."

With Set the Expectation, Tracy works with college athletics programs teaching sexual assault prevention. There is also a pledge players and coaches can sign. Tracy has worked mostly with college football programs, and some teams—including Michigan—have had her back for multiple sessions.

During the workshops, Tracy shares the story of her rape. But then she tells her audience one important thing: "I'm not here to say I think you're the problem. I'm here because I know that here's the solution."

The majority of men don't commit these crimes, but the workshops are targeted at those who don't intervene to stop them. She gives participants actionable steps, such as hosting a Set the Expectation game, signing the pledge, supporting on-campus resources, not victim-blaming, and calling out and checking their friends who devalue women.

Tracy has still faced some pushback.

"I've really had to decide that this is a marathon, it's not a sprint," Tracy said. "And that is really important for me to meet people where they're at…. When you meet people where they're at, and you're open to having conversations with them and educating people, you hope there is this continuum of, 'I started here but now I'm here.'"

Per the CDC's technical packet to prevent sexual violence, developed in 2016, social norms against violence must be promoted by mobilizing men and boys as allies, promoting social-emotional learning, and teaching healthy and safe relationship skills to adolescents. The document also states: "SV prevention has always centered on issues related to gender, and gender equality is central to SV prevention."

Coaching Boys Into Men (CBIM), a part of Futures Without Violence, trains high school coaches to teach their athletes healthy relationship skills.

CBIM's community manager, Jesse Mahler, played hockey from the ages of five to 14. He said by the time boys are 14, they already have their minds made up—but there are plenty of age-appropriate conversations that can be had about consent, one of the most misunderstood topics. It could be speaking to kids about being okay with being hugged or holding hands.

"That is unequivocally about consent, and about making sure that there's informed, enthusiastic, and non-coercive communication between multiple parties, which is ultimately what consent is about," Mahler said.

There is a major lack of understanding of what consent actually is, especially when it comes to sexual assault.

"People don't understand the dynamics, or they don't understand that flirting with a guy at work doesn't mean that you said yes to sex," Tracy said. "Prior consensual sex doesn't mean rape can't happen. Even just a not guilty verdict—people really think [a] not guilty verdict means the victim lied. No, it means that the jury decided that they didn't meet the level, the burden of proof."

There are also other avenues developed to educate players.

Ed Heisler is the co-executive director of Men as Peacemakers (MAP), a Minnesota-based organization that is a member agency of Violence Free Minnesota, a "statewide coalition of over 90 member programs working to end relationship abuse." He works with college athletics at the Division I and Division III levels. He said that to create these skills, you have to first build the athletes' sense of responsibility. You talk to them about how they would support someone who's experiencing this kind of violence. From there, you can talk about how to act when they overhear harmful words or behavior in the locker room.

And it's important to educate these players because they have influence and, at times, live in their own bubble. In 2015, the Big Ten, college hockey's only Power Five conference (Power Five conferences have the ability to introduce their own legislation), introduced legislation to remove a year of eligibility for each year for anyone enrolling in college hockey after 20 years old. Part of the conference's reasoning was that the age difference between hockey players distanced them from the rest of campus, and schools did not want that.

"There's a lot of Division III schools around here and...cultures where there's a lot of predatory stuff going on, like the party scene," Heisler said. "They're all old enough to supply alcohol, throw house parties. The students that they're interacting with, we're talking about women and girls. Research shows it's the most risky time for freshmen girls in that first few months. There is such a different realm of experience from these guys."

Jeffrey O'Brien, the vice president of the Institute for Sport & Social Justice, said there needs to be a focus on teaching players what harmful behavior is and then teaching them skills to intervene and prevent abuse. O'Brien thinks building real relationships between teammates is key—it gives players an avenue to challenge beliefs and actions that are harmful.

But this can't only be on the students. "These organizations run on parents," Heisler said. "And it's the parents who are doing the role modeling. It's the parents who have influence over the kids. And sometimes we do a disservice when we expect kids to be the change that we want to see. When we expect even college students can be the change that we want to see. And we don't invest in expectations for the adults or for the staff who are around them. While prevention education is paramount to stopping gendered violence and domestic violence, the question remains of what should be done when an athlete is accused or convicted of either sexual assault or domestic violence."

Rita Smith worked as a crisis counselor for more than 30 years, 20 of which she spent as the director of the National Coalition Against Domestic Violence. She and her colleagues had realized they needed good men as allies and thought the NFL would be a perfect example. So in 1998, she began pursuing them to create a policy.

In 2014, a video of Ray Rice punching his fiancée surfaced. Smith's team looked at the policy and saw it said the NFL would wait for a ruling from the criminal justice system before making a decision.

"We were very clear with them to say you can't do that, because domestic violence and sexual assault almost never end up in court," Smith said. "Even if there are charges made, it's rarely convicted. You cannot have that be your standard, because it's just not acceptable.... Those of us who've done this work forever, we will not accept it. It has to be you need to look at whether or not you agree that this behavior is acceptable behavior in your organization."

Smith got the call. She started working as an advisor to the NFL, which moved gendered violence to the personal conduct policy, allowing the league to hold independent investigations to determine if the conduct violated the personal conduct policy and to take action. She hoped it would spur similar policies for all sports leagues.

"I'm disappointed that they all just kind of hide behind the NFL and make the NFL be the one who has to carry all the weight, because they all have problems with this issue," Smith said. "They all do. And yet, very few of them are going at it from the perspective of actually making a difference. Most of them are just trying to stay under the radar."

It's a tough topic, because there are many factors at play. The leagues and teams may often wait for the legal system, but as noted earlier, that is not reliable and an acquittal does not mean someone is not guilty.

"Everyone has rights. And [allegations] should be investigated. But there are times where it's pretty darn clear what has happened," Glenn said. "For instance, you may have a player that this is not the first time he's been accused of that. Or you may have a player who could be observed being inappropriate.

"It is tricky, because I know that organized sports really do like to do their own investigations and they tried to have those coincide with any criminal investigation. But here's the thing: not all domestic violence is going to be criminalized...they all have to be dealt with individually, but to say that you have to wait for a criminal investigation, or that domestic violence has to be criminalized so that you can do something about it, is problematic. That's why responsive procedure is so important. It really is, and it does take time to work it out. And not just when there's a case, but to use all those scenarios that might come up and how are we going to deal with that when they do."

There is debate about whether zero-tolerance policies are useful. A zero-tolerance policy states that when someone commits domestic or sexual violence, they are no longer in sports. Glenn said once a league decides on a zero-tolerance policy, implementing it can be challenging.

"It could be really messy," she said. "For instance, you have a player who may be committing domestic violence, then, the NHL as an example, comes out with a zero-tolerance [policy]. Is he going to escalate when he goes to commit violence because he knows there's zero tolerance?" Glenn said. "If that's what we're talking about, what others have alluded to, that's a fallacy. You know abusers are gonna abuse, and they make a choice about that. And I don't think something like that necessarily will increase the violence."

Per the RICADV, outside influences do not trigger someone's behavior and make them violent. "It is important to remember that domestic violence is a choice, regardless of whether or not a person uses drugs or alcohol," the RICADV's domestic violence online guide reads.

"The people who think about zero tolerance, you need to catch it early, you need to make sure the consequences are heavy in the front end," Smith said. "We just can't tolerate any of it. And then there are people who believe that zero tolerance is really hard to achieve. So it also creates problems, particularly in communities of color, where they don't really have expendable people; you don't put them in jail because they need each other. So it's hard to know. I don't have a particular tendency toward either one. I prefer to listen to what people think and how it might impact them in their communities. Individual communities should make decisions together on both lists with survivors always, always, always at the table, but advocates and law enforcement and the criminal justice system and probation and parole, you have those conversations with everybody that might be impacted by it."

Playing sports at an elite level is a privilege, not a right. But it becomes difficult to tell when or if someone has been rehabilitated.

O'Brien referenced the MLB's policy for domestic violence, child abuse, and sexual assault and what results in a suspension. "If this player does this counseling, does this anger management, does this batterers intervention program...are they clean now? And the answer is, 'Who knows?' It's really hard to know that."

The RICADV's guide states that batterers intervention programs are criminal justice interventions and not solutions to violence, and that changing behavior patterns is a lifelong commitment. "Six months of batterers intervention that someone is forced to attend can only begin to plant the seeds for change. Recidivism is very difficult to measure, since arrest rates only capture a small amount of the domestic violence that takes place. What we do know from the research is that batterers intervention programs do decrease an offender's violence while he is in a program. Long-term effects are less likely to occur unless the offender is actively working to change his behavior."

"If somebody is not committed to the work, to improving themselves and their reaction to conflict, or any other type of relationship, they could easily end up reverting back to their other tendencies and how they dealt with conflict," O'Brien said. "And I appreciate that, from the league standpoint, it's hard to know. Because to me, if somebody has done none of those things, you can tell they're not really interested in trying to grow and learn and get better as a human."

5

Bullying, Hazing, and Abuse

As mentioned earlier, all these topics—racism, sexism, sexual assault and violence, bullying, hazing, and abuse—are connected. Sexual assault is also a component of bullying, hazing, and systemic abuse—three topics grouped together in this chapter because they are tethered.

Systemic abuse refers to sexual abuse of athletes by coaching. Hazing is the trials and "rituals" used to initiate new members. Bullying can manifest in both hazing and sexual abuse.

The NCAA defines hazing as "any act committed against someone joining or becoming a member or maintaining membership in any organization that is humiliating, intimidating or demeaning, or endangers the health and safety of the person."

Per Hockey Canada's Bullying Harassment and Abuse Policies:

> Some behaviours which are defined as abuse, when a child
> or youth's protection is at risk, can also constitute harassment

or bullying, when the behaviour breaches human rights or appropriate relationship/conduct boundaries.

Bullying involves a person expressing their power through the humiliation of another person. Bullying may be a form of harassment but also has some of its own defining characteristics. The sport setting is one setting in which bullying occurs. In some cases coaches and players use bullying tactics deliberately to motivate performance and to weaken opponents.

HOCKEY CANADA LISTED the following as common bullying tactics:

1. Unwarranted yelling and screaming directed at the target
2. Continually criticizing the target's abilities
3. Blaming the target of the bullying for mistakes
4. Making unreasonable demands related to performance
5. Repeated insults or put-downs of the target
6. Repeated threats to remove or restrict opportunities or privileges
7. Denying or discounting the target's accomplishment
8. Threats of and actual physical violence

Coaches have been accused of abuse, physical and emotional. Both child and adult players are targeted.

"I won't name names, but I've had a coach actually say to the whole team, 'Maybe one or two [of you] will play in the NHL but I got all your balls in my hand.' Like he just made an insinuation that he controls our lives," Kurtis Gabriel, a current professional player, said.

Historically (and sometimes still currently), the belief was that if a coach is berating a player, the coach is making the player tough. He's building "character."

Stories of coaches bullying their athletes are now being revealed. In 2019, Toronto Maple Leafs alternate captain Mitch Marner told TSN that former head coach Mike Babcock made Marner rank his teammates from hardest-working to laziest when he was a rookie. Johan Franzén told Swedish newspaper *Expressen* that Babcock was a "bully who was attacking people. It could be a cleaner at the arena in Detroit or anybody. He would lay into people without any reason."

Franzén said, "He would lay into a couple of the other players. The nice team players, the guys who don't say very much. When they left the team he went on to focus on me. It was verbal attacks, he said horrible things.

"From 2011 on, I was terrified of being at the rink. That's when he got on me the first time. I just focused on getting out of bed every morning from that moment. Last year I could sleep naturally for the first time since then.

"It was just his attacks, playing in my head. Each and every day."

ESPN reported that Maple Leafs president Brendan Shanahan said Babcock's coaching tactics were not appropriate at the NHL Board of Governors meeting. After Marner spoke out, Akim Aliu tweeted that he wasn't surprised by Babcock's actions because of similar conduct by his protégé. That protégé was Bill Peters, who allegedly used racial slurs against Aliu. Aliu's former teammates Simon Pepin and Peter MacArthur corroborated the allegation. Former Carolina Hurricanes defenseman Michal Jordán told TSN that Peters had kicked him "pretty hard in the back during a game." Current Hurricanes coach Rod Brind'Amour, who was an assistant at the time, confirmed.

This isn't limited to professional players. Jordan DeKort remembers when he was around nine years old and returned to hockey after spending the summer at a cottage with his dad. He had been active, but he wasn't in excellent shape.

"I remember getting shamed for that and I remember thinking to myself, 'I'm never going to put myself in this position again because I feel terrible.' It was the shame of, 'I didn't do enough,'" DeKort said.

When John Cyfko was playing youth hockey, a coach wanted Cyfko on his AAA team. But Cyfko wanted to stay in AA, which was an easier situation for his parents. He caved.

"It really got toxic to the point where I remember in training camp when I had so much anxiety [to] go play for him and go to the training camp that I was physically sick, throwing up and I couldn't go to training camp," Cyfko said. "And he still wanted me there. My parents called him and said, 'Our kid's sick, he can't come,' and he said, 'Bring him anyway,' and I showed up and I was pale and looking very pukey and he said, 'I didn't realize you were that sick, you can go home.'"

There was the time they ran laps around a baseball diamond and he was second to last. His coach berated him for being out of shape.

"I remember him just ripping on me, like, 'You told me you were working hard this summer. I wouldn't expect that out of you,' and just very much looking to any tiny little fault," Cyfko said. "It felt to me like a personal thing. And then any little drill that anyone would mess up, he'd absolutely yell at them...a kid in minor midget. I found that kind of negative reinforcement and berating kids for making small mistakes wasn't very effective or reasonable. And I don't know if he thought he could get away with it because there were no parents watching because it was training camp and parents would be at work during those days. But that was a big part of the reason why I had that anxiety attack and didn't want to go in that one day of camp."

Cyfko remembers doing push-ups once and his shirt exposing a small section of his stomach.

"The trainer started making fun of my belly, saying, 'You'll never get anywhere...you got to start working out more.' It's a very toxic motivation to implant in an impressionable kid," Cyfko said. "I've seen NHL players shirtless. They're not exactly seven percent body fat. It's not like the standard has anything to do with how good you are at hockey. But it's something that that was implanted...if you wanted to go outside while you were working out, the rule was like you had to have a six pack or you couldn't."

Riley Fitzgerald, the coordinator of sports psychology services for Boston University athletics, entered this field partly because of poor experiences playing youth hockey. One of the experiences he remembers is his coach being angry at the team for not blocking enough shots. He was 11.

"He put us all in front of the net one at a time and ripped slap shots at us," Fitzgerald said. "He was shooting hard enough that he broke the shin of one of my teammates. Another coach, I think I was 11 at the time, was breaking clipboards over guys' heads on the bench."

Fitzgerald remembers a particular practice during regional championships when he was about 16 years old.

"Everyone goes, 'Why does it look like anytime you're on the ice your girlfriend just broke up with you?' At this point it's been a couple of months of dealing with, looking back, pretty serious depression," Fitzgerald said. "And part of that is stemming from hockey, and [that was] kind of the only thing that really stood out to my coach after a couple of months. You look like you hate being on the ice. And [in] those moments, in my head, I'm like, 'No shit, I don't want to be here.' But I think part of it is just, you know, the worry of what are your teammates going to think of you and say about you. What your coach is going to think and say about you. Even if you don't necessarily like them, they're such an impactful person on both the short term and the long term, especially if you want to keep playing, or you think you do.

"And so instead of just kind of shrugging it off and laughing, all this is just me being focused and continuing to play through. I think part of that too is that identity piece of not wanting to admit it out loud or admit it to anyone else, because it would make it real."

And after games, one coach asked benched players to raise their hands and say why they thought they were benched. As one of the targets of this exercise, Fitzgerald assumed he was a bad player.

Bullying by players can also be targeted toward non-players, as we discussed in Chapter 3 with Mitchell Miller. Miller bullied a disabled Black boy at his high school. This kind of bullying also needs to be recognized, but is seldom—if ever—talked about in hockey.

HAZING IS AN escalation of bullying, either toward members of the hockey community or others, and can constitute sexual assault.

A 1999 national study conducted by Alfred University found that 80 percent of NCAA athletes said they were subject to hazing. Right now, 44 states have laws against hazing.

The NCAA's hazing handbook maintains there is a difference between hazing and team building—team building is a positive experience and hazing is a power trip.

In June 2020, former NHL players Daniel Carcillo and Garrett Taylor filed a hazing lawsuit against the Canadian Hockey League (the OHL, WHL, and QMJHL).

The lawsuit read, in part, "Canadian major junior hockey has been plagued by rampant hazing, bullying, and abuse of underage players, by coaches, team staff, and senior players. Survivors of such Abuse have come forward and continue to come forward to this day. However, the Defendants have stubbornly ignored or failed to reasonably address this institutionalized and systemic Abuse."

The lawsuit also said the organizations "perpetuated a toxic environment that condones violent, discriminatory, racist, sexualized, and homophobic conduct, including physical and sexual assault, on the underage players they are obligated to protect."

The lawsuit also alleged that senior players, coaches, staff, administrators, and employees knew the hazing was occurring and that players had repeatedly reported the abuse to higher-ups, but the teams and leagues create a culture of silence where speaking up is discouraged.

"I think it's part of the culture that hockey is a sport where there's a definite hierarchy, even things like, on a bus with a team, there's a very specific seating arrangement," Sunaya Sapurji said. "It doesn't matter what team you are, what level of hockey, the hierarchy is always the same.... Because there's that hierarchy, veterans and captains have way more power. That's the other thing, is the power dynamic. If you're a rookie, what can you really say to anyone? And I don't know if that power dynamic has shifted now."

The lawsuit listed several examples of hazing. Rookies had to sit naked in the middle of the shower room as other players urinated and spat on them. At least on one occasion, the head coach saw this happening and just laughed. Rookies were hit on their buttocks with a sawed-off goalie stick. They were stripped naked and forced into the bathrooms on road trips. In one instance, a rookie was taped to a table and was whipped with a belt. The coach also whipped the boy with a belt. Older players also organized orgies where rookies were required to participate in sexual acts. Racist, sexist, and homophobic slurs were directed at the players.

The lawsuit states that the OHL investigated a report made by Carcillo and other players but released no findings or punishment. It read: "Carcillo's experience during his rookie year left him permanently traumatized. He suffered severe mental health issues which were not present before the abuse he endured. He continues to suffer from these mental health issues to this day."

The abuse didn't end in Carcillo's era. Garrett Taylor, who played for the Lethbridge Hurricanes of the WHL in 2008–09, said the head coach gave the players a team credit card to buy alcohol for the rookie party, where the younger players were forced to binge drink and dress in women's clothing.

The lawsuit also lists examples of sexual assault hazing—players being forced to sexually assault teammates, to consume bodily fluids of other teammates, to masturbate in front of coaches and teammates, having objects inserted in their anuses, and more.

This line from the lawsuit said it all: "The Defendants have failed in their duties to protect the children under their care."

In 2000, the University of Vermont canceled what remained of its men's hockey team season due to hazing. The *New York Times* reported it was cancelled due to players lying during the hazing investigation. The article said "recruits to the team had been coerced into drinking large amounts of alcohol, parading naked while holding one another's genitals and engaging in other degrading activities." Corey LaTulippe, a goaltender at the school, had already left the team and filed a lawsuit regarding the hazing.

John Cyfko described his experience to us. "We'd have rookie parties and in juniors for the rookies, and it was just all about women and getting underage kids alcohol poisoning and there is no real way out," he said. "There's this unspoken rule that you have to go to a party. And if you don't, you're not part of the team. What these rookie priorities are like, they make all the guys dress up in a bikini or go to the sex shop and get a really weird costume. And then they just get them hammered and invite over only girls. It's a very weird and super, super hypermasculine."

The behavior also creates a toxic cycle, Sapurji said. "If you were a rookie and you were treated poorly by your veterans, the better the chances are when you become a veteran, you will do the same to the rookies. I had to go through this, and it was shitty and humiliating. You have to go through it."

USA HOCKEY SAYS the goals of its youth programs are "to provide an innovative grassroots foundation for the growth and development of USA Hockey, designing programs aimed at increased participation, improved skills, and a responsible environment for the conduct of youth hockey."

Under the coaches' code of conduct, one of the bullets calls for coaches to "be concerned with the overall development of your players. Stress good health habits and clean living."

In 2019, a CBC investigation revealed that at least 222 amateur sports coaches in Canada had been convicted of sexual offenses in the last 20 years, affecting more than 600 victims younger than 18. The offenses spanned all sports, but hockey had the most charges (86) and convictions (50) between 1998 and 2018. The sport with the next most instances was soccer, with 40 charges and 27 convictions. In almost all cases, athletes were training with their coach.

CBC reporters Lori Ward and Jamie Strashin wrote, "For years, experts say, sports organizations at all levels have created anti-abuse policies without actually knowing the full scope of the problem."

The CDC lists four categories under child abuse and neglect: physical abuse, sexual abuse, emotional abuse, and neglect. This chapter focuses on sexual abuse. The CDC reported that roughly one in four girls and one in 13 boys experience sexual abuse as children at some point, and 91 percent of the time the perpetrator is someone known by the child or the family. Per the National Children's Advocacy Center, false allegations of child sexual abuse happen less than 10 percent of the time.

The U.S. Center for SafeSport reports that one in eight athletes will experience sexual abuse or assault in their sport by age 18. Athletes with disabilities are four times as likely to be harassed or abused as those who are able-bodied.

University of Toronto professors Gretchen Kerr and Peter Donnelly wrote a paper reviewing Canada's harassment and abuse policies. Speaking to fellow faculty member Jelena Damjanovic, Donnelly said, "These 222 cases are the tip of the iceberg. For every case that went to court, there were probably many others where prosecutors decided there was not enough evidence or the complainant withdrew from the process. And, as we are well aware with regard to sexual offences and gender-based violence in general, the vast majority of cases are never reported."

The most well-known case of abuse concerns convicted serial rapist and sex offender Larry Nassar, who abused at least 265 young women and girls over three decades. Penn State assistant coach Jerry Sandusky abused at least 10 boys over a 15-year period. More stories have surfaced at other institutions and within other sports.

In 2006, former NHLer Sheldon Kennedy described the abuse he suffered by his coach, Graham James, in the 1980s as a junior player on the Moose Jaw Warriors and then on the WHL Swift Current Broncos in his memoir *Why I Didn't Say Anything*.

Kennedy revealed that he had troubles with his father. As a child, Kennedy and his brother were dropped off at the Andy Murray Hockey School in 1992 to play under James. Kennedy wrote, "As he said goodbye, Dad reminded us to listen to the coaches and treat them with respect.... Your parents send you and tell you, 'Do whatever he says.' At that age, you listen, especially when you've had an upbringing like mine where you never talked back to the person in charge. You listen to the coach because he is in charge and because he is your first step to playing pro hockey."

James had coached the Junior Fort Garry to the Manitoba provincial title and was a well-known WHL scout, accolades that resulted in hero status. Kennedy said, "Men like Graham were put on a pedestal. They held the keys to the kingdom we were all dreaming about: the NHL.... Piss off someone like Graham or get on their bad side, and you might as well stay home."

Once the abuse started, Kennedy said he didn't tell anyone because he was afraid his dad would call him weak or blame him for not resisting. He thought maybe he had actually enjoyed the sex, or perhaps that he gave Graham consent.

"The worst part is that this questioning and self-loathing and doubt happens in total isolation and loneliness," he wrote.

Kennedy was first separated from his brother when he joined Moose Jaw, where James was able to control Kennedy's life, despite Kennedy having a billet family. James quickly labeled Kennedy as a "problem" within the community. And everyone believed James.

"In junior hockey, your coach is like a god," Kennedy wrote. The coach deals with teachers, mediates between a player and the police, and corresponds with their parents.

"Minor league hockey in Canada is a tight closed community of men who have worked and played together, often for decades. If one of the fraternity decides that a player is 'difficult,' soon everyone in the league knows."

But James' abuse wasn't a total secret. People at least suspected it. Players and coaches and opponents called Kennedy James' "girlfriend" and "wife." Swift Current citizens knew he was hurting, but no one intervened. No one questioned his flunking grades.

Even after James confessed, people still defended him.

James was ultimately convicted of molesting five of his players. He faced charges two more times. In 2016, he was paroled.

In 2019, The Athletic's Katie Strang published an investigative piece on former players' allegations of sexual abuse by Thomas "Chico" Adrahtas, a coach in the Chicago area.

Strang wrote, "The Athletic has uncovered allegations of manipulation and sexual abuse by Adrahtas, who, players say, weaponized their dreams and exploited their trust in order to take advantage of them sexually. His efforts to groom both players and parents are eerily reminiscent of recent sexual abuse scandals in sports. Similar to the abuse scandal in the Catholic Church, when allegations of wrongdoing surfaced, Adrahtas relocated to another post—a new set of young players put under his charge."

Adrahtas' coaching life was filled with second chances. In 2018, he left Robert Morris University in Chicago quietly, with no reason publicly given. But he left because he was being investigated by the U.S. Center for SafeSport, the federally sanctioned authority that responds to allegations of sexual misconduct and abuse within the United States Olympic & Paralympic organizations.

When Adrahtas coached the youth hockey Budweiser Jets in Illinois, he befriended one of his players, Mike Sacks. He found reasons for the two of them to spend time together. He didn't like Sacks spending too much time with his teammates. He praised Sacks. He introduced him to scouts. He endeared himself to Sacks' family. Adrahtas isolated Sacks from his father by telling him that his friends were a bad influence and eventually became Sacks' legal guardian.

Adrahtas told Sacks about a woman he knew, Sheila, who gave oral sex. He asked Sacks if Sacks was interested, with one caveat— he would have to be blindfolded. Sacks agreed. While Sacks didn't know anything was wrong, he still felt relief when he moved away from Adrahtas.

But then Adrahtas landed the assistant coaching job at the University of Minnesota. He continued pressuring Sacks to allow "Sheila" to perform oral sex.

"I think it was starting to affect me and I didn't know it. You don't trust [anyone] and you just don't know what's happening to you," Sacks told The Athletic. "I just didn't care about anything anymore, I just stopped caring. If I was hurting other people's feelings, it didn't register."

Adrahtas gave his Minnesota players the same offer with "Sheila." Eventually, some got suspicious and watched his apartment on one of the nights "Sheila" came over. No one entered or exited. The players told then athletic director Paul Giel of Adrahtas' alleged actions. An NHL scout, Chuck Grillo, told Adrahtas to leave if the rumors were true.

Rumors about Adrahtas spread, but he continued getting coaching jobs around Chicago. He coached the Franklin Park Jets, the Chicago Patriots, and the Chicago Young Americans.

The owner of the CYA, Ira Greenberg, hired Adrahtas despite the stories—believing Adrahtas' version that the stories were part of a vendetta campaign. At one point, Greenberg asked the players why they were spending time at Adrahtas' place and one broke down crying.

Adrahtas was fired. Greenberg shared why he was fired, but Adrahtas ended up coaching with AAA Team Illinois. Strang later reported that multiple men were suing USA Hockey, the University of Minnesota, and the Amateur Hockey Association Illinois (AHAI). The lawsuit made several claims, including that authorities failed to protect players despite concerns being voiced. Another claim states that current USA Hockey president Jim Smith was told by Greenberg—when Smith served as president over the AHAI—that Adrahtas was sexually abusing players, but that Smith did not report it or investigate. The Athletic said Smith said he did not recall being told that. The lawsuit also claims that a letter drafted by former player Chris Jensen in 2010, which detailed how he was sexually abused by Adrahtas, was shown to Smith. The letter petitioned Adrahtas' selection to the Illinois Hockey Hall of Fame. Adrahtas was not selected but continued to coach.

Strang wrote, "Adrahtas did not show up for an AHAI hearing to address the allegation and, despite being indefinitely suspended by the organization as a result, he continued to coach the Robert Morris University [Chicago] men's hockey team for the next eight seasons. It is unclear if anyone from AHAI told RMU officials about the letter or the hearing or alerted law enforcement. AHAI has not responded to questions about its handling of the 2010 letter and ejected a The Athletic reporter from its March board meeting."

Strang reported in May 2020 that Smith was under investigation by both SafeSport and by USA Hockey (through an independent firm) as a result of the allegations. USA Hockey executive director Pat Kelleher told The Athletic via a spokesperson, "The U.S. Center for SafeSport has advised us they have taken jurisdiction and are investigating allegations that people within AHAI, including Jim Smith, were aware of sexual misconduct by Thomas Adrahtas and did not take action."

In May 2021, The Athletic reported that Smith—who served two terms as president of USA Hockey—would not seek re-election for a third term.

Adrahtas denied all allegations to The Athletic. The Center for SafeSport ruled a lifetime ban for Adrahtas.

Later, Strang reported that an independent investigation found that there was no action taken by the University of Minnesota and that an independent investigation carried out by a law firm revealed that Minnesota's athletic department knew about Adrahtas' conduct but failed to take action.

In a statement, the school told The Athletic, "Collectively, based on credible and corroborating firsthand witness accounts, Perkins found that sexual abuse allegations like those reported in The Athletic were known by individuals within the University's Athletic Department at or around the time of the former assistant coach's departure from the University. Despite this knowledge, available evidence shows no action taken by the University to conduct an independent investigation or report the allegations to the authorities. That is not what the University would do today.

"We are committed to learning from this inquiry into the University's past, an inquiry that will strengthen even more our University's commitment to having a culture and practice that responds promptly and seriously to allegations of sexual misconduct."

Laura Robinson, a former competitive cyclist, started working with CBC's *The Fifth Estate* in 1993 and was involved in creating a documentary on coaches and sexual abuse in sport. "In cycling... cross country, skiing, there was a lot. It was endemic, the amount of sexual abuse of female athletes," she said. "Any coach could take any 16 or 17 year old girl he wanted, and I thought that I had gone into the wrong sport. Every sport was like that. So I understood sport as a place where being a predator was acceptable...and definitely in my sport, [they] didn't really even try to hide that."

The U.S. Center for SafeSport has a Centralized Disciplinary Database, which informs the public if individuals in the U.S. Olympics or Paralympics committees "have either been found to have engaged in—or are alleged to have engaged in—forms of misconduct that present a potential risk to other members of the sport community." Not all decisions are published, but published ones include temporary restrictions and certain types of sanctions. The temporary restriction cases involve allegations so severe that they pose a threat to others in that community (like child sexual assault allegations). The cases with sanctions included are those that have some period of suspension following an investigation.

Cases not published in the database involved "respondents" who were minors. Sanctions do not limit participation in a sport where temporary restrictions are "specific to a particular party" instead of the sport community. There are four different levels of sanctions: limited participation, suspension, ineligibility, and permanent ineligibility.

The database lists more than 100 adjudicated people affiliated with USA Hockey. The reasons and sanctions vary, but there are a few who were members of USA Hockey and committed criminal sexual assault acts outside of the team. There are also those who have used their positions of power and abused their players.

There's Douglas Nail, a former youth hockey coach who was accused of sexually assaulting a former player while he coached in Colorado under the Saints Hockey Club in the 1980s, registered through USA Hockey.

In 2012, Anthony DeSilva, the coach of the Massachusetts Maple Leafs, was arrested for trying to seduce two 16-year-old boys, who turned out to be undercover detectives, online. The *Enterprise* reported that one of his former players and his player's father had warned USA Hockey officials about DeSilva's behavior two years prior. He alleged that DeSilva made unwanted advances to him when he was 18, and it resulted in him leaving the team before the season was over. The *Enterprise* reported that the player alleged DeSilva "cuddled" with him, sent him inappropriate texts, and also tried to put his hand down his pants.

Alex Rivers told the *Enterprise*, "He would just show up randomly at our house. He'd text me at 3 AM asking me what I was doing."

"He was a good hockey coach. He was the best hockey coach I've ever had," Rivers said. "I didn't want to ruin [my teammates'] season over a problem I was having with the coach.... I didn't want to ruin friendships."

The *Enterprise* reached out to USA Hockey Executive Director David Ogrean via email, which generated a vacation autoresponder. Attempts to contact other executives at USA Hockey on a Friday afternoon were not successful.

Henry Lazar, president and CEO of the Eastern States Hockey League, to which the Massachusetts Maple Leafs belong, referred comment on the DeSilva incident to Commissioner Andrew Richards, who could not be reached. However, Lazar said that USA Hockey's rules require screening of all adults who have contact with players.

Canadian defender Saroya Tinker, currently playing for the Toronto Six of the NWHL, routinely speaks out against racism in hockey and has shared her experiences as a multiethnic player in several interviews and in written essays about inclusivity in hockey. (Vaughn Ridley/Getty Images)

On February 28, 2021, history was made as Madison Square Garden hosted its first professional women's hockey game. Billie Jean King spoke with members of both teams. (Sarah Stier/Getty Images)

'Attention' bugs black pro hockey player

Mike Marson, just like any other sports hero, wants to be recognized not only by his peers, but by fans and non-fans alike.

Outside the visiting lockerroom in Madison Square Garden, when his team had finished a losing effort, there were TV cameras, sportswriters galore, and a host of onlookers.

It's something that the lone black player in the National Hockey League is getting used to, but not a point of attention that he particularly likes. The reporters weren't looking for an excuse as to why the Washington Capitals lost another game. Mike Marson was the news, not his team.

That's the way it was for

the burly 19-year-old last year. Everywhere he went, he was asked how it felt to be the only black player in the National Hockey League and was reflecting on his troubled first year and the start of a sequel that, in its own way, was perhaps even more disturbing.

"I received a lot of publicity last year before I did anything on the ice," said Marson, who was an object of curiosity, rather than bigotry or hatred. "This created a lot of animosity, a lot of jealousy. There were guys on the team talking behind my back.

"I guess I just put too much faith in people and

teammates but refusing to be more specific.

"Maybe I'm too sensitive," he went on. "Maybe I let too many small things bother me, like other guys talking about me.

"At this point in my carrer, I'm just very mixed up."

Publicity and the resulting resentment weren't the only problems Marson faced in his rookie season. He reported to training camp 25 pounds overweight. Then he tried to lose the extra pounds too quickly and he found his strength sapped.

Marson went the first six weeks of last season without a goal or an assist. He

"Sure, there were times I felt added pressure," the 5-ft. 9-in., 200-pound winger said recently. A month into his second NHL season, Marson was the first man of his race to play in the NHL since Willie O'Ree in 1960-61. And Marson, an articulate Canadian whose father emmigrated to Scarborough, Ontario, from Jamaica, tried to answer as best he could.

"I don't think of myself as any kind of pioneer, like Jackie Robinson or Frank Robinson," he told one interviewer. "Frankly, I don't feel I'm any different than a white player." To another, he confided: "It's no great

compiled by Bobby Orr, but ones that put him among the leaders on an expansion team that was the worst in NHL history. Thirteen of those goals came in the second half of the season. "I didn't really get on track until January," he said.

Though hardly a brawler, Marson was suspended by NHL President Clarence Campbell. The suspension was imposed after Marson threw his stick at the Toronto bench during a preseason game in retaliation for being struck with a stick by the Maple Leafs' Dave Dunn.

In 13 games since then, he has scored three goals and one assist, compared to zero to assists at the point last year. But his

play has been spotty. And while he took his place on a regular shift last year, this year he spends most of his time on the bench.

"Right now, I'm at a low point," Marson confessed. "I'm not getting the ice time because I'm not scoring goals. I've had the chances. The puck just won't go in the net."

Milt Schmidt, the coach and general manager of the Capitals, said, "The problem with Mike Marson definitely is mental. I try to impress upon him that he is a part of us, regardless of what color he is. Sometimes he has the thought going through his mind that he has to be a gentleman. He seems afraid of creating an incident and consequently he lacks

aggressiveness.

"If worse comes to worse, I'm going to have to send him down to a lower level. He lacks confidence right now and he's got to gain that confidence."

In the meantime, Marson engrosses himself in Agatha Christie mysteries and in decorating the suburban Maryland condominium he and his bride of six months just bought. He also vows to work on his game until he improves.

"Making it as a pro is one thing," he said. "Making it as a good pro is another. Everybody likes to excel in whatever field they're in. When I'm finished playing, I'd like to be able to look back on my career and say I made a mark."

For Mike Marson, that mark involves more than being a footnote to hockey history, the trivial answer to the trivia question, "Who was the only black player in the NHL between 1961 and 1975?"

"Someday," he said quietly, "I hope to be a 30 or 40 goal-a-year scorer."

Mike Marson

CAN NEGROES CRACK BIG LEAGUE HOCKEY?
czar of top pro circuit insists ice sport maintains no color bars

---

THE PEOPLE'S VOICE
PV SPORTS

THAT TERRIFIC ALL NEGRO FORWARD WALL (l to r): Ossie Carnegie, Herbie ... and Manny McIntyre

Canadian Hockey Doesn't Draw Line
All Negro Line Sets Precedent, Pac

Three Negro boys are not only making history in Eastern Canada's Inter-provincial Hockey League, one of the top circuits in the Dominion, but they are also proving to be a superlative drawing card that is carrying this newly-formed loop over their special surplus...

Future Seen in Hockey

Blacks Taking to Ice

By Andrew F. Blake
Globe Staff

Black hockey players. What?

At the end of this decade and beyond, experts predict, the Greater Boston area could produce for the first time in abundance:

● America's first generation of black, college hockey players.

● A black player on the U.S. Olympic hockey team.

● Black figure skaters, men and women, in international competition.

● Black professional figure skaters in theatrical ice shows.

● America's first black speed skaters in Olympic and international competition.

The entrance of black athletes in what have been almost exclusively white Winter sports is due in large part to the tremendous general interest in hockey and skating in Greater Boston, availability of ice rinks, organized instruction and competition in ghetto areas according to coaches.

HOCKEY, Page 3

I'm Not a Freak: Black Hockey Player

(c) New York Times

"I'm not a freak. I'm just another 19-year-old rookie coming out of junior hockey and trying to make it in the big leagues. I need what any player needs in the NHL, good coaching and playing time. What I don't need is someone pointing at me and saying, 'Hey, look! There a black hockey player.'"

To Mike Marson of the Washington Capitals, the color of a man's face is not a statistic. The number of goals scored, assists tallied and body checks dished out are. Nevertheless, when the new expansion team played its first game in the National Hockey League last Oct. 9 and the helmeted Mike Marson skated out on the Madison Square Garden ice, the fact remained: Here was only the second black to play in the 58-year history of the league.

Willie O'Ree was the first. The record book says he played a total of 45 games with the Boston Bruins, appearing in two games in 1957-58 and 43 games in 1960-61. He scored four goals and 10 assists and then returned to the minor leagues where he is reported still playing.

"Yeah, I heard of Willie O'Ree, but I never saw him play," Mike Marson said. "That was way before my time. But I think it's time to end all this ridiculousness: The first to do this, the second to do that. Not only for blacks, but for a Russian going to the moon or a Chinese pole-vaulting or whatever. It's childishness."

A second-round draft choice, Mike Marson is one of just two rookies retained by the Capital. Greg Joly, their first draft pick, is the other. A look at last season's records of all the Capital players, however, reveals this statistic: The 94 points amassed by Marson as a left wing with the Sudbury Wolves were more than anybody else scored wherever they played.

"If I was brought up because I'm black," Mike said, "I wouldn't want to be here. I'm here because I can play. I don't want to be singled out as something special. I don't think of myself as any kind of pioneer like Jackie Robinson or Frank Robinson. Frankly, I don't feel I'm any different than a white player."

When he was 5 or 6 years old and dragging around the skates his parents gave him, Mike Marson felt no difference either. In the Toronto suburb where he grew up, his buddies played hockey, so Mike played hockey. Though he was a black and playing a sport supposedly alien to blacks, even in Canada, nobody told him he was doing something wrong.

"Why do so few blacks play hockey, anyway?" Marson asked. "Because of their parents, I'd say. There's no hockey in the background of blacks. Most are from a warm climate like the Caribbean or Africa where there's no ice. Their sports are soccer, baseball, basketball, things like that.

"If I moved to Italy, for instance, how likely would I be to want my kid to be a bocce player? It usually takes a generation to change that kind of thinking. Though my mother was Bermudan, my father is Canadian. And he believed I should play what everybody played in my area."

So far, life in the National Hockey League has been good news and bad news for Mike Marson. He signed a "substantial" three-year contract with Washington but went through a "poor training

NHL Standings

	W	L	T	Pts	GF	GA
DIVISION 1						
Philadelphia	11	3	2	24	55	33
Atlanta	8	6	2	18	48	42
N.Y. Islanders	7	4	3	17	52	32
N.Y. Rangers	6	5	3	15	47	41
DIVISION 2						
Vancouver	9	4	2	20	57	41
Chicago	7	5	2	16	57	37
St. Louis	4	6	3	11	41	45
Minnesota	3	7	3	9	31	52
Kansas City	1	11	1	3	33	64
DIVISION 3						
Los Angeles	9	1	5	23	1	26
Montreal	7	4	5	19	62	44
Detroit	5	6	2	12	38	55
Pittsburgh	4	7	2	10	47	55
Washington	1	3	1	3	28	74
DIVISION 4						
Buffalo	10	3	2	22	63	47
Boston	6	3	5	17	64	43
Toronto	4	6	3	11	51	55
California	2	10	1	8	37	75

Games Tonight

Atlanta at Washington
Chicago at Vancouver
Boston at St. Louis

PRO CLUBS SCOUTING NEGRO PLAYERS IN CANADA LEAGUES

[illegible]

SATURDAY, APRIL 2, 1960 — CLEVELAND CALL and POST — PAGE FIVE—C

Negro Youths Like Tough Hockey Game

By William (Sheep) Jackson

The Negro youth of America have advanced rapidly in baseball and football over the past thirteen years, but here in Cleveland, through the efforts of City Recreation Commissioner John Nagy, they have taken to the Pee-Wee, Junior Hockey League like "ducks" in water.

In 1956, two brothers, Don and Bernard Cade, played their first hockey game, at the Arena before a group of interested parents.

Like other lads on the ice, they skidded, fell and bounced off the boards.

They were the first Negro hockey players to crash a regular lineup.

Today there are five Negro youngsters preforming on the ice in the City Recreation Pee-Wee and Junior Hockey League.

Another brother combination has pushed their way into the hockey picture, with their eagerness to learn the game.

They are the Arrington brothers, Jerry, goalie and Ed, wing, who did a commendable job for the Pee-We Bisons.

The third Negro player on the Bison was Jerry Scott.

Don, the older of the Cade brothers, and a splendid athlete at Holy Name High School was one of the top scorers, for the Indians of the Junior Loop while Bernard, according to Bill Reppa, supervisor of the leagues was just plain terrific.

Some day we may read about these youngsters performing in big time hockey. Who knows, it could be with the Cleveland Barons.

There have been but several Negro players in big time hockey, with Art Dorrington, a skillful, left-handed stick handler, who has starred with the Philadelphia Ramblers of the Eastern Hockey League.

DORRINGTON is a Canadian, and was a sure-fire bet to make the grade when he graduated from the Amateur Junior Loops across the border to the hard, rugged sport. Only in New England is the Negro youth participating in the game in Highland.

But here in Cleveland we should feel very proud of the development of the two hockey leagues.

In talking to John Nagy about the boys, he said that the backing of Jim Hendy, general manager of the Cleveland Barons, Bill Lavery of the Cleveland Arena, hockey clincis conducted by Baron players, Captain Arthur Roth of the Cleveland Police Department's Juvenile Bureau, local industry, business, and even parents have worked quietly and efficiently promote the gigantic hockey program.

"The interest of the boys in Greater Cleveland have cause to erect two outdoor skating arenas of our own," said Nagy.

"They are located in the West Side, at the Holloran Park, and on the East Side, at Woodland Park, and with the Arena having increased our enrollment two-fold," Nagy added.

AS FOR Don Cade, we predict a great future for the lanky skater, who is rough, an excellent skater and can dish it out on defense. He packs one of the hardest shots in the Junior League.

Jerry Arrington is the first Negro youngster to perform in the nets, the toughest position on the ice. He can move laterally very well and stands in the net firm, ready to stop any attack.

This game of hockey is tougher then football, basketball or boxing. It takes intestinal fortitude (guts) and grim determination to play the gamme.

EVERY SINGLE youngster performing in the two leagues has all the mental and physical equipment to play this hard game on ice.

The development of the leagues and its effect on the hundreds of youngsters caught the protective equipment for all in '56.

This story would not be complete without tabbing others, who have aided commissioner John Nagy in this gigantic project.

THE LIST would include, Assistant Recreation Commissioner Bill Willis; R. B. Kline, superintendent of public relations & Research; Bill Reppa, supervisor, amateur hockey; Lou Zontini, assistant supervisor; Al Drew, Steve Jankowski, John Broski, and volunteer coaches, Marvin Axelrod, Robbert Ehrman, Warren, Flenga, Mark Goldstein, Ken Hershfield, aJck Roach and IRchard Witt.

Saperstein Kills Wilt LA Report

CHICAGO. — Owner Abe Saperstein of the world famous Trotters denied a report last week that Wilt Chamberlain would join the Los Angeles entry in a new pro basketball league planned by Saperstein.

"There is no basis in the least for this rumor," said Abe for whose independent Trotters Chamberlain played before joining the Philadelphia Warriors of the National Basketball Association.

"For one thing, we don't even have a league organized yet," added Saperstein.

Representatives of nine cities earlier this week conferred with discussing the possibilities of a new pro loop.

Newcombes Divorced

EL PASO, Tex.—Don Newcombe, Cincinnati Redlegs hurler

Blacks taking to ice; experts say they've a future in hockey

★ **HOCKEY**
Continued from Page 1

Asked why black hockey players have been a rarity, most replied, "It's just not their game."

Others, however, including several players, agreed on the same contributing factors:

• Economics — it costs about $60 to outfit a boy for hockey, not including the cost of sharpening skates, paying for ice time and other items.

• Identity — while there are many black standouts in boxing, track, football, baseball and basketball, there is no black Bobby Orr for black youngsters to identify with.

• Opportunity and exposure — until the construction of MDC rinks in the inner city, ice time and exposure to local organized hockey and skating was nonexistent.

Four years ago, Mrs. Sally Jones of Brookline founded organized hockey teams and figure skating for youngsters in Roxbury and Dorchester.

"Each year it's gotten bigger and bigger," she said. "Out of about 100 players this year, about 40 are non-white. As a result of this play, several have gone on to play for high school teams and we tell them hockey is another way to get scholarships to college."

Two of the teams founded by Mrs. Jones play in the Neighborhood Hockey League, a city-wide league initiated this year and headed by Tim Taylor, an assistant hockey coach at Harvard University.

The program is open to all boys up to 17, and they pay $2 per week. In return they are provided with all the equipment, which is returned at the end of the season.

Taylor and Mrs. Jones said there are several talented black players, and given the exposure and opportunity there is no reason why a local black player could not be an Olympic candidate a decade hence.

Jack Kelley, Boston University coach, has coached several black Canadian hockey players.

In 1950, he played at Boston University on the championship team with Lloyd Robinson of Wellesley, one of the few local black hockey standouts.

Kelly said, "This neighborhood hockey league is really going to pay off for black and white players.

"Given the same opportunities as white players, I can see the day when a local black player will make it as big in hockey as anyone else.

"I don't know of any other area in the country, except perhaps Detroit, that has a hockey program anywhere near as good as Greater Boston's.

"More and more good black players are going to come out of the city. Right now, the few who play are from the suburbs."

There are three black players in high schools around Boston now, at Melrose, Everett and Weymouth. Rindge Tech in Cambridge probably has produced more black high school hockey players than any other high school in America.

Rick Hensey, at Everett High, and Richie Harris, at Melrose High, are two talented and well-known black players who chose hockey over basketball as their Winter sport.

Hensey said, "I used to play basketball, but I live in a white neighborhood and all my friends were crazy about hockey.

"It got to me too, so I started playing. Around here it's THE sport in Winter.

"I saw Richie Harris play at Melrose and he was an inspiration. If he could do it, I figured I could too."

In the National Hockey League there has been only one black, Willie O'Ree, who played 45 games for the Boston Bruins, 2 in 1957-58 and 43 in 1960-61.

O'Ree, now with San Diego in the Western Hockey League, is one of three black players, all Canadian, in professional hockey. The others are Alton White, a rookie with Providence in the American Hockey League, and Stan Maxwell, a player coach at Toledo in the International League.

In the upper echelons of figure skating, one black skater already is making his way toward a gold medal — Atoy Wilson, a West Coast college student well known in competition.

Locally, Mrs. Jones singled out Kingsford Swan, 15, of Jamaica Plain, as a likely future candidate in figure competition.

The two recently constructed MDC rinks in predominantly black neighborhoods are Washington Park and Franklin Field.

Speed skating, which has attracted several talented black youths, is offered at Washington Park.

When the hockey program started, many black youngsters saw live hockey for the first time. Several asked the name of the little disc everyone was chasing.

Last week, said Wayne Embry, former Boston Celtic star and now the city director of recreation, a black youth of about 12, "told me he was going to be the first black hockey star in the National Hockey League."

Newspaper and magazine clippings throughout the decades demonstrate the longtime racist treatment of Black players in the NHL.

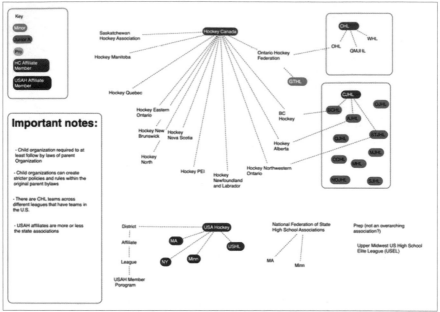

This flowchart explains the structure of professional hockey in North America. (In April 2021, the BCHL announced its intention to leave the CJHL.)

On August 3, 2020, the Dallas Stars' Jason Dickinson (18) and Tyler Seguin (91) and Vegas Golden Knights' Ryan Reaves (75) and Robin Lehner (90) became the first NHL players to kneel during the U.S. and Canadian anthems prior to an NHL game. The game was played in the Edmonton bubble during Covid-19. (Jason Franson/The Canadian Press via AP)

Chicago Blackhawks fans make racist taunts to Washington Capitals player Devante Smith-Pelly during a game in February 2018. Four fans were later removed from the United Center. (AP Images)

Chicagoan John Moore (third from top left) heard Bobby Hull (fourth from top left) make racist remarks during a charity golf tournament. According to Moore, who is Black, Hull made multiple jokes about "darkies." A member of the group informed Hull's son, Brett (fifth from top left), that Moore was Black, and the jokes stopped, but neither Bobby nor Brett apologized or acknowledged the slur again.

(Courtesy of John Moore)

*Co-author Evan
Moore playing
hockey in Chicago.*
(Courtesy of Evan Moore)

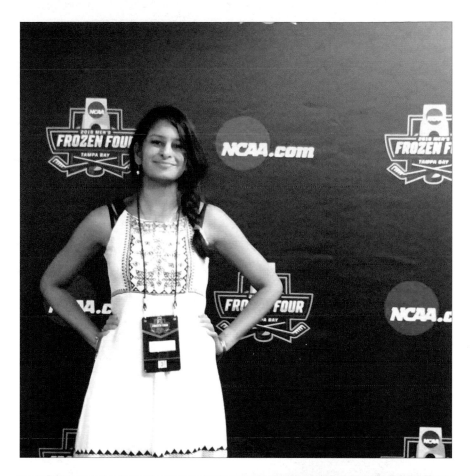

Co-author Jashvina Shah reporting on NCAA hockey. (Courtesy of Jashvina Shah)

The Chicago Gay Hockey Association aims to provide a non-discriminatory environment and an all-encompassing experience within the recreational adult hockey community in Chicago. (Courtesy of Chicago Gay Hockey Association)

P.K. Subban wears a pride jersey in honor of Pride Night in a game against the Pittsburgh Penguins at Prudential Center on April 11, 2021, in Newark, New Jersey. (Andy Marlin/NHLI via Getty Images)

HOCKEY CANADA HAS guidelines on dealing with bullying and harassment, but it slashed its budget for bullying from $30,500 in 2017–18 to $18,500 in 2018–19, saying "next year's expense decrease reflects lower professional services expenses associated with the rewrite of Bullying, Harassment, and Abuse Policy and Complaint Procedures that occurred in '17–18." The authors requested but did not receive a copy of this document and were unable to find it online.

Part of combating bullying (and even sexual assault, as discussed in Chapter 4) requires converting passive bystanders into active bystanders.

According to the U.S. government's campaign against bullying, this happens by teaching people to question the behavior, redirect the conversation, use strength in numbers, engage parents and youth, create rules and policies, and create a reporting system.

For hazing, the NCAA has several prevention strategies. One of them is good leadership from captains. Cornell lists the following steps to prevent hazing via bystander intervention: recognize the behavior and that it's a problem, take responsibility, know how to act, be empowered to act, perform a cost and benefit analysis, and then act.

Strong leadership and emphasis from the coaches is what kept hazing out of North Dakota's Jasper Weatherby's junior team, the Wenatchee Wild of the BCHL.

"I will again go down saying that it's the best run [junior] franchise I have ever seen," Weatherby said. "It was unbelievable, from the way the coaches treated us, to the way the fans treated us, to our beliefs, to the way we traveled, to the coaches. Really being nurtured...and that I went from being a rookie to being one of the leaders on the team. And I remember saying, 'You know what, no one treated me disrespectfully when I was a young new kid. And I'm not gonna let anything happen like that.'"

AS BOTH SHELDON Kennedy's and Mike Sacks' stories show, the culture around hockey—hero worship, the values of respect and obeying your coach—are factors in cultivating, incubating, and protecting sexual abuse. It is all too easy for coaches to cut children off from their parents and exert an abnormal amount of control. For coaches, their ability to win supersedes all else—so they will be considered heroes and, as Graham James was considered, the trusted adult.

Abuse is a problem in all youth-serving organizations. Kennedy's and Sacks' stories demonstrate some of the reasons why this is so dangerous in hockey. The junior system, be it major juniors or Junior A in Canada or Tier 1 in the U.S., lends itself to a structure in which athletes are put in close contact with coaches in a largely unsupervised environment. Players, in many cases, have just moved away from home for the first time. They're living with strangers. The coach is their point of contact, as Kennedy described, to the world. And the culture of hockey creates the subordinate and obedient athlete. You don't question the coach.

And the community will often look the other way. There were rumblings about James' and Thomas Adrahtas' behavior—people knew something was wrong. Yet no one—at least, not the authorities—did or said anything. If they thought something was wrong, the coach might have gotten fired. But they would not report either coach. And some simply turned the other way.

In the book *Sexual Abuse in Youth Sports: A Sociocultural Analysis*, Michael J. Hartill relays several examples of incidents in which some adults knew about ongoing abuse and did nothing or concealed it.

Hartill writes:

> Sport, since its inception, has persistently functioned as a
> site of masculinist intergenerational 'filial devotion' and 'love',

where the initiated (typically adult males) have constructed certain practices (or rites) as central to the achievement of recognition for the uninitiated.

Sex is simultaneously ever-present and utterly denied in dominant discourse, where sport is resolutely about character development, teamwork, discipline, responsibility, achievement, health, etc. Indeed, organized sport is about anything (and everything) but sex. Despite decades of feminist and pro-feminist critique, advocacy and policy development, arguably, the hyper-masculinist sports enterprise has never been stronger. Yet while sex is central to the male changing room/bar-room environment, the rules of the game are clear: what happens in the dressing room/locker room stays there.

A UNICEF review published in 2010 titled "Protecting Children from Violence in Sport: A Review with a Focus on Industrialized Countries" argues that competitive sport tends to treat children as adults, which is a root of the problem:

Too often, however, children with exceptional athletic potential are treated as adults. This has serious consequences for the realization of their human rights and their access to legal processes and mechanisms of protection and defence—which might be more accessible to them in non-sporting contexts.

There has been a drift, however, toward professionalism in competitive sport, which has become increasingly commercialized. This has been seen as associated with a loss of amateur values such as involvement in sports for pleasure and satisfaction, rather than for compensation or for winning at all costs.

A person who perpetrates violence against a child athlete may be dealt with internally through a particular sport's

157

disciplinary procedures covering complaints, grievances, appeals, suspensions and reinstatement.

Peter Donnelly and Gretchen Kerr, in their paper "Revising Canada's Policies on Harassment and Abuse in Sport: A Position Paper and Recommendations," give four main reasons abuse happens in youth sports. First, sports culture is a problem. It considers itself good, which leads to a refusal to admit any problems. That leads to a "code of silence." It's also authoritarian—follow the coach. Second, sports organizations are autonomous and believe in self-governance as opposed to outside oversight. Third, this belief in autonomy is inherently a conflict of interest. And fourth, "The existence of complicit bystanders raises questions about whether stakeholders in sport are aware of their legal duty to report child abuse or suspicions of child abuse, and how the barriers to reporting may be alleviated."

It's difficult to provide oversight or control because one body does not oversee all. Hockey Canada and USA Hockey handle sports associated with the Olympic and Paralympic movement. As illustrated earlier, major juniors and the NCAA don't fall under that umbrella. And Canada does not have a watchdog nonprofit equivalent to the U.S. Center for SafeSport.

In practice, there is no support system for the players. There is fear of being ostracized, the same current that runs through this whole thing—including toxic masculinity.

The culture of silence does exist. People do believe the hockey culture is pure and good and teaches boys important skills and how to be good men, so much so that they would never believe a winning coach who is nice to people in the community could ever do such a thing. Proof enough is that people still defended James after he confessed to abuse.

The culture does police itself—leading to the lack of bystander intervention. It's a very insular community and it does claim authority, hence not really letting anyone else in. (This isn't just a hockey problem—Jessica Luther wrote about this in her book *Unsportsmanlike Conduct: College Football and the Politics of Rape*, explaining how this happens in college football.) Safe to Compete, created by the United States' National Center for Missing and Exploited Children, wrote that the youth sports community is "a context which is conducive to sexual abuse." This is because coaches hold authority over athletes and are respected figures in the community who won't be questioned. There are additional risk factors:

- Sports stakeholders (e.g., athletes, parents, coaches) who are uninformed or poorly informed about sexual abuse prevention policies and procedures
- Local-level sports franchises that are unaware of prevention measures implemented by their national or regional organizations
- Administrators who have difficulty implementing prevention policies and procedures (e.g., background checks) and who lack training and resources about child sexual abuse
- Ambiguity about appropriate and inappropriate behavior
- A subculture that normalizes harassment and exploitation

The NCMEC's tip sheet for making youth sports safer lists red flags that do not necessarily indicate abuse but cross appropriate boundaries:

- Signaling youth out for special attention or gift-giving
- Spending one-on-one time with children such as in private practice sessions
- Touching children in ways not related to training for the sport
- Telling youth sexual or inappropriate jokes and stories
- Commenting on children's appearances when not related to the sport

Hockey checks a lot of these boxes.

There are some policies in place to fight systemic abuse. The U.S. Center for SafeSport's Minor Athlete Abuse Prevention Policies (MAPP) provides training requirements and policies to limit one-on-one interactions—a key hallmark of abuse prevention policy. It ruled that all organizations covered were to implement policies regarding one-to-one interactions, messages and athletic training modality, locker room and changing areas, social media and electronic communications, local travel, and team travel. The required policies are a minimum standard.

USA Hockey also emphasizes mandatory reporting. It uses SafeSport core training, which is valid for one year. It's an online course that "is available to help our members become aware of the information necessary to help prevent abuse from occurring in our sport. We are pleased to announce that all USA Hockey registered coaches, officials, players, employees, and volunteers are entitled to take the training at no cost."

Canada is looking to create an organization that will similarly standardize policy implementation to prevent and address maltreatment in sport.

Hockey Canada uses Respect in Sport, an organization co-founded by Sheldon Kennedy. Per Hockey Canada's website, the training will "Empower and educate youth leaders/coaches on the prevention of abuse, bullying, harassment, and discrimination. Build a holistic culture of respect within the sport community. Provide fundamental training tools which enable ALL coaches and youth leaders to become even better role models for the young athletes in their care."

Respect in Sport is also there for the parents.

SafeSport is a relatively new body, so whether or not it helps stop abuse is still to be determined. The CDC says preventive measures are the most important aspect of combating child abuse in sports.

For any organizations that serve youth, there has to be an extensive vetting and monitoring process. The truth is, coaches are not vetted well. The problem is teams just need bodies there to coach the kids.

The CDC recommends six areas to focus on to prevent abuse in youth sports: screening employees, guidelines on interactions between individuals, monitoring behavior, enduring safe environments, responding to inappropriate behavior, and training about child abuse prevention. The CDC goes more in depth into each area and what is required, but the takeaway is organizations must create the right guidelines and policies and share them, talk about these topics, and heavily screen whomever they admit.

6

Women's Hockey

THIS BOOK FOCUSES MOSTLY ON MEN'S HOCKEY ONLY BECAUSE it is more expansive than women's hockey (itself an example of the sexism inherent in hockey) at both the professional and amateur levels. The structure of women's hockey itself is much less complex. But when examining hockey culture, it is also crucial to examine women's and girls' hockey, both to illustrate sexism in hockey and the culture of women's hockey itself.

Women's hockey is often dismissed or talked about disparagingly, such as when Mike Milbury remarked that there were no women around to distract the players in the NHL bubble and compared empty arenas to the crowd at women's hockey games. (That was not Milbury's first offense, but it was the one that got him removed from NBC. However, the network opted to replace him with Mike Babcock, who bullied his players.)

One needs few examples to understand the lack of equality for those who are not men and who want to play the sport. There is no professional women's league in which players focus on playing hockey full-time. In 2019, the longest-active professional women's league, the Canadian Women's Hockey League (CWHL), folded. Now the only North American professional league is the National Women's Hockey League (NWHL), where the players do not receive full-time salaries and must also juggle full-time jobs. These players don't have time to dedicate to training or weight rooms. They don't have strength and conditioning coaches.

There are half as many Division I women's hockey teams as men's. At the grassroots level, there are much fewer options for girls. And while girls now have more options to play on girls-only teams, some still opt for boys' teams if they believe competition will be better. Then there are the classic tales of girls playing on boys' teams and having to dress in broom closets, which hasn't changed in the past 20-plus years.

Kelly Townsend, an athlete from West Virginia, played boys' hockey for three years before she changed to an all-girls team. One time, where there were about eight high school games in one rink, 12 of the girls had to change in one small room with four chairs.

"There are way too many of us in here. This is not normal. They don't all fit," Townsend said.

There is no question women's sports are always treated as secondary. It's always "hockey" and never "men's hockey," but it's always "women's hockey," as if women are less-than, as if it's a qualifier for the product of hockey. Women's sports receive secondary treatment from mainstream media and harassment from Twitter trolls; they're always deemed "not as exciting" as men's sports. Even in USA Hockey's 2020 Annual Guide, a separate girls' and women's registration date is specified, while the more general "players'" registration date is meant to encompass boys' and men's hockey.

In 2017, the entire U.S. women's national hockey team organized a boycott to fight for fair wages. It was quite a picket line—the national team members reached out to non-national team players, the possible replacements, who all gave up a national team appearance to support the mission. This despite the women's national team, much like U.S. Soccer, having more success than the men.

In 2020, when COVID-19 hit, the International Ice Hockey Federation canceled important women's tournaments while creating bubbles for the men's U20 World Juniors.

The topic of women's hockey and women's sports in general could be a book in itself. How to achieve equality for women's athletics is an expansive topic, and how to fight for equality for women's hockey is a long discussion. It is more than just having a professional league where women can play full-time post-college; it also involves better grassroots programming for girls. It involves a junior hockey league sanctioned by USA Hockey. It involves a program like the National Team Development Program, a program focused on developing the elite 16- and 17-year-olds.

It's hard to see how USA Hockey is "growing the game," since it does not publicly break down money spent on women's/girls' hockey, instead using the too-broad categories of adult, youth, and junior.

Hockey Canada's 2018 Spring Congress Report and Budget showed a $277,100 total spend on "Female." The categories are program development, programming, support and supervision, and general. There was no money spent on program development. The total increased from $259,200 in 2017–18. Hockey Canada spent $485,000 on "women's player's support," which includes "professional services, scouting, strategic planning costs, meetings, and staff development." (Video scouting is an expense that's broken down in the men's budget.)

The total spent on women's hockey operations was $4,168,850. The total for men's hockey operations was $6,325,150. (We need to take into account that the women's system is less expensive than the men's—for example, there is no World Junior A Challenge for the women.) In 2017–18, Hockey Canada spent almost twice as much on Men's Olympic hockey than Women's Olympic hockey.

The report tabbed women's/girls' hockey registration in Canada as 102,959 in total across all levels.

Within USA Hockey, girls' and women's hockey registration has been growing—in 2019–20, it was 84,102 as compared to 69,744 in 2014–15. (Girls' and women's hockey registration experienced bumps after both the Vancouver 2010 Olympics and the Sochi 2014 Games.) But if we're talking about making an impact on women's hockey and focusing on the grassroots level, we need to know how many girls, specifically, are registering.

Take these numbers in context, as women's and girls' hockey is so vastly underdeveloped that it lacks many of the junior leagues and international tournaments that the men and boys have.

There is also internalized misogyny in women's hockey. In October 2020, the NWHL tweeted out its new governance model. The Twitter account for *Token CEO*, Barstool Sports CEO Erika Nardini's podcast, quote-tweeted the NWHL's tweet:

> LET'S GO. Alright @EKANardini now let's get you in on the NWHL.

The Twitter account for *Spittin' Chiclets*, Barstool's hockey podcast, retweeted Token CEO's tweet. NWHL forward Madison Packer retweeted that and then her wife, Anya Packer, who is the director of the National Women's Hockey League Players' Association (NWHLPA), liked the tweet. When it was "exposed," Anya Packer said, "I would be more than open to conversation, but I feel like screenshotting my likes, and calling me toxic is a far cry from who I am as a person and an advocate." When asked why she would like a tweet mentioning an association with a CEO of a sexist and racist website, Packer did not respond.

WHEN TOWNSEND PLAYED on her high school boys' team her senior year, the first year of the team's existence, she felt unwelcome.

"I was one of the better players on the team. It was a very, very mixed range of levels just because it was a starter team, so we didn't really have a lot of players to draw from," Townsend said.

Townsend's biggest opponent was her own brother.

"He told me he didn't think I should be playing on numerous occasions, like I didn't belong on the team," Townsend said. "It was really weird. I felt a step removed from everyone else on the team because I had to change in a separate locker room. So I didn't have that pre-game time spent with the rest of the team."

In youth hockey, Townsend felt no issues playing with the boys. But when she turned 12 and started changing in separate locker rooms, she started to lose that connection.

"There were times where I didn't want to get into high school games," Townsend said. "But it also felt like that was just a part of what hockey was for a girl trying to play on a coed team."

A lot of pushback, Townsend said, comes from the parents.

"I'd like to see it be more common for girls to be able to play on coed teams if they want and not be forced out of it," Townsend said. "A lot of times you'll see a girl play on a coed team up through 14 years round here, and then the next year they'll switch to [a] girls' [team] and it's because either they were forced out, by parents or coaches, or there was just a lack of comfort."

Madison Gay Hockey Association board member Avery Cordingley (they/them) had a similar experience when they played hockey in West Virginia. There was a JV/varsity hybrid with just enough players to make a team, and they traveled around the state and sometimes to Pennsylvania.

"Back then what I experienced was sexism, because I didn't have the language to describe gender dysphoria at the time. So I was just unhappy," Cordingley said.

Cordingley's coach during their sophomore year was just out of college. While it was never expressly spoken, Cordingley would earn playing time only if they proved they could keep up with the boys.

"That usually amounted to playing dirty or taking hits that would be dirty," Cordingley said. "Otherwise, are you familiar with a drill called the goblet? It's a fun time. Most coaches don't do it anymore. The American Development Model from USA Hockey doesn't encourage this kind of teaching because it's not teaching, it's just brutality. You line everyone up...like 30 feet from the boards. And one by one everyone will skate down between the players and the boards and everyone has to hit the person skating by. It's supposed to teach checking, but it doesn't teach shit."

When Cordingley participated in the drill as a junior, they ended up with a broken collarbone.

"I did get to play after that. As shitty as that sounds, I wanted to play. But it was basically, 'If you don't do this drill, why would I play you, because you obviously can't play hockey,'" Cordingley said.

IN MAY 2019, after the CWHL folded, players formed the Professional Women's Hockey Players Association (PWHPA). In a press release, the organization said, "While we have all accomplished so much, there is no greater accomplishment than what we have the potential to do right here and right now—not just for this generation of players, but for generations to come. With that purpose, we are coming together, not as individual players, but as one collective voice to help navigate the future and protect the players' needs. We cannot make a sustainable living playing in the current state of the professional game. Having no health insurance and making as low as two thousand dollars a season means players can't adequately train and prepare to play at the highest level.

"Because of that, together as players, we will not play in ANY professional leagues in North America this season until we get the resources that professional hockey demands and deserves."

The PWHPA began a barnstorming tour in 2019–20 before COVID ended the events for the season.

"Taking a stand and wanting to push for more is really fighting for not only us and our future but also the future of women's hockey, and it was the only way to do that, because if we would have sidestepped to the other league [NWHL], we would have been back to mediocrity," said Canadian Olympian and former Wisconsin Badger Sarah Nurse. "And so we wanted to bring awareness to what professional women's hockey players had to deal with and have to deal with."

It's a catch-22 of sorts—what comes first, grassroots development and minor organizations, or professional women's hockey?

Nurse said grassroots has improved since she played as a girl, but most players still cap their careers around high school. Hockey requires money, time, and commitment, and if there is nothing to get out of it, players question whether putting up with the sexism is worth it. She said she has known many players, good players, who stopped playing after college because there was no place for them to go.

"I was one of the best players in Ontario and Canada and I didn't know that I was going to get a scholarship playing hockey," Nurse said. "Who knows if I would have stuck with it? Because what was there for me to do in hockey? I've been told that there's no place for me in hockey and I was actually told one time that the closest I would ever come to professional hockey was if I married a professional hockey player, because that's the cap that you put on females in hockey, and you don't show them that they can actually amount to be professional hockey players."

SINCE WOMEN ARE marginalized and women's hockey is a marginalized sport, there is a misconception that it is free from bigotry. In some ways, women's hockey is more inclusive. There are trans players. There are players who are openly LGBTQIA+. In fact, Olympians Caroline Ouellette and Julie Chu famously have a child together, despite their USA-Canada rivalry. But much like the women's suffrage movement, there are white women fighting for themselves while ignoring the rights of their non-white, non-straight, and non-cis counterparts.

When Nurse was asked in 2019 about racism in women's hockey, she was stumped.

"Racism is something that isn't discussed really at all, because, honestly, there aren't enough people of color...in hockey so it's not something that's really even brought up," Nurse said.

Nurse is one of a few current prominent Black or Indigenous players. The others are Brigette Lacquette, who was the first First Nations player to be named to Canada's women's national team; Saroya Tinker; and Blake Bolden.

"It really made me think, because women's hockey obviously is pretty open and accepting of people, regardless of walk of life, especially with sexual orientation and sexual identity. So looking at where we are now in women's hockey, I don't see why we wouldn't be open and accepting of people of different races," Nurse said.

Bolden was an infamous snub from the U.S. women's national team, which currently has no players of color. USWNT member Kendall Coyne Schofield tweeted that she was "disgusted" with Colin Kaepernick following his protests (she has since said she has "listened and learned"). Brianne McLaughlin also quote-tweeted a *New York* magazine tweet linking to a video captioned "This video of an activist and a local Fox correspondent arguing about race will make you mad," writing:

OR we could address the issue that kids are disrespectful
and killing. But let's keep sittin around arguing color.

(Note: the video in question showed a police officer throwing a
Black female student to the ground.)

"White women, Black women, every color woman under the sun,
we're not always accepted in the hockey world with the men," Nurse
said. "If white women who are given this privilege over women of
color aren't accepted in the hockey world, how in the world are
women of color going to be accepted in hockey?"

Nurse said she didn't want to be at the forefront of the
conversation because she understood the privilege of her light skin
and that others also needed to share that experience.

"But I knew that I need to speak up too because I knew that I had
a platform and I had an audience that didn't understand," she said.
"Because especially in Canada, we tend to remove ourselves from
these things that are happening in the United States…. But people
don't understand that racism is alive and well in Canada, especially
toward our Indigenous population."

Speaking out still carries a risk, especially when politics rules
decisions in hockey. Nurse said she was confident that speaking out
against racism would not hurt her relationship with Hockey Canada.

"I obviously didn't want to come out and start calling out Hockey
Canada on things that I wasn't completely educated on because I
needed to do more learning, I needed to do more research on
everything that was going on," Nurse said.

"They've taken steps in order to kind of put themselves in a
position to help be antiracist, and that's something that I thought
was very important. I didn't want them to just strictly do diversity
inclusion, I really want them to put a focus on antiracism, and I
definitely know that they have a long way to go.

"They're absolutely not perfect. We spoke about the Hockey Canada board of directors that is 10 or 12 white men. That absolutely needs to change. And not only do there need to be women, but there need to be people of different races on there. There needs to be different hiring practices and policies and getting people involved. I've been with the Hockey Canada program for about 10 years at this point and I have been with two Black staff members in my entire career there. And I've played with one other player, Brigette Lacquette, who is First Nations. And that's a lot of people to go through to not have anybody who looks like you."

And it's important to acknowledge and believe players when they speak up about racist incidents.

"As a woman, you don't want to be the stereotypical quote unquote 'angry Black woman,'" Nurse said. "It baffles me, because people say we're calling the race card again. People don't want to pull that card. People don't want to put themselves in that position where they're the only person and nobody understands what they're talking about."

WOMEN'S HOCKEY ISN'T free of transphobia, either.

"As a visibly trans person, I did not feel unwelcome," Cordingley said. "However, having said that…. Despite the fact that I've never openly been discriminated against for being trans in a hockey space, the fact that I am visibly trans and in a space that is so divided by sex, I don't feel as if I can just openly be myself. Because what if someone questions me? What if I get told I can't play? What if, despite the fact that that is illegal for recreational adult roles, and I know this as a referee, they try to kick me out, but they fail anyway? But, it's enough fear that [even though] hockey's a vocal game and I should yell to my teammates, I don't. Because I'm afraid someone the other team would notice and say something like, 'Why is there a dude playing with you? This is a woman's game, right?'

"I've never had someone walk up to me and go, 'What are you doing?' But there's that fear. That fear comes from knowing how hockey is in general."

WHILE THERE ARE some who have been calling out women's hockey's white feminism problem for a long time, the organizations—the NWHL, the PWHPA, the CWHL—have been reluctant to implement change. Even when the PWHPA was first founded, there were no Black women on the board—until Canadian goaltender Liz Knox stepped aside for Nurse.

Those within women's hockey have also been reluctant to stifle the relationship players have with Barstool. And in January 2021, that seriously harmed the sport.

Barstool CEO Erika Nardini tweeted out from her podcast account a video of her "haters"—which was a bunch of tweets that doxxed NWHL fans and even a staff member. (These people were criticizing any sort of NWHL affiliation with Barstool because of its racism and misogyny.)

The first NWHL player to say anything was Saroya Tinker, one of very few Black women's hockey players. She tweeted:

> WE, as a league do not want support from ANY openly racist platform. Point blank,PERIOD. If you,as the CEO cannot recognize that your platform promotes that of white supremacy & only further divides the athletic community, perhaps w need have a conversation. Pls keep your money.

Barstool founder David Portnoy responded with a video in which he said Tinker should be jailed for her comments.

Professional women's hockey players drew lines in the sand, with some outright liking positive responses to Portnoy's video. Yes—they liked comments supporting a video that said their teammate should be jailed. Initially, this behavior primarily came from Kelly Babstock (who has Ojibwe roots—a reminder that marginalized groups can also be bigoted toward other marginalized groups). When called out for her likes, which are public, she did not stop.

Other NWHL players defended Nardini, even though she was doxxing one of their own social media coordinators in the video. It escalated from there as even PWHPA players jumped in to defend Nardini and her "support" of women's hockey. U.S. Olympian Amanda Kessel reposted a picture in support of Nardini on her Instagram stories (Nardini was wearing a shirt that read, TIE DOMI IS MY SPIRIT ANIMAL). Former Boston College goaltender Katie Burt tweeted in support of Barstool, as did former Riveter Courtney Burke.

The NWHL released a statement from Commissioner Tyler Tumminia that said, "On behalf of the NWHL, I would like to respond to the video posted last night by a media platform about the NWHL, investment, fan engagement, and coverage. As Commissioner, my top priority is to protect, promote, and reinforce the values of the NWHL and its players.

"First and foremost, we must remain inclusive and empowering for women. The success of our movement hinges on respect, opportunity, and a strong sense of connectedness across our players, teams, staff, fans, partners, and avid supporters. Let's keep the focus on our athletes and build on the momentum created in the first few exciting days here in Lake Placid. There is no circumstance where it would be acceptable to call out many of the reporters, staff members, and fans who have given so much to women's hockey, especially knowing that these people could be targeted or harassed on social media.

"In this world of social media, I'm concerned about the impact of the video and the aftermath of it on members of the NWHL family.

Together, we will do everything we can to work through it with open communication and transparency."

The failure to even acknowledge Barstool and call them out by name makes this statement meaningless. The call for inclusivity and empowerment of women is vague at best, and such language usually promotes "unity" over antiracism. There's also no guarantee that, if white women—and a staffer—had not been targeted in that video, the league would have responded at all.

Meanwhile, the NWHLPA tweeted:

> This is bigger than hockey, this has sparked days of conversation, mediation, and reflection. Now more than ever the NWHLPA is focused internally on supporting its athletes. We are proud to work alongside the @NWHL and stand firmly with our athletes.

That, again, is vague and does not address what happened or which athletes it is focused on supporting.

It becomes even more sinister when you consider what Tumminia said when asked by a reporter what accountability players would face for engaging with Barstool and its targeted harassment: "Obviously my full support as the commissioner of this league for Ms. Tinker and we'll support her to any extent. But I will also support every single one of our athletes and our staff and our entire community that support the NWHL going forward. It's just unfortunate what had happened, and [I felt] very sad that it was the case.... Based on conversations I have had today, with multiple players and staff, I hope we're headed in the right direction where our focus will now turn back to where the bubble is, and how we're having such great fun here with the players and the environment that we're in."

No reporter present shared this comment until the Victory Press published it two days later.

You can't support a Black player who was targeted for calling out white supremacy while also supporting non-Black players who support the system that targeted her. Those things are mutually exclusive.

Barstool threw around the idea of starting its own women's league. A Barstool women's hockey league Twitter account was set up, with some pro women's hockey players (like the PWHPA's Natalie Spooner) following it.

To be clear, this is not an NWHL issue or just a PWHPA issue— this is a hockey issue, but specifically in this context, a women's hockey issue. As mentioned earlier, women often use their identity as a woman to ignore the plights of other marginalized communities and shield themselves from criticism. Nardini—and the players who support her—represent the "cool girl" brand of white feminism wherein women—mostly white—are so desperate to "fit in with the boys" that they will degrade any marginalized community—including their own.

Baseball reporter and former San Jose Sharks intern Jen Ramos tackled this "Girl Boss" phenomenon in their Patreon piece on Rachel Luba, Trevor Bauer's agent:

> In many fields, whenever a woman gets to a position of power, they're referred to as a "girl boss." The typical idea of a "girl boss" is a woman who is able to create her own successes and move into a position of power. In the big four sports leagues in the United States, MLB has shown itself to be a league where there hasn't been enough non-cis men, including women, in positions of importance and/or power, so anyone who seems to be moving up in that direction gets a lot of attention.
>
> There's one in particular who maybe shouldn't be getting that attention.

In many features published this offseason, Rachel Luba has been personified as such in the baseball industry because of how she's become a player agent, namely to Trevor Bauer.

However, these features gloss over the fact that in her role as Bauer's agent and as she associates with his brand, she is complicit in the enabling of Bauer's harassment of women on social media. In fact, Luba has participated in this mess herself, defending Bauer's actions and causing even more harassment, though she has been credited with Bauer doing this less. In a Complex feature on Luba, there is a paragraph that states, "For starters, there's the fledgling player representation agency she launched in 2019 with a goal of turning an antiquated business model on its head. Unapologetically herself in the historically male-dominated industry of baseball, Luba's maneuvering in ways simultaneously inspiring for her admirers and maddening for her haters."

The problem is that Bauer and co. call those who critique them "harassers" and "haters," in essence people who are worthy of having their army of stans attack them for days on end, if not months. Sure, Luba can be unapologetically herself in a historically male-dominated industry, but she's also unapologetically enabling the harassment of women in a historically male-dominated industry.

Society is racist and misogynistic (among other things), so it makes sense that people would be raised with those ideals—even toward themselves. But the problem is the failure of people to change. Women's hockey has also skirted around this because not everyone has tried to hold them accountable, and that includes reporters and people who dismiss the very real issues in women's hockey (like how the NWHL cut player salaries in half without giving them advance notice).

Moving forward, that becomes a key issue. We need to find the balance between supporting women's hockey and eradicating the bigotry inside it. The track record for these instances hasn't been great across other hockey leagues—fans, media, and those within the sport have been vocally outspoken against racism, but in a few weeks, they seem to forget about the fight.

7

Ableism

When your favorite player on your favorite team is at a game taking a couple of photos with a disabled fan or a fan who uses a wheelchair, the response is typically something like, "Good on them."

But what does hockey culture do to stop ableism?

What happens when someone has a tough time getting to their seat during a game? Or when ableism stops someone from playing the game? What if a kid who is deaf shows up to a clinic and none of the adults know sign language? Or what if someone has a disability that's not readily seen? More importantly, what does that fan do when the game they love doesn't love them back?

Jennifer Southall, a coach, blogger, and deaf hockey player, knows all about the limitations of hockey culture and ableism. In a series of texts, she wrote:

> [Hockey] is very unwelcoming to non-whites/people who
> don't exactly have money, but at the same time it can be

a common language/bonding for both abled and disabled players because the game can be explained/played in different fashion. It is very true that hockey has an ugly moniker of "rich white boy" sport when I have conversations with friends/fellow sports parents outside of hockey. There's almost a look of disdain that comes across their face but is quickly dispelled during conversations. I see it and their tone changes because of the prejudices associated with hockey.

Even though most modern ice rinks have accommodations for the disabled, Southall believes more ought to be done outside of performative listening—which has been a common theme throughout the book:

Yes it's more accessible in some ways for disabled than it was back then but at the same time way even more inaccessible for both the abled and disabled. Because of the culture and the cost associated with it, I've had parents straight up tell me they are not going to fork over $1000-$1500 just for one season of being on a team where their child is the only non-white player while in other sports they have more diverse voices especially with coaching. I'm the only female Latina/deaf coach in my youth metro organization, so I'm the unicorn in a sense as 98 percent of the volunteer coaching staff are male.

We do have female coaches, but they are all with the only all-girls youth hockey affiliate in our state [Oregon].... That concept goes way beyond hockey because it affects every gender and race. I've had discussions with friends regarding that topic especially for the disabled; we know the disabled are very white. Of course the US has a terrible history with how they treat the marginalized. So it becomes a vicious cycle. In order to have any sense of belonging and power they take advantage of the fact they have white skin to enforce further marginalization of the disabled populace by pushing out non White disabled people from positions of advocacy and opportunities.

And Southall says she communicated her feelings to other communities dealing with ableism:

I'm not black myself but I'm a WOC. I've had conversation with black disabled advocates who say ableism is a major problem within their own community, and I can understand where they are coming from as in the Latin culture there is a huge stigma associated with being disabled.

Latinx families don't want to claim that they have disabled members due to the cultural shame it carries under religious circumstances. If you have disabled members it means god has shaped you as you did something horrible to upset god enough to curse your family with a disabled member.

That kind of mind-set with ableism being a major issue within the BIPOC/POC communities; it shuts out the kids who have the desire and motivation to play disabled sports because parents do not want to acknowledge or more than often enough don't have the additional cash flow that white families have to be able to access extracurricular programs/ activities for their child to participate in where they can socialize with other like minded disabled children.

Southall is extremely clear on how hockey culture can curate an acceptance of disabled hockey fans and players:

Hockey needs to be accessible, period. Diversity and inclusion are not true intersectionality if the disabled are excluded from the table. If one has the desire to play even with beer league, don't let your own fears/disability stand in the way. There are wonderful people within the hockey community. I wouldn't be where I am right now if it wasn't for those few who gave me the chances at the right moments.

But some folks want more than lip service from the hockey culture; in some cases, the disability isn't readily seen, which makes folks who fall into that area the target of a specific form of ableism.

South Side Chicago native Jason Wilson plays for the Chicago Blackhawks Warriors, a hockey team with a roster of disabled military veterans. Wilson, who is Black, served 11 years in the United States Army. He has a disability that's not readily seen by the naked eye: chronic back problems from his time serving. Wilson, who served in the Middle East during Operation Iraqi Freedom, said from what he remembers, the Chicago Blackhawks Warriors program started with a group of disabled veterans who got together to play hockey. Because of his back problems, "it's hard to play regular hockey on a regular basis," Wilson said. And his back issues—essentially, he said, multiple torn ligaments—became progressively worse after he was discharged from the Army—a predicament he relived when he was looking for work.

"It was hard to do a regular job, like what I was trained to do," said Wilson. "Sometimes going through these applications, people ask you on the form in every job that I've seen, 'Do you have any disability? Are you a disabled veteran?' It's like, why are you asking me this?" Wilson says it's the difference between a visible disability—like being in a wheelchair—and one that is less visible but still precludes him from working in certain capacities.

Wilson often finds himself explaining ableism to people who don't know any better—particularly family members.

"They don't know what it's like to go through this," Wilson said. "You know how you feel when it comes to being able to do certain tasks—like, some of us coming home, we might not be able to skate as fast. I have balance issues.

"Some of our wounds aren't physically there. I got a guy on my team who one of his arms was blown up. We have some good skaters, but most of us out there are just trying to break the monotony of being caught in a rut when we come home. Most of us wouldn't come out of the house before this program. We go out and skate for an hour and a half, two hours, so this has kind of been a big help for the mental and physical aspect.

"And it's probably more than on a personal level that people would look at me and they won't know what's really wrong."

Boston-area hockey blogger Chanel Keenan was born with a disability called osteogenesis imperfecta, a disease that prevents the body from building strong bones. Rather than the sport doing the bare minimum by briefly showcasing disabled fans or Make-a-Wish children on broadcasts, Keenan would like those in positions of power to do the work required to hockey more inclusive for disabled folks.

"Representation outside of charity would be awesome," said Keenan. "I recently got into the USA sled hockey team. I knew they existed; I've seen a couple games during the Olympics and stuff, but I never really thought to really get into them. And obviously, since I'm American, I see the pride in that and seeing their community, you know, work so hard to come into a sport.

"But at the same time, they're so separate. You don't really ever see a whole lot of mix going on within the media or even a ceremonial puck situation; I don't think I've seen one. That doesn't mean it didn't happen. But yeah, just representation outside of stuff like that."

Due to Keenan's disability, people she meets are at times shocked by her hockey fandom.

"I had a neighbor at school, we were in the same dorm. He just was so surprised that I knew what was going on, in general, and it was just a really interesting interaction, because he was also disabled, but he had been paralyzed in an accident," Keenan said. "So I kind of saw, like, the internalized ableism and a little bit of misogyny going on. And I thought that that was funny. Because, you know, as much as an event can change your life, if you have these internal beliefs, that doesn't automatically change. If one part of your life gets completely turned upside down, you still probably have, you know, similar beliefs as you did before."

Through Keenan's writing and speaking out for disabled hockey fans, she has landed a role with the NHL's newest franchise, the Seattle Kraken, as an independent intersectionality consultant, in which she plans to advocate for the sport's most marginalized fans.

"They're at such a really interesting point of development as far as starting with nothing," Keenan said. "And for the NHL to start with nothing is really refreshing, obviously, because you know, this is a well-oiled machine; they don't really take the change very well. And they don't really know how to embrace it properly, in my opinion. I think I can do more; I want to do more."

What does the NHL, and the venues its franchises operate in, do to provide an accessible experience to disabled fans? The Americans with Disabilities Act (ADA) requires that new arenas set aside at least one percent of seating for disabled accommodations, according to the U.S. Department of Justice Civil Rights Division Disability Rights Section. The ADA document lays out policies and procedures for concession areas, locker rooms, and restrooms, among other areas.

The document says, in part, "Wheelchair seating locations must provide lines of sight comparable to those provided to other spectators. In stadiums where spectators can be expected to stand during the show or event (for example, football, baseball, basketball games, or rock concerts), all or substantially all of the wheelchair seating locations must provide a line of sight over standing spectators. A comparable line of sight...allows a person using a wheelchair to see the playing surface between the heads and over the shoulders of the persons standing in the row immediately in front and over the heads of the persons standing two rows in front."

In 2014, Olympia Entertainment, the group that ran Detroit's Joe Louis Arena, then home of the Red Wings, was forced to update the venue after being sued by a disabled fan who claimed they were unable to attend the game due to a lack of accessibility. The group added 45 wheelchair-accessible seats and improved accessibility in the restrooms and concession stands, *Athletic Business* reported.

Here's the policy the Staples Center, home arena of the Los Angeles Kings, implemented to provide an accessible experience for disabled fans: "Accessible/disabled seating is available on all levels of the Arena. Accessible seating is reserved exclusively for patrons with accessible needs and their companions. Patrons purchasing accessible seating may purchase one (1) accessible seat and three (3) companion seats adjacent to the accessible seat. Depending upon availability, seats for additional guests will be located as close as possible to the accessible space. This policy ensures that we are able to accommodate all those that need accessible seating."

Due to folks like J.J. O'Connor, a disabled hockey player and advocate who heads up USA Hockey disabled hockey programming, the NHL honors all six disabled hockey disciplines—sled hockey, special hockey, blind hockey, deaf/hard of hearing hockey, warrior hockey, and standing amputee hockey.

"I learned after getting hurt and playing the game and loving the game that the next best thing to playing the game is to help others and do what you can so that other people can enjoy the game,"

O'Connor told NHL.com. "There's certainly gratification in watching the sport grow, watching people with disabilities [who] probably never would have thought that they could play hockey, now have that opportunity."

8

Homophobia, Biphobia, and Transphobia

I think men's team sports have this manufactured idea of what masculinity is, and I think that leads to a lot of problems.... I think that leads to men not taking care of themselves—mental health, specifically.

—Patrick Burke, NHL senior director of player safety
and former You Can Play president and co-founder

THE 2019 DOCUMENTARY *STANDING ON THE LINE*, A CANADIAN film about the LGBTQIA+ experience in sports, has a scene in which former hockey player Brock McGillis, the first male professional hockey player to openly come out as gay, speaks with a group of Quebec Major Junior Hockey League players.

The first question McGillis asks the group: "Who here has used homophobic language? 'That's gay. You're a fag.' Words like that."

None of the players raise their hands. McGillis raises his right hand. And then, some of the players in the room reluctantly raise theirs.

"The easiest way to make a change is through language," McGillis tells the players.

McGillis, a former You Can Play ambassador, who often talks to teens and young players about how the make the sport inclusive, likes to get into the weeds of the origins of homophobic behavior.

"This is the only sport I know of that the majority of kids move away from home at 16 years old," McGillis said. "So now you've left this incredibly insular environment, and then you've moved on to an even more insular environment because you move to a new community, away from your family, away from your friends, everyone else.

"And all you have when you move there is 20 teammates, other than friends, your peers. So now you spend eight months with people who came from similar cultures elsewhere who were influenced by coaches and older players who came from the same culture. And now you're in this even tighter bubble. Once the season ends, you go home and you train for hockey. And who do you hang out with and train with? The players you grew up with, because those were your friends."

While sitting in the press box at the 2017 NHL Draft at Chicago's United Center, Evan remembers a particularly vocal group of fans chirping at NHL commissioner Gary Bettman. Every time he announced a pick, they would chant over and over again, "Bettman has a man-gina!"

Gay slurs, unfortunately, are a part of sports—even in 2021. Aggression in sports often has players jockeying for supremacy, and questioning someone's manhood is commonplace.

When Blackhawks winger Andrew Shaw used a homophobic slur in the penalty box late in Game 4 of the first round of the

2016 Stanley Cup playoff series against the St. Louis Blues, he told reporters after the game, "I'm not that kind of guy."

Then Blackhawks beat reporter for the *Chicago Tribune* Chris Hine wrote a column about Shaw's slur—and being a gay man, he said anger is no excuse for homophobic language:

> I was called that growing up before I even realized I was gay. When you're closeted and thinking about coming out, you have nightmares about friends or family members using that word and making you feel like an outcast. It hurts when your friends use that word in a teasing manner. It's a whole different feeling to have people direct that word at you with contempt. I've had that feeling.
>
> Now put yourself in the shoes of a closeted gay athlete. You're in a locker room or on a playing field, and you hear your teammates use that word. You start thinking, "Is this how they really feel about gay people? Is that what they would call me if I came out to them? Would I still be a member of this team? Would my career be over?"
>
> That word is why gay athletes everywhere hide their sexual identity and often live lives of torment. It's why some contemplate suicide and develop emotional and psychological issues they might never rectify.

Fast-forward to 2020, when Bayne Pettinger, a young hockey agent and former player who had recently come out, had the support of some of hockey's big names, such as Sidney Crosby and Connor McDavid.

"I think I'm going to be a better person, a better agent. It's a 500-pound weight lifted off my shoulders," Pettinger told The Athletic. "I'm tired of walking into a room and thinking, 'Who knows and who doesn't?' I'm tired of playing that game."

A lot of folks are sick of this shit—and have been in the thick of the fight so young players like Pettinger can be treated as an equal.

New York City Gay Hockey Association (NYCGHA) board secretary Steve Lorenzo is an Iowa native who grew up near the Minnesota border, so he's witnessed how intense hockey culture can be for the people inside it.

"There's so many different hockey cultures. There's college hockey, there's youth hockey, there's professional hockey," Lorenzo said. "We've been working a lot with the NHL recently on their Hockey Is for Everyone initiative and things like that. And even within the NHL...there's a very big disconnect between the front office and the people who are actually on the ice. I don't know if it's because they want to shelter them and make them think only about hockey during the regular season and during the playoffs. But clearly, the real world insinuated itself [in 2020]. And there was recognition from the players who were clearly personally affected by that. I don't think when it comes to LGBTQ issues we've had somebody who has demonstrated that they are personally affected by the things that have been going on."

Lorenzo's Chicago counterparts are dealing with the same issues.

"Playing in league play around Chicago, [we've] definitely had some issues over the years," said Andrew Sobotka, Chicago Gay Hockey Association (CGHA) board member. "There's the occasional 'faggot,' other slurs for sure. I would say that that isn't unique to homophobic slurs; there's a lot of misogynistic slurs as well.

"I would say for the most part people are respectful, but there's always a few players who, if they do have an issue with us, it's that—I think it's similar to what you said with Andrew Shaw, where he claims, you know, he's not homophobic, he wouldn't use that language, but in the heat of the moment he did use that language."

CGHA member Elliot Gutman remembers hearing a lot of homophobic language when he was playing high school hockey in suburban Chicago's North Shore, an affluent area north of the city.

"Homophobia there is saying that being gay is less than," Gutman said. "That being gay is a weakness or people are just afraid that they themselves are being gay. And that's where there is a lot of uncertainty. Use of slurs and harsh language like that is where a lot of that comes from; I definitely saw a lot of that, not only on the ice but in the locker room as well."

Gutman says the adults around the sport often set the tone for what players deem normal behavior.

"I know that whatever I saw my coach doing or my coach saying, I definitely emulated the same behavior," Gutman said. "I think that's one of the most important things to kind of normalize acceptance and behavior of inclusiveness."

And what type of grown-ass men continue to use homophobic slurs?

"We typically at least once a season would confront some type of issue of homophobia, where someone on the ice would call one of our teammates a 'faggot,'" said CGHA board member Brian Hull. "And we have jerseys that say 'Chicago Gay Hockey Association.' So what I tried to do in most of those instances is, I would go into their locker room after the game, and just ask them, 'Do you guys know that we are a gay hockey team, and player No. 24 called someone on our team a "faggot?" I just want to let you know that that's not something we're okay with.' You know, just addressing it head-on, so that they understand that it's a problem, and to see that if they actually do show remorse and apologize for it, and also to put it on the rest of the team to let their captains and their leaders have a conversation about it.

"And in the vast majority of those instances we would get messages from the captains or the players saying that they apologize for that and they had a conversation about it, to let them know it's not okay. And it's kind of similar to the Andrew Shaw situation, where the teams that don't respond, or do it again next time, you understand where they're coming from, too. But I think the more that teams are able to address this head-on with each other and let them know it's not okay, it just helps [the] culture at large, too."

Lorenzo gets right to it when it comes to why homophobia continues to be an issue in hockey culture.

"I think there is a genuine concern that people might treat straight men the way straight men treat women. And they're scared of that, because they know just how much they marginalize and disempower women, and gay men are the only people within society [who] could do that to a straight man," Lorenzo said. "And I think that's a power that is asserted over straight men that makes them feel the need to react. You know, if we're talking about teenagers, teenagers are just kind of awful.... They form these cliques and anybody who isn't seen as a part of that is instantly othered or ostracized or demonized. And there are certain characteristics that are easier to point out than otherness, whether it's race, whether it's gender, whether it's kids who were obviously gay."

These characteristics are "low-hanging fruit" players use to make themselves feel better, Lorenzo says. And kids are often a product of what they are taught during their upbringing.

"These are the kids who are taught from an early age that they are special and that they deserve the best. And anybody who challenges or threatens that for them is going to be put in jeopardy. You know, in one way or another, and you see this at all levels of society—hockey is just a microcosm of the bigger hole. And, you know, unfortunately, with regards to hockey there is a socioeconomic barrier to the sport," Lorenzo said. "The gear is expensive. It's difficult to find ice time. So there are all these barriers, you know, to the entry within the sport. So the kids who were privileged are already entering this arena with an advantage. And you know anybody who's coming at it who may be, you know, not from a wealthy family, whose gear is beat up or secondhand or whatever, that's an obvious difference and that's where bullying can start. You know, if it's a young woman, because there aren't enough women skaters to form a hockey team, if there's a woman that's trying to break the gender barrier and get in and escape, that's another obvious difference. So there are all these easy places where people can say, oh, you're different than I am and different in this setting means less than."

The group that has the most power to stop racism, homophobia, xenophobia, sexism, and the ilk? The parents.

"It's bad enough just in regular society, but when you introduce that element of competition, it really starts to bring out the worst in people," Lorenzo said. "You know, people have to feel that their team is the best. And when that is the case, they start looking at things that make them the best. And, unfortunately, things that might be perceived as weakness or otherness can detract from that.

"So I see how it would be very easy for youth leagues—unless there is somebody who is playing an active role in countering these prejudices and trying to do team-building exercises that account for otherness—this stuff is just going to run like wildfire, because you're looking for ways to put other people down and, unfortunately, a lot of the insults that fly around on the ice tend to be sexual in nature. I mean, I don't hear a lot of racially motivated insults happening on the ice. And I don't know if that's because hockey culture has been predominantly white for so damn long, or...I don't feel like I'm capable of commenting on that. But I go to Islander games, and you hear them calling the other goalie a 'cocksucker.' And these are people in the stands, and it's like okay, are you a role model for somebody and you're sitting there and calling the goalie a homophobic slur just because you don't like the team that they play for? It's really amazing how these lowest common denominators emerged just because they're things happening in a competitive environment."

Cordingley believes parents can do more to stop hockey's intersectional issues, but there's context to that, since parents are often separate from the players when they're getting ready to step onto the ice.

"I think hockey almost allows it to be worse because it's not... as easy for parents to observe. You have locker rooms [where sometimes] players have to go to a lower level of the rink, and the parents aren't allowed there," Cordingley said. "It's one of those things that makes [hockey] unique; once you step on the ice, it's like it's a different world. You have to put on all this gear and step on a frozen surface and play surrounded by, you know, glass and boards, and it's different. It feels like a separate place. It feels different than other sports. I played lacrosse; I was the only girl on a boys' team in high school too.

"But the long and the short of it is transphobia is rampant in hockey. I am a trans person. Sometimes I [would] go to random rinks...and just drop in for pickup, [and] wearing my team trans jersey would be a statement.... The thing is, though, if I'm willing to stand there and just casually bring it up, most people aren't going to be dicks in that moment. Because I'm standing there in their face. And just normalizing it, like, 'Yeah, I'm trans. Here I am. You've been playing on the line with me for an hour. You didn't die, but here we are.'"

Jessica Platt is the first trans woman to play in the CWHL, along with being a You Can Play ambassador. While she loves hockey as much as—or possibly more than—anyone who grew up in a town where the game is considered everything, she says she knew she was different from the other kids. And those thoughts held her back from transitioning as early as she initially wanted to.

"I realized in high school that transitioning was something that I wanted to do. I didn't know if I was going to be able to do it. Or how to do it. But hockey held me back on that because I had grown up playing hockey; I had a set idea of how I had to act and how I had to be because of the people that I was surrounded by, so I felt I needed to be someone else and I pretended to be that person," Platt said. "And it wasn't until I stopped playing hockey that I really started to learn that it was okay how I felt; that it was okay to transition and, you know, find happiness being who I am instead of having to suppress that.

"I grew up in a predominantly white, heterosexual city...a conservative town. So I didn't see a lot of diversity. But, you know...I'd meet people at hockey tournaments; man, that has a great potential to bring people together. Unfortunately, it also has the potential to drive people apart because...those people who are not exactly open to things they may not understand don't really branch outside of... what they're comfortable with."

Looking back at her upbringing, and things she heard, the steps Platt took to feel comfortable in her own skin were worth it.

"I loved playing hockey. It was great. But the atmosphere surrounding it was awful," Platt said. "That's why I waited until I was done with hockey to transition.... And from there, I had a couple of rough years where I started really finding myself, but the turning point was, you know, I wanted to have a life. I think it was a year to find the right doctors and get everything shut out."

When she made the decision to transition, Platt received support from her family, friends, and some of the hockey players she had faced off against.

"I had an overwhelmingly positive response. I don't think anyone in my family said anything bad," Platt said. "I had people who reached out to me on social media and congratulated me and said how happy they were and they were happy that I was doing well. That was really nice and unexpected. I didn't expect any people that I had previously played with to reach out. That was really nice. I will say that the women's hockey community is amazing and something that people can look at for how to do things better."

Lorenzo says hockey and the LGBTQIA+ community could do more when it comes to inclusion. Since 2013, the New York City Gay Hockey Association (NYCGHA) has had a strong relationship with You Can Play, Lorenzo says. The NYCGHA had its first scrimmage on professional ice at a You Can Play night with the Bridgeport (Conn.) Islanders (formerly the Sound Tigers), the farm team for the New York Islanders.

"We've had a good working relationship with the [You Can Play cofounder] Burke family and the people that continued the mission in their place," Lorenzo said. "I don't want to say anything that jeopardizes our relationship, but it does feel like when You Can Play started, it was very much about hockey. And it was very much about fighting casual homophobia in the locker room. And it feels like as time has gone on, the organization's mission feels a little less focused.... That that's not to say they aren't doing good, because they are working at a number of different levels within college sports, and they are making resources available to institutions that want to work on improving these issues. But I don't feel that the initial drive of the organization has been sustained.

"Prior to 2016, you know, things seemed to be going pretty well for the gays. And in a way things weren't going well for people involved with Black Lives Matter or for immigrants or things like that...there were much more deserving areas of focus for outrage and for activism. I don't think that You Can Play has...broadened out to encompass all of these things, though intolerance is intolerance and hate language is hate language. So there were ways these issues could be addressed without a major modification of their mission statement. But there has definitely been a shift in the political landscape...and, while a lot of subcultures are feeling singled out and under attack, there certainly are groups that have borne the brunt of that much more so than the gays have."

Don't we want people who've committed transgressions to not only learn from their mistakes, but also be proactive in stopping gay slurs in their tracks? Or do we want folks to stay in that box forever?

Shaw went on to become the Blackhawks' You Can Play ambassador, and deceased basketball legend Kobe Bryant, who also used a gay slur in anger, went well beyond mere performative allyship after the incident.

"If they seem sincere in the moment, and they've taken the steps where they actually care and realize that they messed up, then you have to just come at least initially from a place of positive regard and use it as an educational moment," Hull said. "And for people like that, that shows such a great turnaround and makes it a part of their life story. I think that's a really powerful thing where you can turn a negative into a positive just like Andrew did.

"I think, especially given our current state of politics and the rise of far-right groups and white supremacist organizations and things of that nature, that you hear more of that stuff. If it's from people where it's a repeated offense and you can tell that's just a part of their character and who they are, then in my mind that's a very different situation to be dealt with. It's more structural, and the institutions like the NHL and the Blackhawks...this is where they need to put their weight behind it to let people know that this is not okay. It's not a mind-set that's allowed to be around."

WE'VE ESTABLISHED HOMOPHOBIC incidents happen in life and in sports. What's the impetus behind such behavior? Where does it come from? How do kids pick up this language? And, more importantly, how do we stop it?

"From my perspective...it could be coming from the family, it could be from coming from the leadership within the team or the organization, and I think a lot of it comes from online too,"

Sobotka said. "I think kids nowadays are exposed to content that is inherently racist or homophobic or misogynistic without realizing the impact of it, and it perpetuates the cycle where people use slurs to put people down and they don't even necessarily realize it. And so I think just having the conversation about it and engaging with the teams, engaging with the NHL. Everyone has to understand the impact of it, they have to understand if they've been complicit or if they've been actively working against it. And I think, you know, now is the time; like, there's two sides of history and which side do you want to be on?"

Sobotka says the NHL can do more to influence minds outside of performative allyship.

"I think it's getting there. I think they know now...the thing where everyone turns their logo rainbow and Pride Night, they're checking a box—'We're inclusive'—and I think they realize now that that's not enough, they need to enact real change," Sobotka said.

"There's never been a professional NHL player who came out. There has to be at least one, maybe dozens, over the years. And you have to look at the reasons why that hasn't happened. They do surveys with the NHL Players' Association [and players] will say, 'I'm okay with having a gay teammate.' They asked that question point-blank, and you have to wonder what else it is. The fans. I think that's a large part of it, is they need to make sure that they don't alienate their fan base, but also they need to educate their fan base and I think they realize that now. Based on conversations we've had with the Blackhawks and with other NHL teams [in 2020] alone, I think they're sincerely invested in trying to figure out what they can be doing better—they know deleting the comments on Facebook or Instagram doesn't help. How do you engage with your fans to have a conversation, even over social media, to make something that is educational and not just sweep it under the rug or check the box?"

Lorenzo agrees that the NHL—and other groups—can do better than performative allyship.

"I do appreciate the fact that the NHL has had Pride Nights, but it does feel strange to be singled out that way; it doesn't snap necessarily of tokenism, although certainly people have said it," Lorenzo said. "But as a beneficiary it hasn't felt like, oh look, they're putting the gays out on the ice so they can say, 'We had gays on the ice.' It never felt like that with the Rangers, with the Islanders, with the Devils, because there are people within [those organizations] who are legitimately interested in these issues and pushing forward a social agenda. But, that said, when you make these individual nights, and then that's kind of it, it doesn't really bring about cultural change, because it's only bringing certain people to the table at one time and one time only. So it's not just saying let's have a night for people but it's actually saying, 'What can we do to work with the community to make sure that that people feel like there is a place for them at the table and that there is a place for them on the ice?'"

Lorenzo says hockey needs to realize that LGBTQIA+ people aren't a monolithic group.

"That's the million-dollar question," Lorenzo said. "I think part of it is a notion that is difficult for organizations like the NHL to grasp, and that is intersectionality. People have multiple identities—you know, people who are people of color who are also LGBTQ. You know there are people who are dealing with socioeconomic issues. There are people who are dealing with immigration status, there are all these different things. If hockey is for everyone, you can't just start putting people in specific columns and then targeting things toward that one segment of their identity. I think that the solution is something where you start addressing things from an intersectional perspective.

"I didn't grow up a person of color, but I grew up as a gay person in a rural community. My parents were schoolteachers, and we were definitely on the lower end of the socioeconomic scale. So, even if there had been hockey in the community, I don't know that I would have had access to it because I don't know if my parents would have had the money for the skating lessons and for the equipment."

And McGillis believes the hockey governing bodies often stop short of going to places where they can have the most effect on changing the narrative: locker rooms.

"You can have a Pride Night all you want," McGillis said. "But how is that shifting things in a locker room for a queer hockey player who's struggling and hearing homo-negative language on a daily basis, or the biases that exists for people of color.... How are you reprogramming your staff and whatnot so that you're not doing that?"

Ultimately, the change needs to come from within the organizations that compose hockey's power structures—at the top.

9

Why It Happens
and How to Fix It

How do you fix something that has been around for more than a century, something that is so insular and stubborn? It's not easy, and it takes commitment from people in the community—especially those in charge—to work on it themselves and change things from the inside. While we addressed the causes and fixes for each individual issue, there are some overarching causes that apply to more than one issue. Things like toxic masculinity, cost, billeting, hero worship, and the insular nature of the sport all contribute to keeping the topics we've tackled features of the system, not bugs. And tools like education must be used to combat all these issues within the culture, not just one.

Why It Happens

Toxic masculinity at the foundation of hockey contributes to transphobia, homophobia, and sexism in the sport. Toxic masculinity is the emphasis on traditional male gender roles that stigmatize emotions and elevate toughness. It also frowns upon anything perceived as weak, which is usually deemed "feminine."

In 2018, Tim Skuce conducted a research study on toxic masculinity in elite-level hockey. He interviewed three former NHL players, three current NHL players, and three major junior players. Skuce said the biggest fear his interviewees expressed was that of being perceived as effeminate. "Some of the men said they never thought about how hockey really shaped them and what they thought it was to be a boy and a man," Skuce said. "If you were deemed feminine, you couldn't play through it. That was a real death knell. Unless you're a gifted goal-scorer. And then the rules start to change a bit, right? Because you can score goals."

Hockey's love of fighting is rooted in toxic masculinity, as is the disregard for mental health or taking care of any health. It pushes athletes to play through injuries they should not be playing through. (Look no further than the many narratives praising players for playing with torn ACLs.)

"I had the men telling me that by eight or nine, they understood what it is to intimidate and put the fear of God into somebody," Skuce said.

Some of the players he spoke to who are 40 to 50 years old—and some who are even in the NHL right now—are starting to question the idea of toxic masculinity and what they're taught. But there's trauma associated with it—they thought this was something right, that this is what being a man meant.

"There's men who really want to resist this; they just don't know how to do it," Skuce said. "They feel so threatened that they start questioning themselves. 'Well, maybe it's me and I behave this way. And I've got to be part of the club.' The man card is the phrase that a lot of them talk about. It's just a very powerful binding there. And then there's policing tactics. And you alluded to that they get policed in certain ways, too, right. From the discourse of abuse to hazing to you're not tough enough. It just goes on and on, about getting policed into a particular kind of narrative."

Sunaya Sapurji once wrote a story about kids faking their way through baseline concussion testing so they could still play, despite having concussions. There are countless stories of players who play through injuries, ranging from broken bones to torn ACLs.

Jesse Mahler, who works with prevention program Coaching Boys Into Men (CBIM), said the sport creates a defined box of what it means to be a boy and a man. CBIM is trying to create space for different kinds of masculinity.

"I was looking for other kinds of brotherhood or other types of sibling relationships with other young men around me, and they weren't there," Mahler, who played youth hockey, said. "Creating a little bit of space for the athletes who might be on the outside, who might actually be a really great ally or a great proponent of healthy relationships, of anti-sexist behavior, of a more healthy, more caring, more empathetic masculinity, creating space for that athlete. It's not just about the athletes who might be the most aggressive, it's about those who are looking for something else."

Going almost hand-in-hand with toxic masculinity is hero worship, which is created by hockey but also by the media and fans. We place our athletes on pedestals and think because they are good at a sport, they can never do anything wrong. It makes us run to denial instead of accepting the truth that, say, our favorite player may have assaulted someone.

"We take it as a personal thing," Brenda Tracy said. "All of this adoration...you put all that together and it's a recipe for disaster."

In his memoir, Sheldon Kennedy describes hero worship from his experiences in 1982 when his major junior team, the Swift Current Broncos, were winning: "The players were treated like kings. People also said hello to us wherever we went. Women wanted to sleep with us and be our girlfriends. Men wanted to buy us drinks. We were welcome at every party and social function."

Everyone wants to be friends with the star, the popular winner. And for even that slightest chance, we will ignore any negative signs. Everyone wants to win. And for even that slightest chance, organizations and coaches will ignore the sexual assaults and the systemic abuse. Just to win. Players who are especially good at a sport are most likely to be given passes.

"Why does playing hockey make you a good person? You know, where's the correlation?" Laura Robinson said.

This is something we see in all sports and at levels from juniors through professional. In hockey, that includes college and major juniors, where both Brock McGillis and Jordan DeKort experienced the intense fandom and the feeling of being hounded for autographs. DeKort said whenever something negative happens—like Ben Johnson's arrest—everyone rushes to defend the alleged accuser.

"Because we do things in the community, we're seen as a good person.... It's obviously bigger than a hockey issue, but hockey creates this vacuum," DeKort said.

Sapurji said hero worship comes from the small-town atmosphere of most major junior teams, where the league is the biggest thing in town. And when you're a top prospect, people rush for their brush with fame.

This happens in college hockey and the minor leagues, as well. Star-struck fandom doesn't only happen with "professional" players. This happens to kids who are as young as 14. But there are times it happens to children even younger than that. "There's this thing that we do with athletes specifically where we identify that a young man has athletic ability," Tracy said. "And so we have this high school boy who is not acting appropriately. Maybe it's small things, but it's not okay. And we cover it up because we don't want to ruin his future, because we value perpetrators, not survivors. But we don't want to ruin his chances to play in college, and so we cover things up and we minimize it. Then he's in college and he does something worse. And we cover it up because we'll ruin his chances to go pro. And then he's in the pro leagues and we have these databases. And then we're like, oh, he has a problem. Well, not really. They were that way when they got there."

Rising costs of hockey are also a barrier to cultivating a diverse player base. In 2017, *Time* reported that hockey was the most expensive youth sport among lacrosse, baseball/softball, football, soccer, and basketball, costing a maximum of $19,000 per year. On average, it costs $7,013. But hockey isn't just expensive because of the equipment and ice time. If you are serious about playing hockey and wish to play competitively, play for a scholarship, play in the major juniors, or play for a chance at the pros, you have to invest in much more than just your equipment. Prep schools in the U.S. and hockey academies in Canada are popular but expensive options for children who want to keep eligibility to play college hockey. And if you are serious about being recruited, you need to enroll in showcases so that coaches, who recruit, will notice you.

"I remember when I was going through it, my dad was like, 'I'm not paying $600 for you to go play a weekend of hockey...if you're good enough, they'll find you,'" Nurse said.

But most players aren't as good as Sarah Nurse. And even for the players who are good—the ones who make it to college hockey, the ones who get a scholarship—they still enroll in skating and skills camps for that extra edge. That's a significant barrier that keeps many people—especially those from underprivileged communities—out.

"My family, we didn't have much growing up," Nurse said. "My parents worked multiple jobs to put all of us into hockey, and we're not going to have stories like that anymore because now hockey costs tens of thousands of dollars a year. My parents today wouldn't have been able to put me in hockey. And so you look at that storyline and it's going to die out very soon."

There are organizations that bring hockey into under-resourced areas, including Ice Hockey in Harlem, Snider Hockey, ICE (Inner City Education), Hockey on Your Block, and SCORE Boston. The goal of these organizations is to lower or eliminate the cost of components like equipment and ice time.

But once we get past how expensive it is to play youth hockey, if you want to play at a higher level, it's almost impossible to do so without money—unless you are elite.

"Maybe this is just me lamenting the end of my hockey career, but I wish there was more of an equal opportunity," John Cyfko said. "I don't know I would have made it farther, but I know a lot of people who made it just because they had that privilege of being a very wealthy white male."

Cyfko, who trained at an elite gym in Canada, was only able to do so because of a discount.

Organized hockey is a scam (some lower junior leagues have tried to charge players to play), a money-making machine where you need to have the assets to pay to help your child succeed—something that further keeps hockey culture the same.

"You can get your newly immigrated family into Timbits hockey relatively easier, then they can start to fall in love with the game," Courtney Szto said. "But we've created this stupid hurdle that has made it extremely elitist and far more selective. There's far fewer opportunities there and nobody has to take you for any reason because it's not house league, so there's just all these additional layers that filter color out of the system through the academies. I don't really know how we can roll those back, but it is certainly made it a lot harder to make, in Canada, the national team look like Canada."

Billeting is a major reason hockey culture is so hard to change. In the U.S. at least, the system is fairly unique to hockey. Players leave their homes to play on a team and live with another family—their billet family. That family takes the place of their own. While it's common for players to billet in juniors and major juniors, there are some players who leave home as young as 13, or even as early as 12.

Daniel Carcillo's and Garrett Taylor's lawsuit against the CHL stated, "The majority of these children leave their homes and families to play hockey for a team in a different town or city, far from their parents. They are billeted with a local family and attend the local high school. They are young, impressionable and vulnerable. They are completely inculcated into the culture of their Team and the Leagues. They are deeply incentivized to comply with League and Team culture by the potential to be drafted to the NHL."

Trey Lewis said he was terrified of leaving home when he was 16.

"I'd never lived anywhere besides my grandparents,'" Lewis said. "And it was just overwhelming. And it was like a real relief. At 16, and even at 17, I was so lucky. I had an unbelievable billet family; they were the most down-to-earth, nicest people you could ever meet. They're still best friends with my grandparents to this day and I see them a couple times a year minimum. But if I look back, I'm like, 'Well, maybe if I didn't have such possibilities, maybe I would have given up too.' I had a lot of friends that were playing Junior A back home and that was a very appealing thing for me. If I didn't have my abilities, and was on a good hockey team, I probably would have quit. I can't imagine being 16, going into a new city, being traded a couple of times."

It's a lot for a 16-year-old, or even someone younger, to be thrown into a new system with people they aren't familiar with, subject to being traded at whim. Moving to a new place and a new team leaves them primarily with their billet family, their team, and their teammates as their entire social world. And as we saw with Kennedy, it further separates players from positive outside influences and can be used as a means to control them and their lives. And players don't always get good billets.

"I'll admit there are a lot of issues within hockey culture but you're also sending 16-, 17-year-olds off to essentially live away from their family, maybe be put in a situation where they don't have great billets and are really at the coach's mercy," Lewis said. "How do you feel about the whole system of just the concept of moving away at such a young age? I don't know if getting rid of it will be better or worse. It's difficult because I look at the person that I am now. And a lot of stuff, socially, I would have learned through hockey. You know, how to talk to people, how to do an interview, you know how to act professionally. I cherish those skills that I learned through that. But not everybody gets those skills. And not everybody has that same experience as me."

One player, Radek Faksa, lived in a hotel room at 11 years old so he could play at a high level.

"This is where we need to really bring child development specialists into the sporting system," Szto said. "Is this what we should be doing? And if they say, 'No, you should not send your children away at 13,' then we could just say, 'Okay, we won't do that anymore.' But that seems so outside of the box to be listening to, say, a social worker or something like that with regard to kind of athlete well-being."

Billeting strengthens the insular nature of hockey. Players are sometimes only playing hockey. Some take classes at the same time. Some don't. But it's a new environment. Arizona State's Dominic Garcia was one of the players not taking classes—so his family decided he would get a job.

"That helped me personally gain experience dealing with all types of different people," Garcia said. "A lot of people will attest that the restaurant business as a very early job is one of the best to work in. Just because you have to deal with so many people and some people are rude. Some people are really nice. From that standpoint, I think that helped me a lot."

It's hard for anyone to move to a new place, especially a young teenager. Some players have had good experiences; some, bad. But is it possible to remove this system?

"It feels like it's like the only affordable way to keep the pace with your sport like I did when I was 16 years old," NHL goaltender Ryan Miller said. "For three years, I went to Sault Ste. Marie, Michigan, to play in that time as an independent media team, sponsored by the Kuwaiti casinos, so we were called the Soo Indians. I then had moved on to their junior team and became the starting goalie under the junior team.

"And, you know, we met lovely people. Luckily I moved there with like six of my buddies I grew up playing [with]. So it's sort of like a mini hockey academy for us. But it was hard. It was the only way we could stay at the level we were at and continue playing."

Billeting doesn't have to be removed, per se. But as we've seen with coaching, hockey lacks proper vetting and oversight. It's unfathomable to think that we are not protecting our children by sending them away like this and leaving them open to abuse, bullying, and more. But this is commonplace in hockey. And when it's part of the game, you have no choice to participate.

"I was also the kid that wanted to go to voluntary IMG Academy at the age of 14, 15, and I was very happy to find myself away to just hit thousands of balls across the continent, away from my parents," Szto said. "So I get the desire to do everything you can to succeed in your sport, and the kids' love of the game forces a lot of parents' hands. It's that culture of, in order to succeed, this is what you have to do. We would have to get rid of that so that you have to play—kind of like your local association, until you're at an older level. I think Sweden has something like that...Swedish players basically play on the same team for their entire junior development. So when they get traded to the NHL, it's really kind of disconcerting for them because [it's] the first time they have to interact with new people in a new environment and they're not used to this idea of being traded and changing teams all the time. There are certainly other countries, smaller countries that have the ability to keep kids in a much more normal home environment for a lot longer. I'd be interested to know how that affects their general development."

Looking back, Lewis said he wishes there had been more sports psychologists in the youth system.

"It's definitely something that, I won't say haunts, but it worries me," Lewis said. "A majority of junior hockey players that are coming in at 16, 17 years old, these guys are just kids and they're scared, whether they want to admit it or not. I was scared when I was that young, and I wish that there was somebody there to reassure me to just be myself over anything else."

Hockey may be a fun sport to play that teaches teamwork and physical exercise. Organized hockey, however, is entirely different. It's a factory. It's designed to input the best ingredients to yield the maximum output. The input is the top players and coaches; the output is winning.

Think back to the structure. Think of all the Junior A leagues and Junior B leagues, or the junior leagues popping up consistently in the USA—some of which are just scams. Think of all the skills camps, of hockey academies and prep schools. Think of billeting.

"We're basically creating a child labor system," Szto said. "When we're sending them away at 14 years old, that's the reality of it."

Because organized hockey is designed this way, players go from being people to being objects.

"You can buy and sell and trade a boy when he's 14 in Canada," Robinson said. "That's pretty much all you need to know."

This is true even for adult players. You don't need to look further than during COVID-19, when athletes were expected to drop everything and enter the bubble, and players like Tuukka Rask were villainized for picking their family and others for picking their health and safety over the team. The businesslike, factory nature of organized hockey means people cease being people and become objects. It enhances many of the cultural issues we've already highlighted and, in many cases, prevents real change. If focus were placed on the players as people, as children, it would help protect them from things like bad billets or sexual abuse. But the bottom line is what matters, and adding more oversight hinders that bottom line.

It also creates an environment in which, at the pro level, players are susceptible to drug abuse. Fighting is still a hallmark in hockey, and we've seen the effects it has on players. In *Boy on Ice: The Life and Death of Derek Boogaard*, John Branch details Derek Boogaard's life as an enforcer in hockey. Because of pain, he became addicted to drugs, and an overdose led to his death. Because he was valued only for his contributions on ice, he was pressured to be an enforcer and to continue that life.

And when players' on-ice worth dries up, they're cast aside, not to be cared for again.

How to Fix It

There are solutions, some obvious, when it comes to fixing these issues. A couple big solutions we mentioned above are vetting billets and coaches, increasing oversight, and emphasizing education. The focus of what we want hockey to be has to change. It can no longer be a money-making machine.

When it comes to defraying the costs, the solution may sound simple, but reality is far more complicated. Equipment and ice time have to be accessible, as organizations like the Snider Hockey Foundation and SCORE Boston show. Renee Hess of the Black Girl Hockey Club has raised scholarships for Black girls who need money for equipment or tournaments. But because of the systems in place for players who wish to play at a high level, a scholarship model would most likely not be enough to pay for skills camps, showcases, equipment, prep schools, and more. The prep school and hockey academy model needs to change. How players get to college hockey needs to change. Like billeting, it's not easy to swap the entire system for something new.

Education is fundamental for all levels—be it the pros or youth hockey. It is also important for the coaches, parents, and players. Education in hockey already exists—there are required modules in both Hockey Canada and USA Hockey in order to earn a coaching certificate. However, there are questions surrounding their effectiveness. There are tales of coaches not taking the courses, instead passing them along to a partner. Even if coaches do participate, there's no measure in place to see if they are actually applying that knowledge. And as we've seen elsewhere, there simply isn't enough oversight. With a need for coaches and bodies to fill spots, it becomes hard to force people to spend more time on additional education. Trey Lewis took Canada's required coaching courses when he started at the helm on an Indigenous team, and the requirements were minimum. Riley Fitzgerald now works with coaches, trying to educate them.

"There are so many coaches that mean well that don't necessarily recognize some of the behaviors that they're exhibiting and the impact that they have, right, because they don't have the training," Fitzgerald said. "It's tough because, even then, when you look at the whole sports system, a lot of times parents play into it passively because they also don't know better and they don't feel like they have a choice.

"Hockey's one of the extremes of…what are the qualifications for somebody to be a coach? I do some coach education for Massachusetts hockey, and I think part of that is recognizing I want to do anything I can to help break that cycle. But it's basically a coaching seminar, and then a test that you have to take, and good enough. It's tough. It's tough on both sides in terms of the resources and the infrastructure to really educate coaches long enough, but looking at the stark difference between what teachers have to go through in terms of training and knowledge base and expertise versus coaches, when you're working with the same populations."

Coaches can make or break an athlete's experience. Especially in hockey and especially in higher levels like juniors, major juniors, and college hockey, coaches are crucial to how players develop not only on the ice, but also as people.

"Absolute power corrupts," Kurtis Gabriel said. "People just change when they get to control something. When did the ego of the coach ever come before the team?"

More attention needs to be paid to who gets hired as a coach, as these are the people society is entrusting with their children. As mentioned earlier, there must be specific guidelines to follow when hiring a coach. Although there are already measures in place to educate coaches, getting the coaches to pay attention to that educational material is another battle.

"Some level of education needs to be mandatory, but I don't think that everybody needs to take it purely because we know that making people take things they don't want to take doesn't work very well," Szto said. "Like that gender identity training that they have to take in Ontario that's so outside of many parents' wheelhouses. But at the same time, I think if you are in a leadership position in hockey, you have to have extra responsibility put on you because you have so much power. So I think coaches unfortunately do need to be mandated. And maybe that's a way of weeding out people who shouldn't be in the game."

Education has to be expansive and it has to be about more than hockey. It needs to cover life and social justice situations. Because hockey does not exist in a vacuum. It is part of society and in order for players who are non-white, non-cishet, or non-straight to be welcomed, those at the head of the team imparting values to kids need to understand the challenges marginalized players face and how to empower them. One place to start would be educating coaches on pronouns and getting them accustomed to saying their pronouns. It will take work, but once USA Hockey and Hockey Canada can create a curriculum that tackles racism, homophobia, transphobia, sexism, and xenophobia, it will go a long way toward changing the culture.

While we can educate our coaches and our coaches can pass that knowledge on to our children, coaches are not always teachers and children are still influenced by their parents. So players must be educated, even when they're young. Children are capable of understanding the concepts of right and wrong, of accepting and empowering. They also pick things up very quickly at a young age. It would be helpful if—and this goes back to caring about players as people first—specialists came in and talked with the players about these topics, therefore crafting educational concepts suited to each age group. (Jashvina's mother specializes in early education and Jashvina also served as a mentor, tutor, and teacher.)

"The whole culture needs to shift, because it's not just the players," Sapurji said. "Coaches and everyone who they come in contact with at the rink, that has to change too. I remember when I traveled on a bus with teams, *Slap Shot* used to be played every bus trip. And that's not exactly the best movie. It has not aged well in terms of its messaging. It feels like times have changed, but sometimes like hockey hasn't."

It's also important because there are rampant reports of racism, sexism, homophobia, and more within hockey at all levels. And those are moments where coaches and players can—and should—have conversations. It's something that they do in Snider Hockey, Philadelphia's program that serves a mostly marginalized community.

"Ideally you just want everyone to be educated," Garcia said. "I was called the n-word. At the time, like, I don't blame that kid who's

10 years old. He didn't know what it meant. Or what it meant to history…. From that standpoint, educating them that I wish they knew what it meant. But again, that's a hard thing to accomplish. That's the main thing I've been trying to push, in general, is just educating yourself. Not even about all the political side, but just [from] a human being standpoint."

When Liz Knox was playing youth hockey, one of her best friends was called the n-word. When they talked after the game, Knox told her friend that "it's just a name." But there was no conversation on the team about it. She had no clue of how to handle it.

"I was not equipped for that conversation. I should have never said it. Granted, you know, we are kids, and I learned from it how to be a better ally," Knox said. "But we, as white people, do not understand the weight of being called a n-word…. That should have been a learning moment for everybody. And it was just an extremely painful moment for her. And then that was it. Even now when I think about it, shit, man; I wasn't equipped, but I wasn't a good friend in that moment."

Organizations like SCORE Boston and Snider Hockey incorporate this education into their programming. Both organizations aim to teach not just hockey but also life skills. And it is a necessity when you have players who will be called slurs on the ice. When that has happened at Snider Hockey, they have always had a conversation about it afterward. SCORE Boston's educational component consists of twice-monthly classes on topics like racism and bullying. Board of directors member Deniere Watford-Jackson said class attendance is mandatory. If you don't show, you can't skate.

"We get a pretty high attendance that participate in the courses and discuss some of the concerns and addresses some of the things that are happening within the culture of the sport and in life," Watford-Jackson said. "We're able to have age-appropriate conversations with the players about instances or subjects such as racism or bullying and things of that nature. In the years that we've been here, we've had the rare occasion where there were incidents. And we were able to sit down with our players and have a discussion about how some of these things might make them feel or proper responses to things. If you're facing some of these incidents out in the real world, how you could handle yourself, or what's the best way to address certain things like that. We also are fortunate to have a pretty diverse coaching staff, and most hockey programs don't. A lot of these kids come in and they get to see a lot of coaches of color in a sport that's typically not displaying that. That helps break the ice or break barriers down or build a different perspective for people. Both [for] our kids and our parents, I would imagine."

Organizations like Coaching Boys Into Men are educating players. They have faced some pushback, but people like Brenda Tracy and Brock McGillis have learned that it's possible to get the message across to the athletes. Humanizing the issue is key.

"By not only shifting [to] humanizing and shifting language, educating them and everything else, but let's also start sharing things we enjoy and [our] passions," McGillis said. "The hockey world doesn't get that, because it's been ingrained in us from the age of seven that all you focus on is hockey and your identity as a player has slowly been based off hockey."

Trey Lewis, who works as a teacher and is now coaching an Indigenous team, said he would like to see programs for younger children, meant to educate them and tell stories that build empathy, showing them "the devastation that racism has caused and continues to cause."

"Since I'm a teacher, you want to make better people," Lewis said. "It sounds like a cliché, but that should be the goal, whether you're a coach on a sports team or you're a teacher. You should still focus on making better people all around."

But how do you implement that?

"It'd be hard to implement," Lewis said. "But minor hockey should take time to have a meeting about it, or a presentation about it, or something like a seminar, even for younger kids. Because, especially where I grew up, we didn't have any of those talks. I never had any talk about racism with my grandparents, who raised me. You just don't really talk about that stuff. And maybe it's because we're, you know, small town, a rural mind-set, maybe that's it, but everybody's scared to express who they really are, how they really feel, and it's weird. It's strange."

Parents are another potential barrier. Education—any type of education—is only cemented if children receive the same message in all aspects of their lives. So if the parents are using bigoted language, the coach emphasizing not to may not have an impact. Children are very adept at parroting back and internalizing what their parents say. Now, when you are teaching children about social justice, their parents may not approve. The parents must be included—given an explanation of the topics being covered and given educational materials as well. Hand them a packet. Tell them you want to celebrate diversity and ask if there's any holiday or cultural practice they participate in they'd like to share with the team. However, you can't force parents to care about the isms and you can't force parents, already bereft of time from driving their kids to and from rinks, to devote more time to educational purposes.

"So much time that we're asking for parents already just to get their kids to the rink and prepare them for hockey that to say, 'Okay, now you sit down for a one-hour, two-hour sensitivity training,' it doesn't go over well," Szto said. "When you're opting in to just participate in the culture I think that that should be optional, but make it very accessible to people."

Lastly, the players must be educated at all levels. Receiving that education as children is ideal, but there are professional players right now who do not understand racism and bigotry, and they are role models who influence the children who are playing youth hockey right now. Their behavior, such as using racial slurs and being able to continue to play, shows children what's acceptable and what's not. They want to be just like their heroes. (And whether we like it or not, athletes are public-facing heroes to children.)

"I really believe in a top-down approach, because although changes need to be implemented and made at the lower level, it needs to start there," Sarah Nurse said. "You have to have kids learning about what not to say, what's not okay at five years old, so that you carry with them throughout life. But…you need a top-down approach, because at the end of the day when people look and talk about hockey and talk about hockey culture, and all of that, the NHL is, like, god."

Why do the NHL and other organizations have this responsibility, though?

"If the league says nothing about Black Lives Matter at all, then fine. If the league didn't have Pride Nights, then fine," McGillis said. "But if you're going to try and get the PR win and have events or have Black History Month events and have Willie O'Ree travel around… then, at that point, it is your responsibility. Otherwise what you're doing is performative."

The University of North Dakota's Jasper Weatherby thinks it is the league's responsibility. Weatherby has been meeting with UND to discuss how athletics can support social justice and LGBTQIA+ rights.

"At the end of the day, when the top organizations are showing their players that they care about these issues that might not affect the guys at the top, it resonates through the entire organization," Weatherby said. "It shows people that they are allowed to take the stance for the things that are right in this country and in this world. I encourage the NHL to make statements, I encourage college hockey to make statements."

Nurse agrees.

"I look at the NHL and they need to be leaders in this fight, and ultimately it's like, get on the bus or get left behind," Nurse said. "If you don't want to hear about racism in hockey, if you want to say…keep politics out of sport. It's not politics. It's human rights, not politics at all. I'm really looking for the governing bodies to be leaders, and Hockey Canada, USA Hockey play a huge role in this. But at the end of the day, when people look at hockey they look at the National Hockey League."

After Akim Aliu shared his story and other players also came forward, the NHL announced it would create a tip line. However, whether that's been used and how it's been used are a mystery. There has to be strong external oversight in all aspects of hockey. In youth hockey, it's critical to keep that oversight on coaches and their interactions with athletes. At the pro level, it applies to much more. There still isn't a real avenue for players to air complaints. Or, as we saw with the Pittsburgh Penguins, there's no guarantee you won't get punished if you do express a complaint.

"It has to be external oversight," Szto said. "There needs to be some sort of a hotline or an external complaint system where people can go and it can be anonymous. And that they know it has nothing to do with this association or this federation. That's the only way that people can feel safe, really, to say anything and not fear repercussions from it, but that takes money and that takes some level of coordination. Because are you just doing it for the state or are you doing it for the entire country? So it's certainly logistically a problem, but that's the only thing I think that will really change the culture and start making you more accountable."

Vetting standards also need to be made much stronger, at all levels and across all positions, possibly with consequences if there is a failure to do so. In youth-serving organizations, it is critical that anyone working with children is thoroughly vetted. But it's not just coaches—even general managers, trainers, and others need to be vetted. Someone like John Vanbiesbrouck shouldn't be hired.

As we saw with sexual assault and domestic violence, there need to be clear policies in place to deal with all manner of infractions. Similarly, our rulebooks do not have the language to ensure Hockey Is for Everyone. In 2019, Jashvina reported that a racial slur had been directed at a Providence College player during a game against Boston College. No action was taken, as Hockey East deemed it could not figure out who said it. The slur had been reported by a referee who overheard it.

When a player is suspended for an on-ice interaction, such as a hit to the head, the conference makes a statement about the suspension. There was no announcement that Hockey East was looking into this incident, because there was no precedent from the conference to do so since this was not visible to the public, as an on-ice hit would have been. Hockey East should have stated it was investigating the incident. Taking no action at all was unacceptable. But this happened because our rulebooks are not equipped to handle issues like racism. Hockey East did what it did per the rulebook, and were this something like a plain insult, it would have been fine.

But it wasn't. This was a far different and far graver offense. Hockey East said there was no proof of which player uttered the slur, so no one would be punished, but it's up to the coach (BC's Jerry York, in this case) to find out what happened from his players. And if not, the team should have been penalized with York not being able to coach for at least a couple of games. That's what should have happened. That didn't happen, because there are no policies in place for explicitly dealing with racism, sexism, homophobia, transphobia, and xenophobia. (Also, in most cases players do not disclose bigotry because nothing will be done about it and people often question the victim's truthfulness. Always believe the victims.)

A big challenge to these solutions is that hockey is very insular and not many people in power want to make positive change. It results in just a continuous recycling of the same people or those with like-minded beliefs. Look no further than the endless general manager and coaching carousel in the NHL. NHL coaches and general managers can be fired repeatedly and still get a second, third, fourth, or even 10th chance. It is very difficult for anyone new to break in, as new blood is seldom welcome.

"We've had this regurgitation of NHL-level coaches because... you need to have a coach with this kind of experience and this coach has that experience and there's only like 40 of them that have it so we have to pick from this pool as opposed to giving somebody else a shot," Szto said. "You need somebody who's willing to go against the mold and...actually is successful. That would go a long way. I don't really know how you kind of force the issue except for testing and changing those people at the highest level."

Cyfko used the Toronto Maple Leafs' Troy Bodie as an example. Bodie signed a one-year, two-way contract with the Maple Leafs in 2013 and is now a professional scout for the team.

"It also makes sense because the owner of the Leafs at the time was his father-in-law," Cyfko said. "And people say that because he wasn't a good hockey player, but somehow he was on the team."

It's partly because—and this applies to hiring all over hockey, not just in the general manager or coaching positions, but also the team staff, operations, and more—hockey hiring works by word of mouth. People look to their circles to hire. And those circles tend to look like them. What ends up happening, on a larger scale, is that players who come up through the system are taught by people who are cishet white men. They hear things that are sexist, racist. It becomes a part of their culture. It becomes a part of them. These people then grow up to teach the next generation.

"I've seen coaches in major juniors take road trips that shouldn't be overnight trips so they could go party and be with women and different things like that," McGillis said. "On the road. That's influencing kids. When coaches are talking about players' moms, growing up in minor hockey, and there are coaches that do that, how hot a mom is and everything else, that's influencing and reinforcing these kids that that's the behavior. And people will argue all their parents should do differently. They're not around their parents as much as around the hockey coaches and teammates. You get to the rink, you're there three, four hours a night. Plus you've been at school all day. When are you around your parents?"

It isn't just that coaches influence the behavior; it's also that there is no other choice than to do this.

"Parents who want their kids to get that scholarship so badly or to go play professionally so badly…almost internalize it as being the process and the cost, and it all feeds into each other so immensely," Fitzgerald said.

The problem with having the same people at the helm is that it has been very hard to get them to change their views or commit to changing anything within the sport.

"They don't want to accept new ideas as often," Kurtis Gabriel said. "It's such a large issue to tackle…. To think that there are good people is a positive but it always starts with the people who run everything. And it trickles down."

Providence College player Gabriel Mollot-Hill said he considers himself someone who cares about social justice but has still found it hard to say anything against bigoted language he hears in the locker room.

"A teammate dynamic does make it substantially harder to do anything about it," Mollot-Hill said. "Many times I should have said something, I should have done something. I do regret that. I do want to do that better going forward, especially given everything that's going on in the world right now. It's like, damn, I could really have done a lot more. But the team dynamic is so hard to get past because this is your teammate—not just on the ice, but you live with the person, you hang out most of the day, like you don't want to be that guy who's going to Coach about it or something, you know. And that's, I think, by far the hardest part of changing some of that stuff."

It can't trickle down if it wasn't there to begin with.

"I've talked to other people who do CDI work or they feel like they're just waiting for certain people to die and put new people in those positions," Szto said. "It's so crass, but at the same time that's quite literally what it is, or it's certainly what it feels like."

ALL OF THESE factors result in lack of exposure to people who aren't cishet, straight, white men—as players and as coaches, as scouts and in the front offices. There are organizations like SCORE Boston that serve underserved communities and serve children of different backgrounds, which board of directors member Deniere Watford-Jackson says is vital.

"Being able to introduce people of different backgrounds and experiences at a younger age, and then on top of adding the sport is not super diverse, I think a lot of our minority students or players come to the program to try something different," Watford-Jackson said. "And then we have a large population of players and families who are white who are invested in hockey, like that was their lifestyle or maybe their parents played or grandparents or aunts and uncles, so hockey is the lifestyle and experience that they're looking for. So they might not be exposed to people."

Something that seems to increase exposure to those who aren't cis, straight, white men is coming from "non-traditional markets" or newer teams and leagues like the Seattle Kraken or the PWHPA. Although decades apart, former NHLer Ryan Miller and current

Arizona State player Dominic Garcia both played amateur hockey on newer teams in "non-traditional markets," and their teams were more diverse. For Garcia, who is Black, it was while growing up in Las Vegas and then playing hockey at Arizona State, then the newest Division I men's team.

"Just from my college experience, personally dealing with things like diversity on our team, I haven't had to worry about that as much," Garcia said.

Garcia, along with Northeastern's Jayden Struble, released a statement in support of Black Lives Matter after George Floyd was killed.

"People would call when I first put out my statement," Garcia said. "They were wondering how they can get involved with programs and stuff like that. People are talking about making players when they first start playing watch a video about diversity. But it's hard to regulate. I guess the only thing I'm starting to think about is a video from USA Hockey for teams and referees to watch that is mandatory."

Miller grew up playing in California before eventually playing at Michigan State and continuing his career in the NHL. He remembers when a girl joined his team as a goaltender, and he thought it was cool.

"That's a teaching moment for that group of kids right there," Miller said. "At the time it was heavily on there's a difference between us. And there was going to be some special treatment about the locker room and all that kind of stuff, but the topic of respect was brought up, and I thought we all handled it really well. I really wish I had a better memory, but I played hockey for so long and now I'm 40, so I just remember that moment thinking, like, 'That's cool somebody wants to play hockey.'"

When Miller was playing youth hockey in California, his dad was the coach. And the only way they could field a team was if they welcomed every type of player.

"I thought it was cool [that] this young lady wanted to play," Miller said. "And I think that the parents handled it really well."

A highly effective way to change the culture of insularity is by having new teams subscribe to diversity and inclusion when they start, something the Seattle Kraken, the NHL's newest franchise, has been doing. Also key is that people in hockey must be active allies. There are several players who have worked on being allies, including Kurtis Gabriel, Ryan Miller, and Jasper Weatherby. It's been hard for players, as Mollot-Hill said, to speak out against the culture. They may get cut or have ice time taken away. But even if they don't—how will everyone else listen to the one voice of reason?

"If you were worried about the past when now's probably the best time ever, there's been a huge movement against danger in this pandemic," Gabriel said. "I don't think kids are ever going to be super comfortable until something changes at the top; it all starts at the top."

A big example is to give your space to someone else—which is what Liz Knox did when she resigned from the PWHPA board in favor of Sarah Nurse.

"The biggest gift that I have right now is being on the board, actually having a voice at our table," Knox said.

It does take effort from those who are privileged within the hockey community especially. Gabriel comes at it from both sides, serving as a moderator and inviting people into the conversation— because it's not the responsibility of marginalized people to have the polite conversations about why they deserve basic human rights.

"What I try to communicate as an ally is trying to fill in the gaps for people and try to help humanize the issue, but I can't do it as well as you guys can," Gabriel said. "You almost have to challenge their logic. If someone's coming to you and you humanize this to them, how can [they] not see there's an issue there? That's what blows my mind: the lack of accountability. There's the internet, there's every resource out there. Back in the day when we wrote on paper and that, you didn't know anything. [Now] we're connected to the whole world. It's a very clear line of what's racist, what's not, what's the right thing to do, what's not, and it just boggles my mind it's still not that way."

Weatherby uses his social media platform to voice his opinions and stand with BIPOC, even though he knows there might be pushback from fans. Weatherby's grandmother marched in Selma, Alabama, and was sprayed with hoses.

"If I can sit behind my computer, and I can go to rallies, and I can, you know, tweet out how I support this stuff...and [she was] sitting there, getting sprayed by police officers in Alabama with hoses, I think I'm going to be alright," Weatherby said. "And as she always, always told me, it's never the wrong time to do the right thing. So had there been racist people tweeting at me and telling me how wrong I am, absolutely, [I am] gonna do my best to educate them as best I can."

Weatherby decided to go public and eventually knelt during the national anthem at the start of the 2020–21 season.

"There are other people out there who might not have these big platforms but are voicing their opinions," Weatherby said. "I've gotten several messages from people here in the Grand Forks community. [One person] messaged me individually and said, 'Thank you so much for sharing your story. I've been caught within my family who is absolutely against Black Lives Matter and feeling like I'm alone, and being able to say hey, you know what, there's people out there in the Grand Forks community who believe in these things....' I'm gonna start to voice my own opinions and I think that the more people talk about it, the better it can be."

Weatherby said he plans on continuing his involvement in social justice at North Dakota, encouraging all teams and programs to use their social platforms for social justice. He also reached out to Eric Burin, a historian who teaches at the University of North Dakota and edited a book about Colin Kaepernick and kneeling. He spoke with Black student athletes, who want to have a history class about social justice offered for credit at the university.

"I'm going to be trying to encourage them to cut ties with any donors who have supported or engaged in hate speech, discrimination, or racial ideas," Weatherby said. "We're in a very unique opportunity right here with UND being in the middle of a very diverse community in a very red state."

North Dakota was the program that recruited Mitchell Miller. And after his bullying behavior became public, the team initially doubled down and kept him as a recruit before ultimately rescinding the offer.

"You can only talk for so long, and it's about making positive change that can last and that will continue making more and more change and continue the ball rolling," Weatherby said. "It forces a lot of people to say, 'Oh, wait a minute, I can't just post a black box on my Instagram.'"

Ryan Miller is also one of the more outspoken players. His wife, Noureen DeWulf, is a Muslim-raised Indian woman, allowing him a close vantage point from through which to understand her experience.

"I can walk around anywhere, any time of day, and I can kind of do anything. I'm white, over six feet tall, and, you know, of a certain age," Miller said. "I was not not blind to the world, but [being married to DeWulf] was eye-opening that there are a lot of little things I didn't even consider.... It's definitely on the organizations and the parents, or people helping to encourage the parents and organizations, to get ahead of things and educate, so everything is a lot more normal before the situation can occur. That's the only thing we can do at this point."

Players do have a responsibility to advocate for social justice because they are not just players—they are also members of society.

"In a locker room full of privileged white dudes who are just like, 'Oh, yeah, let's just dump and chase,' you're carrying the weight of so much more than just a hockey game," Knox said. "You're in a room full of people that not a single one understands. It's great that there's a diversity alliance to help changes, but also you need to support it. It's victim support, right? You need to reach back to people that have lived through this day after day and have had no support.... That's the other thing. It's great to create change, but are you even helping? Are you even fixing the open wounds that are there right now? Are you just trying to prevent that from happening again?"

The biggest barrier, though, is that it is hard to change the culture without complete buy-in from those in charge. And that is something we don't have yet. Look no further than the New York Rangers and their continued refusal to address Tony DeAngelo's behavior, or USA Hockey hiring John Vanbiesbrouck.

"It is weeding out the people that shouldn't be in the game, hiring different people, holding people accountable for their behaviors," Szto said. "It's like...all the things we've seen with USA Gymnastics, we've seen the enabling of abusers throughout the system. So, it should be a one-strike policy; if you're hired and paid in these organizations and you have misconduct issues, you're not entitled to that particular job. So we need to be willing to let people go instead of failing people upward or just kind of passing them along to some other organization."

Sports can be a great beacon of healing. Think of how sports brought communities together after 9/11, or the Boston Marathon bombings, or Hurricane Katrina. They have the power to bring us all together, but unfortunately they are not always used that way—instead, those in power in sports choose to stay silent on issues like racism and sexism instead of working to be a force to fight against them.

And it is possible to be that change.

Take Belfast, Northern Ireland, for example. Belfast has a team in the Elite Ice Hockey League, the Giants. The history of Northern Ireland is quite complicated, and there are still pockets of division. Instead of shying away from speaking about it, the Giants have gone out of their way to bridge the gap. A newer sport in Northern Ireland, hockey does not have the ties to one side or the other that the other sports have. When the Friendship Four, a college hockey tournament, started, the Giants sent an equal number of teams to both Protestant and Catholic elementary schools. Protestants and Catholics sit next to each other. Certain flags and colors are banned from the arena. It's one thing and one thing only: the Giants.

WE TOOK A look at the NHL's "Committing to Change" website with great interest.

Seeing that Chicago was reportedly on the Stanley Cup Playoffs hub city shortlist, Evan created a Twitter thread on a local version of the CTC's advocacy section on books, articles, and films.

A lot of folks love to advance the discussion by asking about solutions while systemic issues are rarely dealt with in the context they should be. If we're going to diagnose the problem, we have to engage in a deep dive into how we got here. We can't skip over how the problems became problems before talking about solutions.

Amid the protests in the aftermath of the police killings of George Floyd and Breonna Taylor that devolved into looting and violence in several cities across the world, Evan was asked to make an appearance on a Chicago-based radio talk show. The host asked him, "We know [the] problems; what can we do about solutions?" Evan privately bristled at the notion, because we need to know how to identify the systemic issues that got us here.

In the same segment, Evan said, "Check your friends and family who say awful things about Black people, gay people, women, and other folks." Dan McNeil, the show's co-host, said, "I couldn't agree more; zero tolerance."

Three months later, McNeil was shitcanned from his job for an inappropriate tweet toward Maria Taylor, a Black woman and ESPN reporter. He did exactly what Evan warned him and his listeners not to do.

When will people learn?

Here is a list of articles, movies, podcasts, and books to give anyone who is interested in getting a head start.

Movies, Documentaries, and Podcasts

16 Shots
America to Me
A Most Beautiful Thing
Benji
Boss: The Black Experience in Business
Central Park Five
City So Real
DuSable to Obama: Chicago's Black Metropolis
Hoop Dreams
Judas and the Black Messiah
Small Axe
Standing on the Line
The Banker
The Green Book: Guide to Freedom
The Interrupters
The Murder of Fred Hampton
The Trial of the Chicago 7
This American Life episodes on Harold Washington and Harper
    High School
When They See Us

Books

Ghettoside: A True Story of Murder in America by Jill Leovy

Hood Feminism: Notes from the Women That a Movement Forgot by Mikki Kendall

Hoop Dreams: A True Story of Hardship and Triumph by Ben Joravsky

The Defender: How the Legendary Black Newspaper Changed America by Ethan Michaeli

The Red Record: Tabulated Statistics and Alleged Causes of Lynching in the United States by Ida B. Wells-Barnett

The South Side: A Portrait of Chicago and American Segregation by Natalie Moore

Unsportsmanlike Conduct: College Football and the Politics of Rape by Jessica Luther

TV Series

Lovecraft Country

The Wire

Watchmen

Articles

The Atlantic, "The Case for Reparations" by Ta-Nehisi Coates

The Atlantic, "The Lost History of an American Coup D'État" by Adrienne LaFrance and Vann R. Newkirk II

CBC, "Remains of 215 Children Found Buried at Former B.C. Residential School, First Nation Says" by Courtney Dickson and Bridgette Watson

Chicago Reader, "Icing Racism" by Evan F. Moore

Chicago Sun-Times, "Letter to a Young Lord: Remembering Manuel Ramos" by Manny Ramos

Chicago Tribune, "Andrew Shaw's Slur Sheds Light on Homophobia in Sports" by Chris Hine

Globe and Mail, "No, This Is Not a Watershed Moment for Hockey" by Jashvina Shah

Injustice Watch, "Chicago Protests and Looting Confused America. The Media Moved on, but Inequality Remains" by Carlos Ballesteros

New York Times Magazine, "The 1619 Project"

Players' Tribune, "Hockey Is Not for Everyone" by Akim Aliu

ProPublica Illinois, "The Legend of A-N-N-A: Revisiting an American Town Where Black People Weren't Welcome after Dark" by Logan Jaffe

The Triibe, "West Side House Party Exposes the Disconnect between Young Black Residents, Chicago Officials and the News During COVID-19 Pandemic" by Vee L. Harrison

Epilogue

OVER THE YEARS WHEN JASHVINA AND I—AND OTHER FOLKS— have written articles about hockey culture, we've been accused of attacking the game even though we've said on numerous occasions how that premise doesn't jibe with reality.

Let me make this clear: I love hockey. And when I love something, I want to make it better. Any criticism herein doesn't mean we aim to weaponize this book in order to take hockey down.

Keeping things all the way "100," hockey culture needs an intervention—therapy, at least. In those instances, we need to foster an uncomfortable conversation where past incidents need to be described in full detail.

We—which includes fans, journalists, coaches, players, parents, administrators, and anyone else who says they are a stakeholder in the game—need to start doing something simple but revolutionary: listen.

At this point, we'd like for folks who care about the sport to utilize the same discretion they use in their personal lives, whether it's their wives, husbands, children, boyfriends, girlfriends, etc. In those instances, I bet many of them do everything within their power to find a solution and not stick their heads in the sand like some hockey fans do when the sport's issues are discussed in a public manner.

I'm not trying to get rich from this book; I want to kick-start a long-overdue conversation.

—E.M.

When my nephew Niam was born, I bought him a couple BU Hockey onesies. He's older now, but I keep buying him BU hockey clothes. The last time I shipped them to him for his birthday, I explained in his card (he's three, so he can't read it) why I was giving him all this clothing from some random team.

It's because BU hockey is one of the most important things in my life. That is my home and those people are my family. I still keep in touch with people from BU athletics. When my faith in hockey fails, it's some of those former players I turn to for hope. I think about the time after I was sexually assaulted and how the only three people in college hockey I told were three people affiliated with BU Hockey.

I want my nephew to have the same support and love that I do.

But he's also a half-Black, half-Indian kid. And I don't want him to have to suffer the way that others have, the way that I have. I don't want him to fall into the traps hockey creates. I want him to be a good kid who is always loved and supported.

That isn't a reality right now.

I'm still here not because I hate this sport. And as Evan said, we're not trying to get rich. Really, choosing to speak about all these topics for the past four-plus years has definitely hurt my career, and ostracized me for good. People have shut the door in my face. I have a target on my back. But I'm still here. Because I know there is good and I want everyone to be able to experience that good. So many other people love it too. And all we want is for it to love us back.

Can hockey change? Yes; it just takes a little faith and a lot of work.

—J.S.

Acknowledgments

Anthony Holmes (Tony X.); Brock McGillis; Chris Peters; Ryan Miller; Shireen Ahmed; Darren Andrade; Louis Moore; Bill Montague; Brian Hull; Val James; Gloria Wong-Padoongpatt; Renee Hess; Jack Silverstein; Bob Dawson; Riley Fitzgerald; Howard Bryant; Courtney Szto; Eric Gibbs; Kurtis Gabriel; Alan Sutliff; Dominic Garcia; Brenda Tracy; Elliot Gutman; Ed Heisler; Jennifer Southall; Ali Lawrence; Rane Carnegie; the staff at Triumph Books; our editor, Michelle Bruton; Hemal Jhaveri; Jessica Platt; Jason Wilson; Trey Lewis; Chanel Keenan; Courtney Yeah; Jeff Pearlman; Andrew Sobotka, Chicago Gay Hockey Association; Sunaya Sapurji; Jaslyn Lim; Steve Lorenzo, New York City Gay Hockey Association; Kwame Damon Mason; Raychel McBride; John Brown; Tony Rodriguez; Gabriela Ugarte; Avery Cordingley; Jordan DeKort; Jasper Weatherby; Gabriel Mollot-Hill; Sandra Kirby; Jesse Mahler and Coaching Boys Into Men; Ruth Glenn; Rita Smith; Sarah Nurse; Liz Knox; Laura Robinson; Kelley Townsend; John Cyfko; Deniere Watford-Jackson; Ryan Miller; Tim Skuce; Nate Flemming; Seth Askelson; Saroya Tinker; Scoop Jackson; Dave Zirin; Jessica Luther; and Kayla Grey.

—E.M. and J.S.

There are so many people who've helped make this book possible. Thank you to Triumph Books for believing in us, to Michelle Bruton for all her hard work editing. Thank you to everyone who helped look over this to make sure we were using the correct language. Aside from actually writing this book, I wouldn't be in this position if it wasn't for so many people. My friends Erica, Micaela, Sandra, Kim, Laura, Drew, Chris, Namank. My parents. Our family friends in New Jersey and Boston. My Boston University crew—including my former hall director, Valerie Heruska. (No, I have not forgotten about all those times I would come to rant in your office.) And thank you to Brian Kelly, Kevin Edelson, Brian Durocher, Jeff Kampersal, Megan Rowley, Adam Augestine, Brian Smith, Catherine Bogart, Chad Twaro, Jason Hadju, Joe Meloni, and so many other amazing people in the hockey community who've supported me and in some cases have literally picked me up off the floor. You will always be my family. Thank you to my Princeton hockey families and parents— the Kuffners, Michael Hallisey, Kevin Becker, Teri Phinney, and especially Mark Pompi, who told me I'd be famous the first day he met me and has followed my career since. I could not be here without the absolute kindness and support and encouragement from everyone who has done everything possible to help me follow my dreams.

—J.S.

Survivor Resources

U.S.
Adult Survivors of Child Abuse
DoJ Directory of Crime Victim Services
Domestic Violence Survival Kit
National Coalition Against Domestic Violence
National Domestic Violence Hotline: 800-799-7233
National Sexual Violence Resource Center
Rape Abuse and Incest National Network (RAINN): 800-656-4673
The Blue Ribbon Project
The Trevor Project (for LGBTQ+ youth): 866-488-7386
Trans Lifeline: 877-565-8860

Canada
Calgary & Area Child Advocacy Centre
Canadian Centre for Child Protection
CASW Acts
Childhelp National Child Abuse Hotline: 800-422-4453
Ending Violence Association of Canada
Hope for Wellness: 855-242-3310
Kids Help Phone: 800-668-6868
Shelter Safe
Trans Lifeline: 877-330-6366

Sources

Books

Branch, John. *Boy on Ice: The Life and Death of Derek Boogaard*. W. W. Norton & Company, 2014.

Gallagher, Jack, and Valmore James. *Black Ice: The Val James Story*. ECW Press, 2015.

González, Juan, and Joseph Torres. *News for All the People: The Epic Story of Race and the American Media*. Verso Books, 2011.

Gruneau, Richard, and David Whitson, ed. *Artificial Ice: Hockey, Culture, and Commerce*. University of Toronto Press, 2006.

Harris, Cecil. *Breaking the Ice: The Black Experience in Professional Hockey*. Insomniac Press, 2003.

Hartill, Michael J. *Sexual Abuse in Youth Sports: A Sociocultural Analysis*. Routledge, 2017.

Luther, Jessica. *Unsportsmanlike Conduct: College Football and the Politics of Rape*. Edge of Sports, 2016.

Robidoux, Michael A. *Stickhandling through the Margins: First Nations Hockey in Canada*. University of Toronto Press, 2012.

Robinson, Laura. *Crossing the Line: Violence and Sexual Assault in Canada's National Sport*. McClelland & Stewart, 1998.

Magazines, Newspapers, and Periodicals

Arizona Republic
Boston Globe
Chicago Reader
Chicago Sun-Times
Chicago Tribune
Cincinnati Enquirer
Dallas Morning News
Denver Post
Detroit News
Eagle-Tribune
Ebony
Enterprise
Hartford Courant
Jet
Los Angeles Times
Minneapolis Star-Tribune
New Hampshire Union Leader
New York Post
New York Times
Pioneer Press
Pittsburgh Post-Gazette
Sports Illustrated
St. Louis Post Dispatch
Tennessean
Time
Toronto Sun
USA TODAY
Waterloo Region Record
Winnipeg Free Press
Vancouver Sun

Journal Articles

Canadian Journalists of Colour and Canadian Association of Black Journalists, "Canadian Media Diversity: Calls to Action," *J-Source* (January 2020).

Nikolas Dickerson, "Constructing the Digitalized Sporting Body: Black and White Masculinity in NBA/NHL Internet Memes," *Communication & Sport* Vol. 4, Issue 3 (May 2015).

Peter Donnelly and Gretchen Kerr, "Revising Canada's Policies on Harassment and Abuse in Sport: A Position Paper and Recommendations," University of Toronto Centre for Sport Policy Studies (August 2018).

Stacy L. Lorenz and Rod Murray, "Goodbye to the Gangstas: The NBA Dress Code, Ray Emery, and the Policing of Blackness in Basketball and Hockey," *Journal of Sport and Social Issues* Vol. 38, Issue 1 (June 2013).

Ibid. "The Dennis Rodman of Hockey: Ray Emery and the Policing of Blackness in the Great White North," *Commodified and Criminalized: New Racism and African Americans in Contemporary Sport* (2011): 183–202.

Video and Films

ABC News *Nightline*

Across the Line

Canadian Bacon

ESPN *SportsCentury*

NHL Network

Soul on Ice: Past, Present, & Future

Standing on the Line

The Carter Effect

Websites

8newsnow.com

ada.gov

adl.org

allprobailbond.com

apa.org

apnews.com

athleticbusiness.com

audacy.com/670thescore

awfulannouncing.com

blackgirlhockeyclub.org

buzzfeednews.com

cabj.news

cbc.ca

cdc.gov

chicago.cbslocal.com

chicagoelections.gov

chicagogayhockey.org

chicagonow.com

chicagoreporter.com

chicagosidesports.com (defunct)

chl.ca

citybureau.org

cjhlhockey.com

cjr.org

cnn.com

collegehockeynews.com

colorofhockey.com

corporatekin.com

deadspin.com

duluthreader.com

edmonton.citynews.ca

enterprisenews.com

espn.com

fop.net

foxnews.com

freep.com

hawkeyeshockey.pointstreaksites.com

hockeycanada.ca

hockeydb.com

hockeydiversityalliance.org

hockey-graphs.com

howtohockey.com

huffingtonpost.ca

imdb.com

indianatechwarriors.com

influencecommunication.com

instagram.com

jeffpearlman.com

justice.gc.ca

justice.gov

kornferry.com

medium.com

merriam-webster.com

minnesotahockey.com

missingkids.org

mlb.com

morningconsult.com

nahl.com

nbcsports.com

ncaa.com

nhl.com

nhl.com/coyotes

nhl.com/sharks

npr.org

nycgha.org

nymag.com

obrienforcook.com

ohf.on.ca

ontariohockeyleague.com

patch.com

patriotledger.com

pittsburghartscouncil.org

players-coalition.org

profootballweekly.com

propublica.org

quigley.house.gov

rainn.org

safesport.org

safetocompete.org

sbnation.com

soogreyhounds.com

sportsnet.ca

sports.yahoo.com

theathletic.com

thehockeynews.com

theplayerstribune.com

theqmjhl.ca

theshadowleague.com

tshq.bluesombrero.com/kennedyparklittleleague

tsn.ca

twincities.com

twitter.com

unicef.org

unlv.edu

usahockey.com

ushl.com
utoronto.ca
vocativ.com
wbez.org
wbur.org
wgbh.com
wgrz.com
whitehouse.gov
whl.ca
windycitygridiron.com
youcanplayproject.org
youtube.com